Genealogy Online

About the Author

Elizabeth Powell Crowe has been pursuing genealogy for more than 30 years. Her previous editions of *Genealogy Online* have sold a combined total of nearly 200,000 copies. In the past, she has worked as an editor for numerous genealogy- or technology-related publications, including *Computer Currents* magazine, *Valley Leaves*, *LeDespencer* magazine, and the *Computers in Genealogy* newsletter, and she contributed articles to *Digital Genealogist* magazine. Crowe presents and speaks on genealogy throughout the South, when she is not pursuing elusive ancestors. She lives and works in Navarre, Florida.

Genealogy Online

Tenth Edition

Elizabeth Powell Crowe

New York   Chicago   San Francisco
Athens   London   Madrid   Mexico City
Milan   New Delhi   Singapore   Sydney   Toronto

Library of Congress Cataloging-in-Publication Data

Crowe, Elizabeth Powell.
    Genealogy online / Elizabeth Powell Crowe. — Tenth edition.
        pages   cm
    ISBN 978-0-07-184110-8 (paperback)
  1. Genealogy—Data processing.   2. Genealogy—Computer network resources—
Handbooks, manuals, etc.   3. Internet—Handbooks, manuals, etc.   I. Title.
    CS21.C67   2015
    929.10285—dc23   2014027050

McGraw-Hill Education books are available at special quantity discounts to use as premiums and sales promotions, or for use in corporate training programs. To contact a representative, please visit the Contact Us pages at www.mhprofessional.com.

Genealogy Online, Tenth Edition

234567890 QFR QFR 1098765

ISBN   978-0-07-184110-8
MHID   0-07-184110-5

Sponsoring Editor
  Roger Stewart

Editorial Supervisor
  Patty Mon

Project Manager
  Jigyasa Bhatia,
  Cenveo® Publisher Services

Acquisitions Coordinator
  Amanda Russell

Copy Editor
  Lisa McCoy

Proofreader
  Vicki Wong

Indexer
  Karin Arrigoni

Production Supervisor
  George Anderson

Composition
  Cenveo Publisher Services

Illustration
  Cenveo Publisher Services

Art Director, Cover
  Jeff Weeks

Cover Designer
  William Voss

This book is dedicated to my mother, Frances May Spencer Powell
1926–2007

Contents at a Glance

Contents

PART II
Using the Internet for Genealogy

PART III

The Nitty Gritty: Places to Find Names, Dates, and Places

PART IV
Appendixes

Acknowledgments

As with any book, this one was made possible by those who helped and worked with me. First, I thank each and every person mentioned in this book. The people who graciously granted me interviews, sent me success stories, and shared their expertise with me made this book possible.

Special thanks go to all my genealogy friends on Facebook: Amy Coffin, Bill Ammons, Bill West, Cheryl Rothwell, Cyndi Ingle, Dick Eastman, Elizabeth Shown Mills, Elyse Doerflinger, Jeanne Henry, Judy G. Russell, Leland Meitzeler, Linda Mullikin of the FHGC in Navarre, Kay Rudolph, Lisa B. Lee, Liz Kelley Kerstens, Marian Pierre-Louis, Megan Smolenyak Smolenyak, Michael John Neill, Myra Vanderpool Gormley, Pat Richley-Erickson, Randy Hooser, Roger Stewart, Romi White, Russ Worthington, Terry Morgan, Thomas MacEntee, and all the rest. Great thanks to all the staff at McGraw-Hill Education. And immense gratitude is due to all my family and friends who were so understanding while I was in "writing hibernation" and patiently waited for me to emerge.

Most of all, I want to thank my mother, Frances May Spencer Powell, who I know is collaring ancestors in heaven and recording their vital statistics!

Introduction

More than 20 years ago, my mother asked my brother and me, "This Internet thing you all are always talking about: Can it help me with my genealogy?"

My brother and I were already deep into online discussion groups about writing (me), archaeology (Bob), music, astronomy (both of us), and other topics.

Immediately after Mother asked, I knew two things: The answer was yes and I would have to write it all down for her. And that is how this book came to be.

Who Should Read This Book

The early editions of this book assumed you knew how to do genealogy, but not how to use the Internet. Since that time, commercial online services and the Internet have added, expanded, revised, and changed what they offer, as well as how and when they offer it. From having to use a dial-up connection over a modem in 1992, to cable and satellite connections, to today's iPhone, we've come a long way. Social networking and Multimedia Messaging Service (MMS) messaging make sharing your data easy and almost irresistible. So in this edition, the author assumes you know most Internet technologies and programs and that you want to know how to use them to do your genealogy. I've gone from a "what button to push" approach to a "why would you want to use that" one.

The potential for finding clues, data, and other researchers looking for your same family names has increased exponentially in the last decade. Since 2000, push technology, streaming video, blogs, podcasts, social networking, and indexed document scans have radically changed what can be found on the Internet and how we search for it. If you feel you need formal instruction in researching family history, online courses, from basic self-paced text to college-level instruction, can now make that happen.

In short, online genealogy has never been better, and it's a good time to try your hand at it! Let's look at some examples of how online genealogy works.

Bill Ammons' Story

Bill Ammons is a friend of mine who used a few hints on online genealogy from me to break down a brick wall in his genealogy research. Here is what he wrote to me about his quest:

"I started my genealogy research 16 months ago with the name of the only grandparent I knew from my childhood. The journey has taken me from knowing a very small family to discovering an enormously large family. I have learned a lot about history, our society, family secrets, and what not to say in e-mails, even jokingly, to family. I have hit roadblocks and gotten through some, while others are still being researched," Bill Ammons wrote. Some roadblocks will never be resolved, he noted, as you will discover that documents were destroyed in the Civil War or in mysterious fires at courthouses or newspaper offices.

However, on your journey, you, too, will become a collector of websites, books on dead people, and American history.

"Roadblocks are very interesting challenges, in that one must begin to be creative in their research to find clues to get them through the roadblocks," Bill said. "If the information on the Internet leads to roadblocks, then try going to the county historical society office and then to the county courthouse to look for wills, land documents, bible records, newspaper articles, and even personal letters. I have found old bible records at the historical societies that have provided clues to names I was uncertain of and even provided insights into cemetery records. I started my journey with a simple posting to the Horry County, South Carolina Historical Society home page (www.hchsonline.org/).

"From a simple posting on the message board of the four family surnames (Ammons, Denton, Martin, and Tompkins), I received a response the next day that solved the Martin branch of my tree to 1810. My cousin is, in fact, one of the contributors of documents to the Horry Historic Society Site. Sometimes, one can find a new family member and find genealogy at the same time," Bill said.

"The next day brought another surprise when I received an e-mail from a gentleman in Atlanta and he provided the Denton branch of my family tree. His mother was my grandmother's sister. I never met my grandmother's sisters," he continued. "But this posting yielded another new family member and also received information about the Denton family as a bonus. This family member pointed me to documents and newspaper articles that were available online that provided personal insight as to the possibilities that my grandmother and grandfather were Native Americans.

"Then I had to really get into the digging mindset to start finding information and documents on the other surnames. The Ammons surname has taken me from the coast of South Carolina to the Appalachian Mountains and back to Sampson County, North Carolina. I never had any idea that the Ammons family came from North Carolina because I grew up with the understanding that the Ammons were "Black Irish" that migrated to South Carolina. The real surprise has been in the documentation I have obtained that does not support this idea we were "Black Irish."

Census reports from Ancestry.com (www.ancestry.com) were well worth the monthly cost for the subscription, Bill said. These census reports are searchable and easily accessed, even with a dial-up connection. The census reports provide a road map of where the family lived in different decades. Also, the census reports tell something about the family's living conditions, employment, education, and neighbors. From these documents, Bill was able to trace the family from 1780 to the 1920s. He found the Ammons family as early as 1780 in Sampson County, North Carolina. Next, they migrated to Marlboro County, South Carolina, after the American Revolution. In the next generation, the children migrated to Macon and Cherokee counties of North Carolina.

Bill found documents from the American Revolution at Wallace State College in Hanceville, Alabama. This community college has a tremendous records area on the American Revolution and the Civil

War, as well as access to the 2.5 million microfilm reels from the Genealogical Society of Utah. The college also has courses in family and regional history. These records showed Bill that his Ammons family received a land grant in Marlboro County because they served in the American Revolution.

Using Cyndi's List (www.cyndislist.com) to help search the Native American connections, Bill found it a great help when researching roots connected to the federally recognized tribes. The issue of researching Native American heritage is a separate and interesting journey, which can involve discovering your genetic markers, such as Asian shovel teeth, anatomical knot, and genetically transmitted diseases.

Another helpful resource was the Melungeons page (www .melungeon.org/), he said. "Some people are really confused about this group of folks that lived in North Carolina. The more I read about the forgotten Portuguese, the more interesting this hidden part of America's history became in tracking the family history," Bill said.

Bill's journey brought him to the Waccamaw Indian People of South Carolina and the Croatans of Sampson County, North Carolina. He is a tribal member of the Waccamaw. Among the helpful sites were the University of North Carolina at Chapel Hill Library's Documenting the American South page (www.docsouth.unc.edu/). This site has a Hypertext Markup Language (HTML) version of a book called *The Croatan Indians of Sampson County, North Carolina. Their Origin and Racial Status. A Plea for Separate Schools,* written in 1916 by George Edwin Butler.

The online book was a jewel of a find in this surname search. The book discusses the Croatans having a possible connection with the lost colonists of Roanoke, which led Bill to research the census records again. The census places family in the correct place at the correct time to strengthen this argument of where the family originated. Currently, Bill plans to continue the research focused on the county, state, and federal records of the time. A big plus was the photos in the book, with people who resemble family members that Bill knows today!

"In my research for records, I have been to the North Carolina Archives in Raleigh, North Carolina. (A word to the wise: Don't take any ink pens and/or briefcases; you will not be allowed into the records area.) Believe me—it is a tremendous treat to see the historical records that remain. The information you can discover is well worth the frustration," he said.

As you can see, Bill Ammons' journey took him to many different online and offline resources: Bill took what he knew from his own immediate family, plus the family legends and gossip, to begin searching for the original records he needed. He went to some resources in person, such as the North Carolina Archives and Wallace State College Library, but only after online research told him that's where he needed to go. This is an excellent example of genealogy online.

Where Computers Come In

Databases, online services, online card catalogs, and bulletin boards are changing the brick wall syndrome, that frustrating phase of any lineage search where the information needed seems unavailable. Genealogists who have faced the challenges and triumphed are online, helping others.

State governments and the federal government have recently started to put data, such as death records, veterans' records, and so on, in computer-readable databases, which can then be accessible via the Internet. The Bureau of Land Management, the Library of Congress, and the National Archives and Records Administration are just a few examples of government sites that can help the family historian.

The United States alone has numerous genealogical societies that trace people's descent. Some of these are national, but many more are local or regional, such as the Tennessee Valley Genealogical Society or the New England Historical Society. Others are specific to certain names. Many patriotic organizations, such as the Daughters of the Confederacy, limit membership to descendants of a particular historical group. Many of these groups offer courses in genealogy, which can help you with online and offline research.

There's no denying that the computer has changed nearly everything in our lives, and the avocation and vocation of genealogical research is no exception. Further, the Internet has added to the ways a genealogist can research, as with Bill Ammons' example, to find those elusive primary sources that are essential to any family history. This book explores many different networks, services, and websites that can help you in your pursuit of your ancestry.

Stories about how online communities have helped people in their genealogical research abound. The following sections provide some examples.

DearMYRTLE Finds a Patriot

DearMYRTLE, a daily genealogy columnist on the Internet, was helping a friend move files, data, and programs from an old computer to a new one. In the course of the conversation, DearMYRTLE's friend wondered aloud what online genealogy could do for him, but expressed doubt anything useful could turn up online.

Then the conversation turned to the new U.S. quarters celebrating the states in the order they joined the Union, specifically, the one with the Delaware patriot Caesar Rodney on the reverse.

"Who was he?" asked DearMYRTLE's friend.

"All right," DearMYRTLE replied, "let's run a test. Your wife here will look up Caesar Rodney in the *Encyclopaedia Britannica*. You look him up on your old computer using Microsoft Encarta 97. I'll look him up on the Internet with your new computer."

Faster than the other two could use either a book or a CD-ROM, DearMYRTLE found a transcription of a letter from George Washington to Rodney.

Nancy's Story

Nancy is a friend of mine from high school who knows more about computers and the Internet than I do, but not quite so much about genealogy. When her stepmother died recently, Nancy got a large box of her father's memorabilia and photos. She asked me about genealogy, and I showed her some good genealogy sites on the Internet on her laptop computer.

I didn't think much more about it until she called me a few weeks later in considerable excitement. She had not only found the USGenWeb (www.usgenweb.org) site for her father's home county in Texas, but also that the moderator of the site had known both her father and her grandfather. She was scanning in the old photos and e-mailing them to the fellow, and he was identifying people in them left and right. One was of Nancy's grandfather as a child. Another showed her father as a teenager. Every day, the USGenWeb moderator was helping her fill in more holes in her family history.

These are just two examples of how you, too, can do online genealogy.

What This Book Covers

This book covers the techniques used by Bill, Pat, and Nancy, as well as ways to teach yourself genealogy, learn from experts, and create "cousin bait" such as blogs and tweets.

It also takes you on a tour of some specific resources that can help you research your family history online, publish it, and share it.

A Quick Look at This Book

The chapters go from the simplest to more complex facets of genealogy in Part I. In Parts II and III, you will find some "hands-on" guides to using specific resources.

Notes and boxes along the way give you some details that help you do all this more quickly and easily.

Part I: Basics

Chapter 1: Beginning a Genealogy Project For those just becoming interested in how to research family history, this chapter will go over the steps you need to take. If you have been doing genealogy for a while, still glance at the chapter. Please be sure to take this one idea from the chapter, regardless of your experience level: BACK UP YOUR WORK REGULARLY.

Chapter 2: Software You'll Need This chapter will help you learn about some of the software that can make genealogy both online and offline easier to research, save, and share.

Chapter 3: Ethics, Privacy, and Law in Genealogy This subject can get sticky as you pursue your family tree. When you find crime, illegitimacy, and surprise ancestors, you are faced with some interesting choices.

Part II: Using the Internet for Genealogy

Chapter 4: Genealogy Education This chapter covers the online and offline ways to improve your level of genealogy expertise. From simple self-guided tours to formal accreditation, you can pursue genealogy education in many ways.

Chapter 5: Revving Up Search Engines   This chapter will show you how to effectively use any search engine, from Bing to Google to Yahoo!, to find general and specific topics, such as online genealogy pages about a surname or where a state's wills are recorded.

Chapter 6: Talk to Me: Twitter, Skype, IM, and Google   Real-time communication on the Internet, smart phones, and virtual worlds have really changed how genealogists connect to each other.

Chapter 7: Fun with E-mail: Mail Lists, Newsletters, and More   Worldwide, continual discussions on any topic you can imagine is one more resource. And, of course, an electronic query can be your best tool online!

Chapter 8: Social Networking   Professional and hobbyist genealogists alike are using social networking tools to share and educate throughout the Internet. You can, too!

Chapter 9: Blogging Your Genealogy: Sites, Software, and More   The perfect recipe for cousin bait is a lively, fact-filled blog. Here's how to use it to further your research into your ancestry!

Chapter 10: DNA Genealogy   The latest tool in the genealogy box is using mtDNA, YDNA, and autosomal DNA tests to find living and past relatives.

Part III: The Nitty-Gritty: Places to Find Names, Dates, and Places

Chapter 11: Vital Records and Historical Documents   This chapter explores how and where to get those important government documents and certificates.

Chapter 12: The Church of Jesus Christ of Latter-day Saints: FamilySearch.org   The Mormon Church has one of the best online databases and library card catalogs on the Web. Learning to use it can save you a lot of time and effort!

Chapter 13: Ellis Island Online: The American Family Immigration History Center   Forty percent of Americans have an ancestor who passed through Ellis Island. This chapter explores how to find out if yours is one of them and the best tools to use for the search. (Hint: They aren't on the official Ellis Island site!) Learning to use Ellis Island will also help you find ships' lists for other ports.

Chapter 14: Online Library Card Catalogs and Services   This is not your grandmother's library with paper cards in a physical catalog. You can search and use databases from your library or at home; libraries truly are information centers now.

Chapter 15: International Genealogy Resources   All our families come from somewhere. In the United States, when you get "back to the boat," you need to know how to search in the "old country."

Chapter 16: Ethnic Genealogy Resources   As you've seen in this Introduction, certain ethnic groups present special challenges in family history, but online resources can help you overcome them.

Chapter 17: The National Genealogical Society   This chapter explores one American resource that has education, data, networking, and more. Learning about the NGS can also help you understand how local genealogical societies work.

Chapter 18: Ancestry.com and RootsWeb   The oldest online genealogy community, RootsWeb, is part of the largest commercial genealogy company, Ancestry.com. This company also runs Genealogy.com, MyFamily.com, and other sites full of resources for the family historian. This chapter will look at what is free, what is cheap, and what is expensive.

Chapter 19: Genealogical Publishing Houses and Their Sites   This chapter will show you the companies that publish genealogies and how you can do it yourself!

Chapter 20: A Potpourri of Genealogy   A whirlwind tour of sites that you'll want to visit, use, and maybe bookmark!

Part IV: Appendixes

Appendix A: Genealogical Standards from the National Genealogical Society

Appendix B: How to Hire a Professional Genealogist

Glossary

Part I

The Basics

Chapter 1

Beginning a Genealogy Project

An old Chinese saying goes, "A journey of a thousand miles begins with a single step." To paraphrase the Chinese, a journey of a thousand names begins with a single one: yours. If you are just starting your genealogy, with or without the Internet, the process is simple, if endlessly fascinating. This chapter will help you understand that process.

Organize from the Beginning

Friends often call to ask me, "Okay, I want to start my genealogy. What do I do?" The process of genealogy has these basic steps: Look at what you already know, record it, decide what you need to know next, research and query to track that information, analyze the new data, and then do it all again.

Experienced genealogists are more than willing to help the beginner. Longtime online genealogist Pat Richley-Erickson, also known as DearMYRTLE, has a lot of great advice on her site, www.dearmyrtle.com. Here are what she feels are the important points for the beginner: Just take it one step at a time, and devise your own filing system.

Don't let the experts overwhelm you. Use the Family History Library's Research Outline for the state/county where your ancestors came from. They can get you quickly oriented to what's available and what has survived that might help you out.

Don't invent your own genealogy program. Instead, choose one of the commercially available ones. Only use a GEDCOM-compatible software program, because it is the generic way of storing genealogy data. This way, you can import and export to other researchers with common ancestors in the future.

That's the "what" to do, and soon we'll look at that more closely.

"How" to do it includes these two basic principles: document and back up.

From the start, keep track of what you found, where you found it, and when. Even if it's as mundane as "My birth certificate, in the fireproof box, in my closet, 2014," record your data and sources. Sometimes, genealogists forget to do that and find themselves retracing their steps like a hiker lost in the woods. Backing up your work regularly is as important as recording your sources. Both of these topics will be covered in more detail in this chapter.

Your System

Software choices are covered in Chapter 2, where you will see how modern genealogy programs help you to do this. However, remember the good old index card (see Figure 1-1)? These can be useful to record data you find in a library, a friend's book, or even an interview with older relatives until you can get back to your computer.

The handwritten index card also serves as a backup, which brings us to the second most important thing: Back up your data. For most of this book, I assume you are using a computer program to record and analyze your data, but even if you are sticking to good old paper, typewriter, and pencils, as my fourth cousin Jeanne Hand Henry, CG, does, back that up with photocopies. Back up your computerized data in some way: external hard drive, flash drives, or online storage sites (see the following box) are all options, but you must back up. Grace happens, but so does other stuff, like hurricanes, wildfires, and hard drive crashes.

Many genealogists believe that using a good genealogy program with a feature to record sources is the way to go. Paper sources can be scanned into digital form for these programs. (You can also store paper documents in good old-fashioned filing cabinets.) Remember

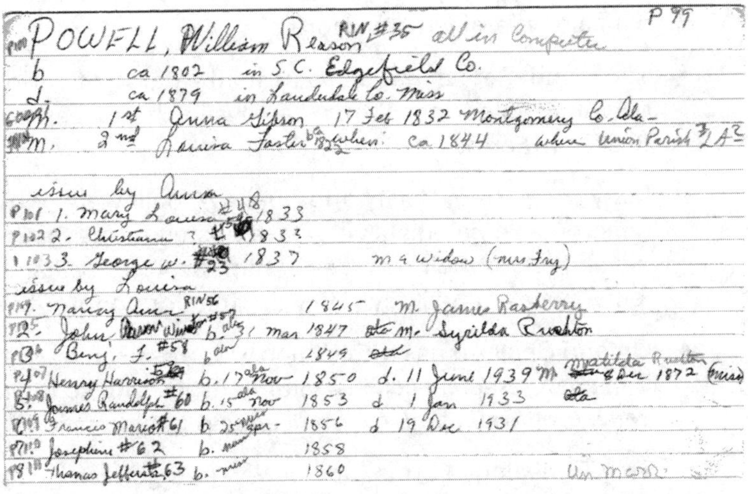

FIGURE 1-1.   *A sample index card with page numbers indicated for the data collected. The name of the book is written on the back.*

to keep a record of all your research findings, even those pieces of information that seem unrelated to your family lines. Some day that data may indeed prove pertinent to your family, or you may be able to pass it on to someone else. Even if you decide to do the bulk of your research on a computer, you might still need some paper forms to keep your research organized. The following box lists some websites where you can find forms to use as you research censuses and other records so that you can document your findings and sources. There's more about documentation later in this chapter.

A Baker's Dozen of Free Forms

You can find free, downloadable forms to record and track your research. Here are just a few places:

- Ancestry.com has Portable Document Format (PDF) files of useful forms, such as a family group sheet, research calendar and research extract summary. Check out http://www .ancestry.com/save/charts/ancchart.htm.

- You can find several good forms at the Midwest Genealogy Center site, including some that can help you research old United States census records: http://www.mymcpl.org/ genealogy/family-history-forms.

- The FamilySearch page has a small catalog of various downloadable forms: https://familysearch.org/learn/wiki/en/ Research_Forms.

- Mary (Hagstrom) Bailey and Duane A. Bailey are two generous genealogists who have posted forms they developed for their own use at http://www.cs.williams .edu/~bailey/genealogy/. They are free for nonprofit use.

- Ontario GenWeb has a collection of forms useful for recording Canadian research: census, vital statistics, and so on, at http:// www.rootsweb.com/~canon/needhelp-genforms.html.

- Free-Genealogy-Forms (http://www.free-genealogy-forms .com/) has forms to help you record data from North America and the United Kingdom.

- Lynne Johnston Westra has gathered a few useful forms at http://www.rootsweb.org/~ilfrankl/resources/forms.htm. For example, you'll find PDF files of family group sheets and a census summary chart to help you trace a family through several censuses.

- Search for Ancestors (http://www.searchforancestors.com/) has a set of tools you can use online, such as a cousin calculator and a way to generate a virtual time capsule for any given year and place.

- Microsoft Office Online (http://office.microsoft.com/en-us/ results.aspx?qu=genealogy&ex=2) has several templates for Word and Excel, including a family history book template for sharing your results.

- *Family Tree Magazine* has a page of forms in text and PDF formats for note-taking, checklists, and more (http://www .familytreemagazine.com/freeforms).

- For researching in the United Kingdom, go to http://www .genealogy-links.co.uk/html/freebies.html for a list of free forms, tools and more.

Good Practices

To begin your genealogy, begin with yourself. Collect the information that you know for certain about yourself, your spouse, and your children. The data you want are birth, marriage, graduation, and other major life milestones. The documentation would ideally be the original certificates; such documents are considered primary sources. Photographs with the people in them identified and the date on the back can also be valuable.

Such documents are considered primary sources because they reflect data recorded close to the time and place of an event.

> **Note** ⎯⎯⎯⎯⎯⎯⎯⎯⎯⎯⎯⎯⎯⎯⎯⎯⎯⎯⎯⎯⎯⎯
>
> A primary source is an original piece of information that documents an event: a death certificate, a birth certificate, a marriage license, etc. A secondary source is a source that may cite an original source, but is not the source itself: a newspaper obituary or birth notice, a printed genealogy, a website genealogy, etc.

Pick a Line

The next step is to pick a surname to pursue. As soon as you have a system for storing and comparing your research findings, you are ready to begin gathering data on that surname. A good place to begin is interviewing family members—parents, aunts, uncles, cousins, and in-laws. Ask them for stories, names, dates, and places of the people they knew. Ask whether some box in the attic or basement might have a file of old documents: deeds, marriage licenses, naturalization papers, family bibles, and so on. A good question to ask at this point is whether any genealogy of the family has been published. Understand that such a work is still a secondary source, not a primary source. If published sources have good documentation included, you might find them a great help.

Visit a Family History Center (FHC) and the FamilySearch site (www.familysearch.org), which has indexes to The Church of Jesus Christ of Latter-day Saints family History Library and access to the new FamilySearch site. This site has data uploaded by members of the church, as well as other genealogists, and extractions of original records, such as marriages, births, deaths, and census records. In Figure 1-2 is my grandparents' marriage license as an example.

Adventures in Genealogy

Family legend can be a good starting place, but don't accept what you hear at face value. I will give you an example from my own experience.

When my husband and I were dating, his family's stories fascinated me. One is that his mother is descended from Patrick Henry's sister, who settled in Kentucky soon after the Revolutionary War. Her Logsdon line was also said to be descended from a Revolutionary War hero. T. W. Crowe, Mark's paternal grandfather, said his grandmother was full-blooded Cherokee.

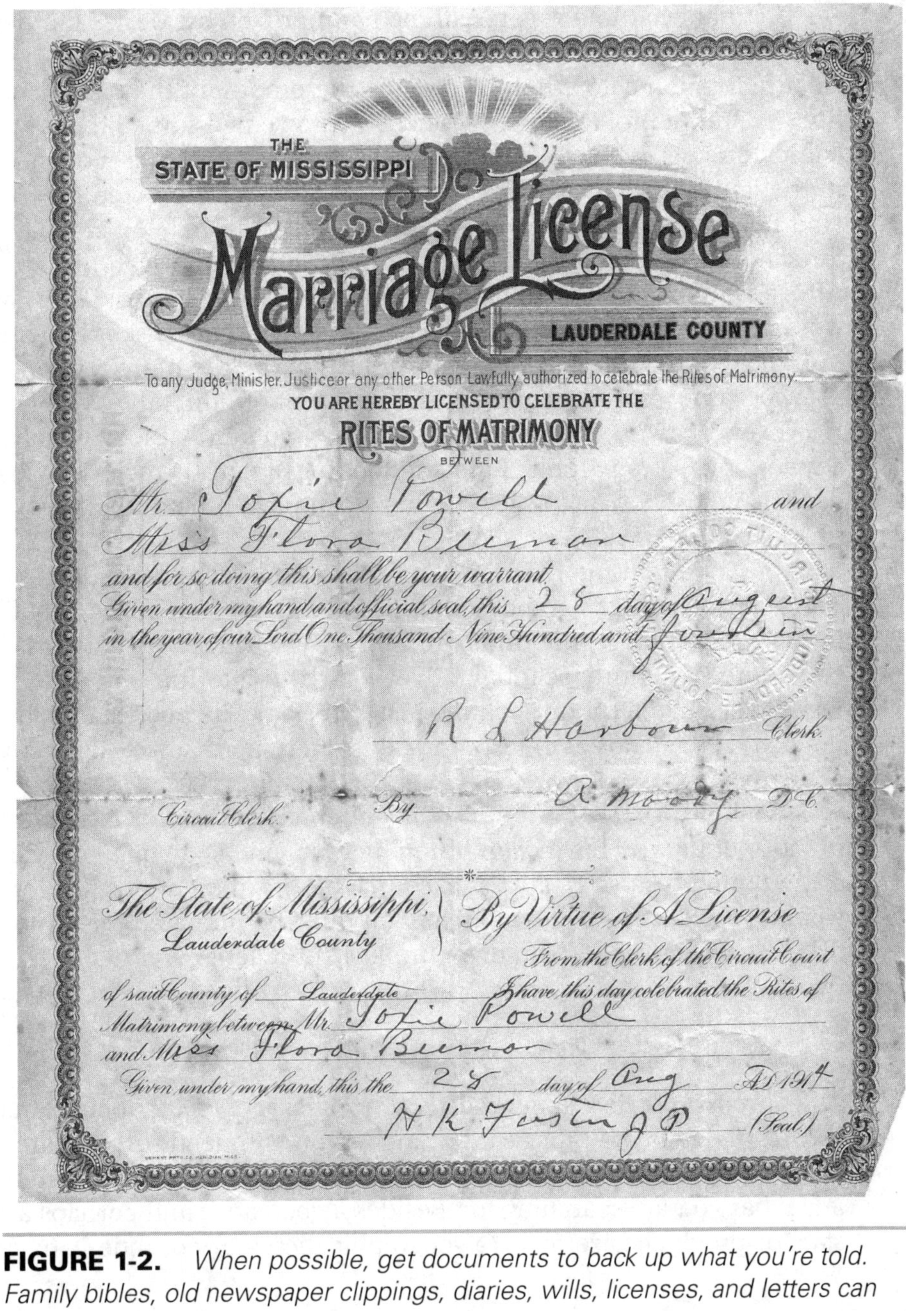

THE STATE OF MISSISSIPPI
Marriage License
LAUDERDALE COUNTY

To any Judge, Minister, Justice or any other Person Lawfully authorized to celebrate the Rites of Matrimony.

YOU ARE HEREBY LICENSED TO CELEBRATE THE
RITES OF MATRIMONY
BETWEEN

Mr. Topie Powell and
Miss Flora Beeman
and for so doing this shall be your warrant.
Given under my hand and official seal, this 28 day of August
in the year of our Lord One Thousand Nine Hundred and fourteen

R L Harbour Clerk.

Circuit Clerk. By A. Moody D.C.

The State of Mississippi, Lauderdale County } By Virtue of A License
From the Clerk of the Circuit Court
of said County of Lauderdale I have this day celebrated the Rites of
Matrimony between Mr. Topie Powell
and Miss Flora Beeman
Given under my hand, this the 28 day of Aug AD 1914
H K Foster J P (Seal.)

FIGURE 1-2. *When possible, get documents to back up what you're told. Family bibles, old newspaper clippings, diaries, wills, licenses, and letters can help here.*

The maternal line was researched and proven by Mark's mother as part of the Daughters of the American Revolution project. Documentation galore helped provide the proof. But the paternal line was more problematic. While T. W. Crowe had some physical characteristics of Native Americans, as does my husband, no one in the family had documents to help me prove the connection. Had I been able to prove it, our children might have been eligible for scholarships and special education in Native American history. After we married and had children, I asked T. W. for the details that would qualify our children for this, but he would not discuss it with me. Indeed, the more I pressed for information, the more reticent T. W. became, and he died in 1994 without my finding the evidence. However, I have kept searching. Using the old family bible, which has a record of T. W.'s parents, I am still looking at census records, wills, deeds, and other data to see whether I can prove one of them was of Cherokee descent.

A relative told me that T. W., in effect, had been testing me: The Native American grandmother was something not talked about in his generation or the one before his. By telling me what was considered a "family scandal," T. W. was trying to find out if I would be scared off from dating his grandson. The poor man had no idea he had chosen to test me with something that would get my genealogy groove on!

Which brings up this point: While all family history is fascinating to those of us who have been bitten by that genealogy bug, to others, some family history is, at best, a source of mixed emotions and, at worst, a source of shame and fear. You must be prepared for some disagreeable surprises and even unpleasant reactions.

References to Have at Hand

As you post queries, send and receive messages, read documents online, and look at library card catalogs, you will need some reference books at your fingertips to help you understand what you have found and what you are searching for. Besides a good atlas and perhaps a few state or province gazetteers (a geographic dictionary or index), having the following books at hand will save you a lot of time in your pursuit of family history:

- **The Handy Book for Genealogists** *United States of America* (9th Edition) by George B. Everton, editor (Everton Publishers, 1999). Pat Richley-Erickson, aka DearMYRTLE, says she uses this reference book about 20 times a week. This book has information such as when counties were formed; what court had jurisdiction where and when; listings of genealogical archives, libraries, societies, and publications; dates for each available census index; and more.

- **The Source** *A Guidebook of American Genealogy* by Sandra H. Luebking (editor) and Loretto D. Szucs (Ancestry Publishing, 2006) or *The Researcher's Guide to American Genealogy* by Val D. Greenwood (Genealogical Publishing Company, 2000). These are comprehensive, how-to genealogy books. Greenwood's is a little more accessible to the amateur, whereas Luebking's is aimed at the professional certified genealogist, but still has invaluable information on family history research.

- **Cite Your Sources** *A Manual for Documenting Family Histories and Genealogical Records* by Richard S. Lackey (University Press of Mississippi, 1986) or *Evidence! Citation & Analysis for the Family Historian* by Elizabeth Shown Mills (Genealogical Publishing Company, 1997). These books help you document what you found, where you found it, and why you believe it. The two books approach the subject differently: The first is more amateur-friendly, whereas the second is more professional in approach.

Analyze and Repeat

When you find facts that seem to fit your genealogy, you must analyze them, as noted in the section "How to Judge," later in this chapter. When you are satisfied that you have a good fit, record the information and start the process again.

Success Story: A Beginner Tries the Shotgun Approach

My mother shared some old obituaries with me that intrigued me enough to send me on a search for my family's roots. I started at the ROOTSWEB site with a metasearch, and then I sent e-mails to anyone who had posted the name I was pursuing in the state of origin cited in the obituary. This constituted over 50 messages—a real shotgun approach. I received countless replies indicating there was no family connection. Then, one day, I got a response from a man who turned out to be my mother's cousin. He had been researching his family line for the last two years. He sent me census and marriage records, even a will from 1843 that gave new direction to my search.

In pursuing information on my father, whom my mother divorced when I was two months old (I never saw him again), I was able to identify his parents' names from an SS 5 (Social Security) application and, subsequently, track down state census listings containing not only their birth dates, but also the birth dates of their parents—all of which has aided me invaluably in the search for my family's roots. Having been researching only a short while, I have found the online genealogy community to be very helpful and more than willing to share information with newbies like myself. The amount of information online has blown me away.

—Sue Crumpton

Know Your Terms

As soon as you find information, you are going to come across terms and acronyms that will make you scratch your head. Sure, it's easy to figure out what a deed is, but what's a cadastre? What do DSP and LDS mean? Is a yeoman a sailor or a farmer?

A cadastre is a survey, a map, or some other public record showing ownership and value of land for tax purposes. DSP is an abbreviation for a phrase that means "died without children." LDS is shorthand for the Church of Jesus Christ of Latter-day Saints, or the Mormons. And finally, a yeoman can designate a farmer, an attendant/guard, or a clerk in the Navy, depending on the time and place. Most of this is second nature to people who have done genealogy for more than a couple of years, but beginners often find themselves completely baffled. And then there are the calendars—Julian, Gregorian, and French Revolutionary—which means that some records have double dates, or a single date that means something different from what you think it should.

No, wait—don't run screaming into the street! Just try to get a handle on the jargon. I have included a glossary at the end of this book with many expressions.

Sources and Proof

Most serious genealogists who discuss online sources want to know if they can "trust" what they find on the Internet. For example, the original *Mayflower* passenger list has been scanned in at Caleb Johnson's site, www.mayflowerhistory.com. Would you consider this a primary source? A secondary source? Or simply a good clue? This is a decision you must make for yourself as you start climbing that family tree.

Some genealogists get annoyed with those who publish their genealogy data on the Internet without citing each source in detail. Once, when I was teaching a class on how to publish genealogy on the Internet at a conference, a respected genealogist took me to task over dinner. "Webpages without supporting documentation are lies!" she insisted. "You're telling people to publish lies, because if it's not proven by genealogical standards, it might not be true!"

And in 2012, many online genealogists were very concerned with the difference between evidence and proof. Websites, books, and long discussions raged across the Web about definitions and methodologies and techniques to the point almost of obsession.

Here, dear reader, I have to admit I have a more relaxed attitude. You do have to read carefully, you do have to get as close as possible to the original record, and you do have to realize that information posted by someone on the Web may well be inaccurate. However, I do not think the information on the Web is any more or less accurate than information in your library in physical form. And you can't let being careful get in the way of the sheer joy of finding a clue, an answer, or a fourth cousin you never knew about before.

Please be aware that many respected professional genealogists disagree with me. I say this as a hobbyist, as someone who simply enjoys the research process and the puzzle solving involved with genealogy. I am not someone trying to impress anyone with my family history, and no important issue hangs on whether I have managed to handle the documents myself. If I wanted to register with the College of Arms or inherit a fortune from some estate, then the original documents would be absolutely necessary. If I just want to know what my great-grandfather did for a living, reading a census taker's handwriting on the Internet will do. And it must be said, secondary sources are much easier to find than primary sources. The main value of these secondary sources on the Internet is in the clues as to where and when primary sources were created. Simply reading that a source such as a diary, a will, or a tax document exists can be a breakthrough.

Some primary materials are online, however. People and institutions are scanning and transcribing original documents onto the Internet, such as the Library of Virginia and the National Park Service. Volunteers are indexing census records and marriage records at https://familysearch.org/indexing/. You can also find online a growing treasure trove of indexes of public vital records and scanned images of Government Land Office land patents (www.glorecords .blm.gov—see in Figure 1-3).

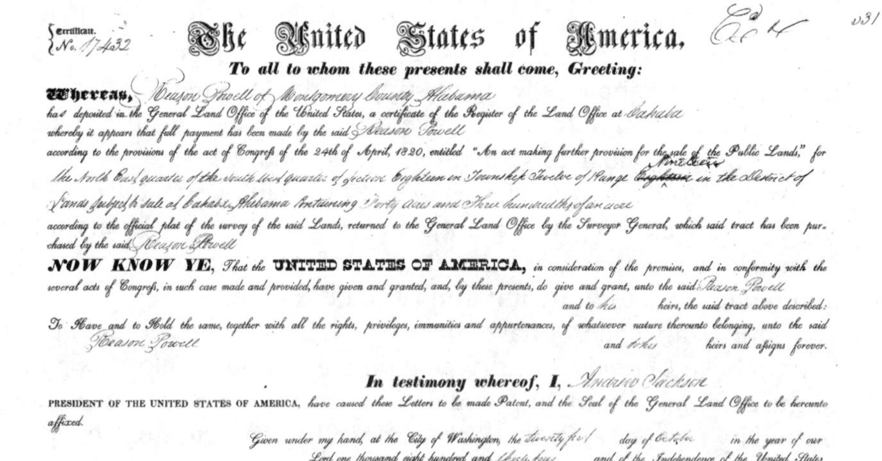
Certificate. No. 17432

The United States of America,

To all to whom these presents shall come, Greeting:

Whereas, Reason Powell of Montgomery County Alabama has deposited in the General Land Office of the United States, a certificate of the Register of the Land Office at Cahaba whereby it appears that full payment has been made by the said Reason Powell according to the provisions of the act of Congress of the 24th of April, 1820, entitled "An act making further provision for the sale of the Public Lands," for the North East quarter of the South West quarter of Section Eighteen in Township Twelve of Range Nineteen in the District of Lands subject to sale at Cahaba Alabama containing Forty acres and Three hundredths of an acre according to the official plat of the survey of the said Lands, returned to the General Land Office by the Surveyor General, which said tract has been purchased by the said Reason Powell

NOW KNOW YE, That the UNITED STATES OF AMERICA, in consideration of the premises, and in conformity with the several acts of Congress, in such case made and provided, have given and granted, and, by these presents, do give and grant, unto the said Reason Powell and to his heirs, the said tract above described: To Have and to Hold the same, together with all the rights, privileges, immunities and appurtenances, of whatsoever nature thereunto belonging, unto the said Reason Powell and to his heirs and assigns forever.

In testimony whereof, I, Andrew Jackson, PRESIDENT OF THE UNITED STATES OF AMERICA, have caused these Letters to be made Patent, and the Seal of the General Land Office to be hereunto affixed.

Given under my hand, at the City of Washington, the twenty first day of October in the year of our Lord one thousand eight hundred and thirty four and of the Independence of the United States the Fifty Ninth

Andrew Jackson,

By the President: By A. J. Donelson Sec'y.

Elijah Hayward Commissioner of the General Land Office.

FIGURE 1-3. *You can view original land grants, such as this one for my ancestor Reason Powell, and order certified copies online. This sort of original record is invaluable in family history research.*

The online genealogist can find scanned images of census records at both the U.S. Census Bureau site (www.census.gov) and volunteer projects, such as the USGenWeb Digital Census Project (www .rootsweb.com/census/).

Therefore, I still believe in publishing and exchanging data over the Internet as long as you remember to analyze what you find and make reasonable conclusions, not fanciful assumptions.

How to Judge

Be aware that just because something is on a computer, this doesn't make it infallible. Garbage in, garbage out has always been the immutable law of computing. The criteria for the evaluation of resources on the Web must be the same criteria you would use for any other source of information. With this in mind, ask yourself the following questions when evaluating an online genealogy site.

Who Created It?

You can find all kinds of resources on the Internet—from libraries, research institutions, and organizations such as the National Genealogical Society (NGS), to government and university resources. Sources such as these give you more confidence in their data than, say, resources from a hobbyist, or even information from an online query. Publications and software companies also publish genealogical information, but you must read the site carefully to determine whether they've actually researched this information or simply posted whatever their customers threw at them. Finally, you can find tons of "family traditions" online. And although traditions usually have a grain of truth to them, at the same time, they are usually not unvarnished.

How Long Ago Was It Created?

The more often a webpage is updated, the better you can feel about the data it holds. Of course, a page listing the census for a certain county in 1850 needn't be updated every week, but a pedigree put online should be updated as the author finds more data.

Where Does the Information
Come From?

If the page in question doesn't give any sources, you'll want to contact the page author to acquire the necessary information. If sources do exist, of course, you must decide if you can trust them.

In What Form Is the Information?

A simple GEDCOM published as a webpage can be useful for the beginner, but ideally, you want an index to any genealogical resource, regardless of form. If a site has no search function, no table of contents, or no document map (a graphic leading you to different parts of the site), it is much less useful than it could be.

How Well Does the Author Use
and Define Genealogical Terms?

Does the author clearly know the difference between a yeoman farmer and a yeoman sailor? Does the author seem to be knowledgeable about genealogy? Another problem with online pages is whether the author understands the problems of dates—both badly recorded dates and the 1752 calendar change. There are sites to help you with calendar problems.

Does the Information Make Sense
Compared to What You Already Know?

If you have documentary evidence that contradicts what you see on a webpage, treat it as you would a mistake in a printed genealogy or magazine: Tell the author about your data and see whether the two versions can be reconciled. This sort of exchange, after all, is what online genealogy is all about! For example, many online genealogies have a mistake about one of my ancestors because they didn't stop to analyze the data and made erroneous assumptions.

In Figure 1-4, you can see a transcription of the 1850 Census of Lake County, Indiana.

The column labeled HN is for household numbered in order of visitation; the column labeled FN is for families numbered in order of

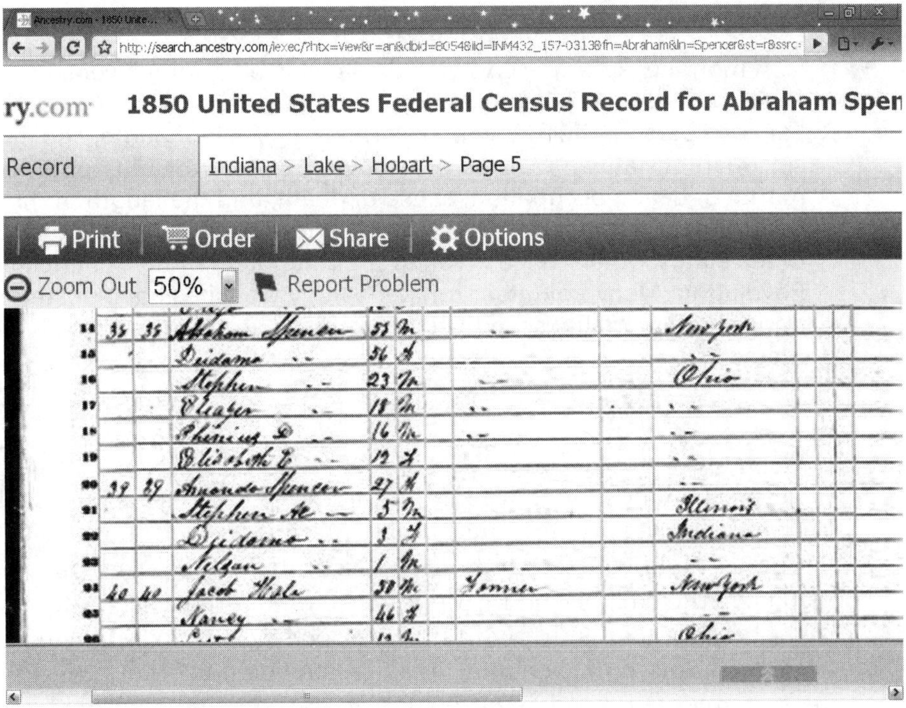

FIGURE 1-4. *Census records sometimes need careful study and interpretation.*

visitation. You can see Abraham Spencer (age 58) and his wife Diadama (age 56; her name is misspelled on the census form) have children Stephen through Elisabeth, and underneath are Amanda, age 27, and then three children under the age of 5. Some genealogies I have found on the Web assume that Amanda and the following children are also offspring of Abraham and Diadama, but if you look at the ages and how the families are listed—with Amanda and the younger children under the youngest of Abraham and Diadama's children—you see this doesn't make sense. On the other hand, if you were to look at the mortality schedule for the county for that year, you would see that Orsemus Spencer (Amanda's husband and Abraham's son) died in February before the census taker arrived in October. Amanda and her children moved in with her in-laws after her husband's death. The three youngest ones are part of the household, but they aren't Abraham Spencer's children; they are his grandchildren.

Note

A mortality schedule contains data collected during a census about those who died before June in the year of the census. For each person, the following information is listed: name, age, sex, marital status if married or widowed, state or country of birth, month of death, occupation, cause of death, and the length of the final illness. In 1918 and 1919, many of these records were returned to the states; others were given to the Daughters of the American Revolution. Many volunteer-run genealogy websites have posted transcribed mortality schedules for counties around the United States.

With this in mind, becoming familiar with the National Genealogical Society's Standards for Sharing Information with Others, as shown in Appendix A, would help. Judge what you find on the Internet by these standards. Hold yourself to them as you exchange information, and help keep the data on the Internet as accurate as possible. After you have these standards firmly in mind, a good system to help you track what you know, how you know it, and what you don't know, as well as the surnames you need, is simply a matter of searching for the facts regarding each individual as you go along.

Sources That Can Help a Genealogical Researcher

- **Vital records**   Birth, death, and marriage records can sometimes be found on state government sites. However, many states did not require these before the twentieth century.

- **Court records**   Wills, adoptions, land and property bills of sale, tax rolls, deeds, naturalization, and even lawsuits.

- **Church records**   Baptisms, marriages, burials, etc.

- **Newspapers and magazines**   Not only obituaries, marriage, and birth notices, but also social news; perhaps parents, siblings, or cousins are mentioned.

- **Military records**   Enlistment, commission, muster rolls, and veterans' documentation.

- **Fraternal organizations**   Organizations such as the Elks, Knights of Columnbus and college fraternities and sororities can be helpful.

- **Ships' passenger lists**   Not only for immigrants to your country, but also for travel within. Also, some rivers, such as the Tennessee, were the site of many pioneer marriages.

- **Family History Centers**   These have resources such as the International Genealogical Index, Ancestral File, and Old Parochial Register.

- **State archives and libraries**   Many of these are online!

- **Census records**   Not only federal, but also local and state.

- **Published genealogies**   Most local libraries have at least a few genealogies in their reference section.

- **Relatives**   This includes aunts, uncles, cousins, grandparents, and folks who knew them before you were born.

Standards of Genealogical Research

Genealogy is a hobby for most of us, and we do it for fun. The average genealogist is not doing this for fame and fortune, but because of an insatiable curiosity about the people who came before us. Given that, this little section may seem a bit too serious, even "taking all the fun out of it." Still, I believe that if you approach this hobby with the right attitude and care, it will be more rewarding than if you just dive in without giving a thought to the best practices and ethics. Despite the fact that there are no official "rules" to this when you are a hobbyist, following guidelines and standards can, in the end, make your experience easier and more enjoyable.

As mentioned previously, in the appendixes to this book you will find the latest standards and guidelines from the National Genealogical Society (www.ngsgenealogy.org), and I suggest you study them. Though you can (and should) take many excellent courses in genealogy, if you review and understand these documents first, you will be better prepared to proceed on your family history quest in the best manner.

Briefly, the NGS standards and guidelines emphasize these points:

- Do not assume too much from any piece of information.

- Know the differences between primary and secondary sources.

- Keep careful records.

- Give credit to all sources and other researchers when appropriate.

- Treat original records and their repositories with respect.

- Treat other researchers, the objects of your research, and especially living relatives with respect.

- Avail yourself of all the training, periodicals, literature, and organizations you can afford in time and money. Joining the NGS is a good first step!

- And finally, mentor other researchers as you learn more yourself.

Another good outline to the best way to practice genealogy is the Board for Certification of Genealogists Code of Ethics and Conduct on their website at www.bcgcertification.org/aboutbcg/code.html. This is also a guide to choosing a professional, should you decide to get some help on your genealogy along the way!

How to Write a Query

Genealogy is a popular hobby, and lots of people have been pursuing it for a long time. When you realize that, it makes sense to first see whether someone else has found what you need and is willing to share it. Your best tool for this is the query.

A query, in genealogy terms, is a request for data, or at least for a clue where to find data on a specific person. Queries may be sent to one person in a letter or in an e-mail to the whole world (in effect). You can also send queries to an online site, a magazine, a mailing list, or another forum that reaches many people at once.

Writing a good query is not hard, but you do have to use certain rules for it to be effective. Make the query short and to the point. Don't try to solve all your genealogical puzzles in one query; zero in on one task at a time.

You must always list at least one name, at least one date or time period, and at least one location to go with the name. Do not bother sending a query that does not have all three of these elements, because no one will be able to help you without a name, a date, and a place. If you are not certain about one of the elements, follow it with a question mark in parentheses, and be clear about what you know for sure as opposed to what you are trying to prove.

Here are some style points to keep in mind:

- Use all capital letters to spell every surname, including the maiden name and previous married names of female ancestors.

- Include all known relatives' names—children, siblings, and so on.

- Use complete names, including any middle names, if known.

- Proofread all the names.

- Give complete dates whenever possible. Follow the format DD Month YYYY, as in 20 May 1865. If the date is uncertain, use "before" or "about" as appropriate, such as "Born c. 1792" or "Died before October 1850."

- Proofread all the dates for typos; this is where transpositions can really get you!

- Give town, county, and state (or province) for North American locations; town, parish (if known), and county for United Kingdom locations; and so on. In other words, start with the specific and go to the general, including all divisions possible.

- If you are posting your query to a message board, it is helpful to include the name, the date, and, if possible, migration route using > to show the family's progress.

- Finally, include how you wish to be contacted. For a letter query or one sent to a print magazine, you will want to include your full mailing address. For online queries, you want to include at least an e-mail address or your user name on that site.

Note

Do not ever send a letter or query that says, "Send me everything you have on the Jones family" or words to that effect. This is not a game of Go Fish. It is rude and unfair to ask for someone to just hand over years of research. When you ask for information, have some data to exchange and a specific genealogy goal to fill. Also, always offer to pay copying and/or postage costs.

Here's a sample query for online publication:

```
Query: Crippen, 1794, CT>MA>VT>Canada
I need proof of the parents of Diadama CRIPPEN born 11 Sept
1794 in (?), NY. I believe her father was Darius CRIPPEN, son
of Samuel CRIPPEN, and her mother was Abigail STEVENS CRIPPEN,
daughter of Roger STEVENS, both from CT. They lived in Egremont,
Berkshire County, MA and Pittsfield, Rutland County, VT before
moving to Bastard Township, Ontario, Canada. I will exchange
information and copying costs. [Here you would put your regular
mail address, e-mail address, or other contact information.]
```

As you can see, this query is aimed at one specific goal: the parents of Diadama. The spelling matches the death notice that gave the date of birth—a secondary source—but because it is close to the actual event, it's acceptable to post this with the caveat "I believe." It has one date, several names, several places, and because this one is going online, a migration trail in the subject line (CT > MA > VT > Canada). If the author knew Diadama's siblings for certain, they would be in there, too. When you have posted queries, especially on discussion boards and other online venues, check back frequently for answers. If the site has a way to alert you by e-mail when your posting gets an answer, be sure to use it. Also, read the queries from whatever source you have chosen to use, and search query sites for your surnames. As you can see from the example, queries themselves can be excellent clues to family history data!

Documentation

Document everything you find. When you enter data into your system, enter where and when you found it. Like backups of your work, this will save you countless hours in the long run.

A true story: At the beginning of her genealogy research in the late 1960s, my mother came across a volume of biographies for a town in Kansas. This sort of book was common in the 1800s. Everyone who was "someone" in a small town would contribute toward a book of history of the town. Contributors were included in the book, sometimes with a picture, and the biography would be a timeline of their lives up to the publication of the book, emphasizing when the family moved to town and their importance to the local economy. One of these biographies was of a man named Spencer and included a picture of him. He looked much like her own grandfather, but the date was clearly too early to be him. Still, she photocopied it, just in case. However, she didn't photocopy the title page or make a note of where she had seen the book, which library, which town, and so forth.

Fast-forward 15 years to the early 1980s. At this point, my mother is in possession of much more data, and in organizing things, came across the photocopy. Sure enough, that biography she had found years before is of her grandfather's grandfather; she had come across enough primary sources (birth certificates, church records, and so on) to know this. And now, she knew this secondary source had valuable information about that man's early life, who his parents were, and who his in-laws were. However, all she had was the page, with no idea of how to find the book again to document it as a source! It took days to reconstruct her research and make a guess as to which library had it. She finally did find it again and documented the source, but it was quite tedious. Just taking an extra two minutes, years before, would have saved a lot of time!

Backup

Back up your data. I'm going to repeat that in this book as often as I say, "Document your sources." Documentation and backup are essential. On these two principles hang all your effort and investment in genealogy. Hurricanes happen. Fire and earthquakes do, too. Software and hard drives fail for mysterious reasons. To have years of work gone with the wind is not a good feeling.

If you are sticking to a paper system, make photocopies and keep them offsite—perhaps at your cousin's house or a rental storage unit. More and more people are using "the cloud" or online backup—that is, using someone else's computer to hold your data files.

Online storage services are a convenient way to store offsite backup copies of critical information. Some services that are free until you reach some level of use are XDrive, box.net, Mozy, DropBoks, iBackup, eSnips, MediaMax, OmniDrive, openomy, and more. If you need more than the basic free space, they all offer additional storage, costing from $5 to $30 a month, depending on how much room you need. Several of these services will let you make some files available to other people while keeping other files secret and secure. Although all of them will work with both Macintosh and PC computers, some of them are picky about the web browser you use. Experiment with several of these services and find the one with the right fit for you. Then use it often!

Publishing Your Findings

Sooner or later, you're going to want to share what you've found, perhaps by publishing it on the Internet. To do this, you need space on a server of some sort. Fortunately, your choices here are wide.

Most Internet service providers (ISPs) allot some disk space on their servers for their users. Check with your ISP to see how much you have. Many other sites offer a small amount of web publishing space for free, as long as you allow them to display an ad on the visitor's screen. Just put "Free Web Space" in any search engine and you will come up with a current list.

Some software programs will put your genealogy database on the software publishers' website, where it can be searched by others. Some websites, such as WorldConnect, let you post the GEDCOM of your data for searching in database form instead of in Hypertext Markup Language (HTML). Finally, genealogy-specific sites, such as ROOTSWEB and MyFamily.com, offer free space for noncommercial use in HTML format.

Some of the programs, however, don't give you a choice of where you post your data. Some will post your data on a proprietary site. Once there, your data becomes part of the company's database, which may be sold later. Simply by posting your data on the site, you give them permission to do this. There is quite a bit of discussion and debate about this privatization of publicly available data. Some say this will be the end of amateur genealogy, whereas others feel this is a way to preserve data that might be lost to disaster or neglect. It's up to you whether you want to post to a site that reuses your data for its own profit.

In short, publishing on the Internet is doable, as well as enjoyable, but you have to do it thoughtfully. By publishing at least some of your genealogy on the Internet, you can help others looking for the same lines. But don't get carried away—you want to publish data only on deceased people, or publish only enough data to encourage people to write you with their own data and exchange sources. Don't publish data on living people.

Success Story: Finding Cousins Across the Ocean

After ten years of getting my genealogy into a computer, I finally got the nerve to "browse the Web," and to this day I don't know how I got there, where I was, or how to get back there—but I landed on a website for French genealogists. I can neither read nor speak French. I bravely wrote a query in English: "I don't read or speak French, but I am looking for living cousins descended from my ancestors ORDENER." I included a short "tree" with some dates and my e-mail address. Well, within a couple of hours, I heard from an ORDENER cousin living in Paris, France. She did not know she had kin in America and had spent years hunting in genealogy and cemetery records for her great-great-grandfather's siblings! She had no idea they had come to America in the 1700s and settled in Texas before it was a state of the Union. So, while I traded her hundreds of names of our American family, she gave me her research back to about 1570 France when the name was ORTNER! About four months later, another French cousin found me from that query on the Web. He did not know his cousin in Paris, so I was able to "introduce" him via e-mail. One of them has already come to Florida to meet us! What keeps me going? Well, when I reach a brick wall in one family, I turn to another surname. Looking for living cousins is a little more successful than looking for ancestors, but you have to find the ancestors to know how to go "down the line" to the living distant cousins! Genealogy is somewhat like a giant crossword puzzle— each time you solve a name, you have at least two more to hunt! You never run out of avenues of adventure—ever!

—Patijé Weber Mills Styers

Caveats

In discussing how to begin your genealogy project, we must consider the pitfalls. This chapter has touched briefly on your part in ethics and etiquette, and future chapters will expand on that. We must also consider the ethics of others, however, and be careful.

In the twenty-first century, genealogy is an industry. Entire companies are centered on family history research and resources. Not surprisingly, you will find people willing to take your money and give you little or nothing in return in genealogy, just as in any industry. Many of them started long before online genealogy became popular, and they simply followed when genealogists went online. "Halberts of Ohio" is one notorious example, a company that sold names from a phone book as "genealogy."

Don't believe anyone who wants to sell you a coat of arms or a crest for your surname. These are assigned to specific individuals, not general surnames. (Although a crest may be assigned to an entire clan in Ireland—the crest is the part above the shield.) A right to arms can only be established by registering a pedigree in the official records of the College of Arms. This pedigree must show direct male line descent from an ancestor who was granted a letter patent. You can also, under the right circumstances, apply through the College of Arms for a grant of arms for yourself. Grants are made to corporations as well as to individuals. For more details, go the college's site: www .college-of-arms.gov.uk.

Always check a company's name and sales pitch against sites that list common genealogy scams. For example, Cyndi Howells keeps on top of myths, lies, and scams in genealogy and has a good set of links to consumer protection sites, should you fall prey to one of them. Cyndi's List Myths, Hoaxes, and Scams page is at www.cyndislist.com/myths. Kimberly Powell's How to Identify & Avoid Genealogical Scams page (http://genealogy.about.com/od/basics/tp/scams.htm) gives a good set of steps to follow too.

If you feel you have been scammed, report it to the Federal Trade Commission (FTC) at www.ftccomplaintassistant.gov/.

Wrapping Up

- Record your data faithfully. Back it up faithfully. These two things will save you a world of grief some day.

- To begin your genealogy project, start with yourself and your immediate family, documenting what you know. Look for records for the next generation back by writing for vital records, searching for online records, posting queries, and researching in libraries and courthouses. Gather the information with documentation on where, when, and how you found it. Organize what you have, and look for what's needed next. Repeat the cycle.

- Beware of scams!

Chapter 2

Software You'll Need

O nline genealogy is simply using new tools to do the same research that always has been required of genealogists. To accomplish online genealogy research, instead of using a photocopier, you might save an image of the document or a searchable Portable Document Format (PDF) file from your scanner. Instead of sending queries in an envelope, you send them by e-mail, post them on forums, or make it your Facebook status. Instead of reading a magazine article on paper, you can read it on your tablet computer. And instead of (or before!) going to the library or courthouse for a document, you can search the card catalog and even the text of whole books from home. In other words, you are doing the same tasks with additional tools.

Please understand—I don't mean to imply that you won't ever do things the old-fashioned way again. Of course, you will! But you'll use these online techniques much more frequently. Often, before you set out to research the traditional way, you will use some online tools to lay the groundwork.

Look Ma, No Wires!

You'll need to learn about the Internet, software, and techniques for online information exchange to get the most out of the experience. This chapter covers such considerations and the software you might want to use. Of course, it is assumed you have a computer with some connection to the Internet. High-speed connections are best, as so many genealogy resources are now available as online images that take up a lot of bandwidth. Some people use a slow home Internet connection just for checking e-mail and surf the Web at a local library to take advantage of a high-speed connection. The disadvantages to that are obvious: In such a setup, you can only work on your genealogy when the library is open, and you certainly can't work in your pajamas at the library, which is part of the fun of online genealogy!

Still, there will be days when you do go to the library, and then a laptop or tablet with wireless capabilities can be useful. For example, at the Family History Library in Salt Lake City (and many other libraries), you can now use your laptop computer, smart phone (such as a BlackBerry or iPhone), or tablet (such as an iPad or Nexus) with Wi-Fi wireless networking to check your e-mail, visit genealogy sites, or otherwise surf the Web. You can do all this without connecting any network cables; the wireless networking card in your device will connect via low-power radio waves to the building's network.

This benefits you and the library in several ways. Often, you will find all of a library's computers reserved on a busy day, but you can pull out your laptop and use that instead when the library has Wi-Fi network capabilities. The library saves money because it does not need to purchase so many computers, and they don't have to worry about possible viruses and malware if you have the right protection software on your computer. And, in many local libraries, the card catalog is all online; with a laptop and Wi-Fi, you can search for the book you need, find out if it is on the shelf, and sometimes check out the e-reader version of it for two weeks!

An all-in-one printer with scanning, fax, and printing capabilities could be useful when asking for vital records from a courthouse miles away, so you may still use your phone line for some genealogy chores. A good color inkjet printer, especially an all-in-one that can scan and copy, can help you preserve images of your original documents and primary sources. And there are other choices in hardware.

Back Up Your Data

Hard drives fail or meet with natural disasters. Sometimes, files will not be transferred properly when you get a new computer. And then there are times when your whole area loses power for days at a time, leaving you with no access to your data. When bad things happen to good computers, backups are the only hope. And bad things always happen.

Most people don't use a CD burner to back up data any more. The old writable CD-ROMs proved to have problems with stability and over the years became unreadable. Most people now use "the cloud" for their backup, although an external hard drive is the second most popular choice. Please note that they are not mutually exclusive choices: I use both.

"The cloud" is a slang term for using someone else's hardware to hold your most important files—images, documents, and sound files of your oral history interviews, for example. Several good cloud storage sites such as Google Drive, Dropbox, and iCloud are free for up to anywhere from 10 to 20GB, and they all claim to have security features in place to protect your data from prying eyes, hackers, and

(*Continued*)

disasters. On all of the free cloud backup sites, you can pay a yearly fee for more than the minimum storage. You simply sign up for an account on these cloud drives, and the software for that service can be set to do the backup automatically at set time intervals.

Note

On Microsoft Office, now the programs as well as the files themselves are on the cloud. Your computer becomes a dumb terminal running the software that resides on a gigantic mainframe, which also holds the results of your work, be it documents or data. This is just like the old days back in the 1980s, when I first started using computers.

You can also consider it a cloud backup when you upload your data into any of the dozens of online genealogy tree sites, from WikiTree to FamilySearch to Ancestry.com. On any online genealogy site like this, you can also later download your data as a GEDCOM. When you use a site like this for your backup, it, of course, makes your data accessible to others, which can be a good thing. However, if you are not sure enough of your data at the moment to put it out there for all the world to see, or if you prefer to pick and choose who gets to use your research, then storing the backup as a GEDCOM on the previously mentioned cloud drives may be your preference.

Another way to back up your genealogy data is an external hard drive that mirrors your computer's hard drive. The one I use came with software that will perform a backup automatically every day, week, month, or any other time frame I choose. The software will copy certain folders, file for file, if I want; back up only certain files with extensions such as .ged, .docx, or .xls; or can even make a compressed file of everything, software and all, if I choose that option. An external hard drive has the advantage of being portable. Should you take a trip to the Family History Library in Salt Lake City, for example, you can back up just your genealogy data file and take it with you. You can get a terabyte backup drive for under $100 at this writing, and that is a very small price to pay for peace of mind.

So no matter how you do it, back up!

> **Note**
>
> Have you backed up today? This week? This month?

Software

Once you have your hardware in place and you know how you're going to connect, you need to look at your software. Many Internet service providers (ISPs) include software as part of the package: the communications software, browser, file transfer program (FTP), e-mail, and other programs you need. The programs you use to access the Web are often called browsers or clients. These programs send commands to other computers, called servers, instructing them to display files and information to you or to run programs for you. The resulting display might be e-mail, a webpage, or a GEDCOM you want to study.

Which Browser Should I Use?

I'm often asked, "Which is the best browser?" In my opinion, this is like asking, "Which is the best car?" It all depends on your taste, habits, and needs. The current leaders in the browser wars are still Microsoft Internet Explorer and Netscape's progeny, Mozilla Firefox. Apple's Safari is catching up, however.

Entire books are devoted to helping you get the most out of Internet Explorer. The major online services and ISPs have lined up with one or the other for their customers to use and install automatically with their software, so you don't have to do any extra work to use it. Internet Explorer is free, and you get it (whether you like it or not) when you buy a Windows system. It works well with Outlook, Microsoft's calendar, contacts, and e-mail program.

Firefox is free, has a nice user interface, and is easy to use. It now has a companion e-mail program called Thunderbird. Some sites, you will find, do not look as "clean" in Firefox as they do in Internet Explorer, especially if the site was created with a Microsoft product.

Google's Chrome browser, which is free, is designed to integrate with Google's products such as e-mail, calendar, document storage, photo storage, and, of course, web search. Tabs and windows work much the same way.

Apple's Safari is the default browser for iPhone, iTouch, and Macintosh. Safari's presentation is much like that of Firefox and Chrome. The status bar and menu bar are hidden by default; you have to click the relevant options to show them. You can make toolbar changes and customizations by clicking the gear icon— another similarity to Chrome. Safari boasts fast performance, a simple user interface, easy bookmarks, pop-up blocking, inline find, tabbed browsing, automatic form filling, built-in RSS (Really Simple Syndication), resizable text fields, private browsing, and security.

If you have disability issues, such as macular degeneration or arthritis, there are browsers that magnify the type on a webpage, read the words aloud to you, accept spoken rather than typed commands, and more. Check out www.e-bility.com/links/software.php for a list of pointers to information and some demonstration versions of alternative browsing methods.

Ninite

Whenever you are downloading a general-purpose program such as a browser, a graphics editor, or a media player, it is a good idea to use http://ninite.com. This page (see Figure 2 -1) is simplicity itself, and a great time saver.

Often, if you download a program from the originator site or an aggregator site, it will come with extra little programs that track you, clog your computer's memory, and put extra toolbars on your browser. Not all of these are malicious in intent, but their presence will slow your browsing speed and add "spyware" to send information to advertisers and marketers.

On the other hand, Ninite will construct a custom installer with only the programs you need—no spyware, adware, or toolbars added. You go http://ninite.com, choose exactly the ones you want, and then download the installer, which will be called Ninite.exe. You simply click the Ninite.exe file and it installs the clean apps, in default locations, in the latest version. You can keep that Ninite.exe on your desktop and run it occasionally to get the latest versions because it will skip up-to-date apps and only download ones that need to change.

Another advantage: It will skip any reboot requests from installers, use your proxy settings from Internet Explorer, and verify digital signatures or hashes before running anything, so the install is not only clean and virus free, it is really fast.

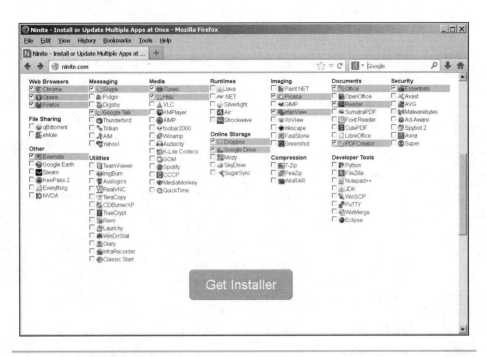

FIGURE 2-1.   *The Ninite site will give you quick, clean, and reliable downloads of browsers, media players and more.*

My advice is to test-drive a few different browsers and see which one suits you best if you don't like the one that comes with your ISP.

Genealogy Programs

Your most important software will be your genealogy program, which is basically a database program for recording, maintaining, and sharing your data. In shopping around for the right genealogy program for you, consider these factors:

- First and foremost, check the program's ability to record your sources. If it doesn't have a way for you to track where and when you found a fact, reject it out of hand. You'll wind up retracing your steps a thousand times without the ability to instantly retrieve the sources you've already used.

- Second in importance, but only slightly second, is the appearance. This may seem trivial, but it's not. Most genealogy programs have some sort of metaphor: When you open the program, the screen looks as if you are working on a scrapbook, 3 × 5 cards, or a genealogical chart. Finding one that presents the data in a way that suits your methods is important.

- Third, consider how you output your data. Don't use anything that can't output to GEDCOM, which is the standard for all programs. A GEDCOM is a text-only file with the data formatted so that any other program can use it. This is important for comparing your research to others', but that's not the only output form for your work. For hard-copy output, think about what you want to create. The output can be simply data; whole books with pictures; or wall charts, a website, iron-on transfers, or even a giant mural for the next reunion. Look for a program that fits your output needs.

Note

Importing and exporting data between programs is often problematic, despite the standard of GEDCOM 5.5. Each software engineer implements that standard slightly differently. For that reason, backing up your data just before importing any other GEDCOM file is critically important!

- Fourth, look at the software package's support, and ask friends what their experience was when they needed support. Read the manual to see how much support is included with the purchase price and for how long. Understand that within a year, the software (any software) will be upgraded. Find out whether upgrades are free or available for a minimal charge. A really good program may cost from $25 to $50 a year to keep it current; some shareware gives you upgrades for $5 or less. Also, ask at the next meeting of your local genealogy club whether anyone has the program you are interested in and is willing to help you with the learning curve.

- Which brings us to the final consideration: the cost. When you find the program you want, can you afford it? If not, see whether the program comes in different versions—some less powerful but also less expensive than others. Sometimes, the cost includes CD-ROMs of secondary or primary material, but perhaps some of this material is available at your local library and you need not buy it.

An important development in the world of genealogy software since the last edition of this book is that Personal Ancestral File (PAF) is no more. As of July 2013, the popular and newbie-friendly program was discontinued by the Church of Jesus Christ of Latter-day Saints (LDS), both in download and support. For several years up to that, as the online FamilySearch became more sophisticated, the software team at FamilySearch focused on building relationships with partner software companies to meet the needs of the twenty-first-century family historian. When most of those products both integrated with FamilySearch and have free versions, after a good, long run, PAF was retired.

The following sections provide a quick roundup of some popular programs that you can at least try for free, and these particular ones will sync your data with one or more online sites such as FamilySearch and Ancestry.com.

RootsMagic 6

This $30 program has worldwide fans: It has a function to create CDs to share with your family, to run the software and data directly from a portable flash drive, and to integrate a feature called WebSearch to help you pursue your genealogy online, especially with FamilySearch.

RootsMagic has five main views, plus a sidebar for easier navigation. You switch between the views by clicking the tab for the view you want. You can navigate using either the mouse or arrow keys. Double-clicking a person's name brings up the data entry screen for that person. You can even open multiple databases side by side.

The RootsMagic edit screen lets you add an unlimited number of facts for every person (such as birth, death, marriage, occupation, religion, description, etc). The edit screen is shown in Figure 2-2. If you want to add a fact type that isn't in RootsMagic's predefined list, you create your own fact types. RootsMagic also allows notes

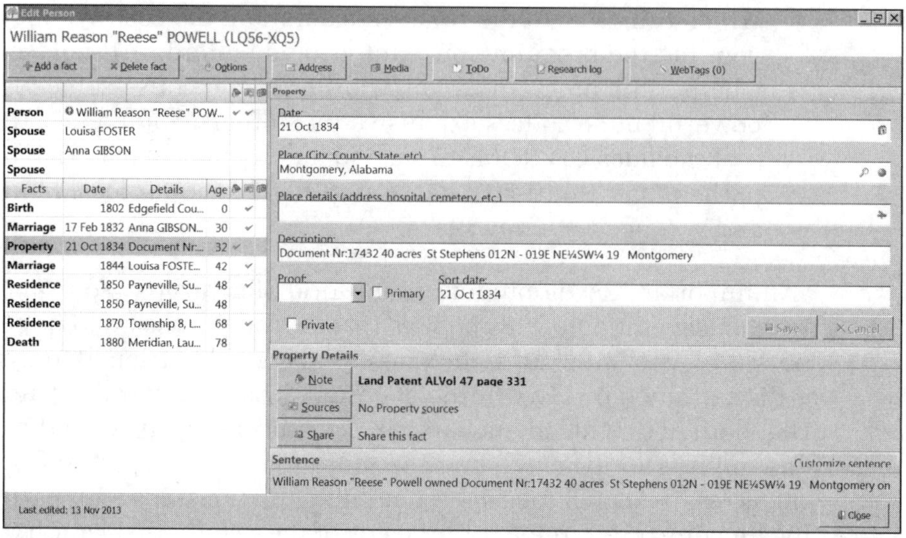

FIGURE 2-2.   *RootsMagic's edit screen lets you see facts about one person and include sources and proof.*

and unlimited source citations for every fact, and you can attach more than one person to a source and more than one source to a fact. You can add, edit, delete, merge, and print the sources of your information.

Every piece of information on a person is available from the main screen: name, parent and spouse info, personal and family facts, DNA test results, alternate names, or LDS information. You can directly access the notes, sources, media, and more for every item.

Output format includes pedigree charts, family group sheets, four types of box charts, six styles of books, 27 different lists, mailing labels, calendars, hourglass trees, graphical timelines, relationship charts, letter-writing templates, individual summaries, five types of photo charts, and seven types of blank charts. Your database can be output into a pedigree chart with Hypertext Markup Language (HTML) links among the individuals in the genealogy.

If you import a GEDCOM and find it has some mistakes, you can correct them, but it can be tricky.

For example: I imported a GEDCOM with my grandmother's family, BEEMAN. In my grandmother's generation, some of her siblings were duplicated because of nicknames. This fix was easy: Simply click the merge sign in the toolbar, bring up both entries, and merge them into one.

But further back, there was a more complicated problem. My great-great-grandfather James Ivy Beeman had what today would be called a melded family: After the Civil War, he was widowed with two children. He married a woman named Sarah or Savannah Cross who was widowed with two children. This resulted in a mistake in which the two Cross children, John Wesley Cross, Jr. and Ransom Patrick Cross, were listed as the sons of James Ivy Beeman. Adding to the confusion is that John Wesley Cross, Sr., the father of these two, was not yet in the database. Then, Sarah and James Ivy had several children of their own.

The fix: First, click each of the children, then click Edit, and then click Unlink. Then add the person who is their father, John Wesley Cross, Sr. Then add the two children as his and Sarah's. Simple!

I also like that when certain the family was correct, I was able to share the good data to FamilySearch with one click of the tree icon in the toolbar. Very handy!

Family Tree Maker

Family Tree Maker (www.familytreemaker.com) is Ancestry.com's product now, and it is closely integrated with the website. You can use Ancestry.com and Family Tree Maker together to get the most out of both by importing your family tree and attached images from the website to the program or vice versa. From the Family Tree Maker program, you can search Ancestry.com and merge what you find into your tree. It also uses the Ancestry.com hints feature to suggest records that might match your data. I included this program in this brief list because Ancestry.com is so important to online genealogy, but this is the one program that does not have a try-before-you-buy policy as of this writing. You have to buy it to try it, which puts it at a real disadvantage in my mind; however, you probably can find a genealogy buddy or library that has a copy of the program you can test-drive.

You can scan documents and photographs and then organize your photos, document images, and other graphics into slideshows, books, and other formats as well (such as sound and movies). The source function has standard source templates to help you save the right information about a source and rate each source on how useful you found it.

Once you have your data in, you can view relationships within the context of your entire family tree, with timelines and interactive maps highlighting events and places in the lives of your family.

The user interface lets you quickly switch between important features and import data from any program that can produce a GEDCOM. It has tools for merging duplicate individuals, calculating dates, creating to-do lists, and more. It retails for $39.95 and requires at least Windows XP or Vista to run.

The Master Genealogist

The Master Genealogist (TMG) (www.whollygenes.com) does everything the previously mentioned programs will do, but more—it helps you organize your search. Cheryl Rothwell, who writes three genealogy blogs, said, "I have used TMG since before it was officially released. I don't know how to do everything and I never will. There are some features I will just never need. But it is flexible enough to do what you want the way you want." A screen shot is in Figure 2-3.

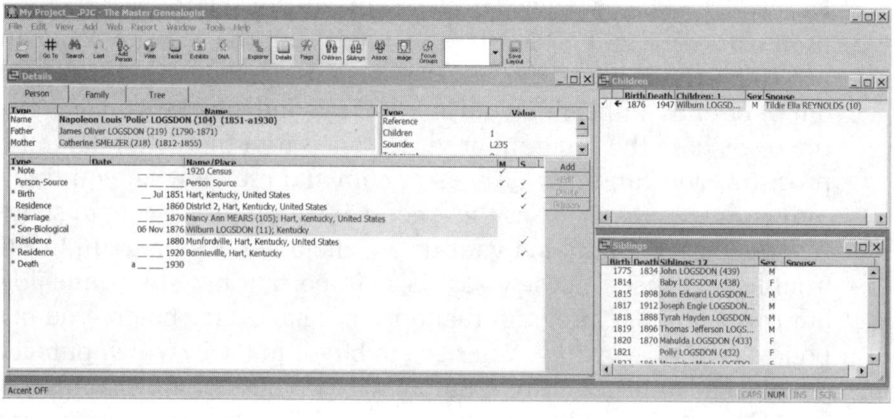

FIGURE 2-3. *The Master Genealogist is the favorite of many long-time genealogists.*

You can tie many more facts and historical context to your ancestors with TMG, as it is affectionately known, as well as output in almost any format you like. Mind you, it has a learning curve, and the program is written with professional genealogical standards in mind. That should not deter you, however. It comes with a tutorial and has much more flexibility than its easy-to-use competitors. It is designed to let the novice get started quickly and grow into the more advanced features. Wizards, "cue cards," data-entry templates, ditto keys, macros, and other features make TMG easy to learn and use.

It is this flexibility that makes people feel that TMG is worth the effort to use. The program allows for an unlimited number of people, events per person, names per person, relationships, user-defined events, freeform text, photographs, citations, and repositories. You control the data. It also has features to help you track what you need to find and a to-do list of genealogy chores.

Referencing source data is TMG's strongest point for the serious genealogist. Each entry provides space for documenting an unlimited number of citations, including a rating scale for their reliability, which is an important point. Newspaper articles, family bibles, and interviews with your relatives all have different reliability, which can be recorded with TMG.

For $40 for the Silver edition and $80 for the Gold, TMG is a popular program with experts in family history.

Heredis

Available for desktops, tablets, and smart phones, Heredis is fully revamped for 2014, and it is impressive. Very popular in Europe, it has versions for Mac, Windows, iPad, and iPhone. At about $50, it is a feature-full program with a great user interface. You can download a trial version at http://heredis.com.

What I like most about Heredis are the different views of a family. The Immediate Family tab displays all the members of the immediate family (parents, spouses, children, grandparents). One click, and you access the quick entry screen to add members (see Figure 2-4).

New to this version is the Melded Family view: siblings, remarriage, stepchildren, stepbrothers and stepsisters, children from other unions of the different spouses, noting whether or not when they belong to the direct lineage. This makes situations such as I described earlier much clearer.

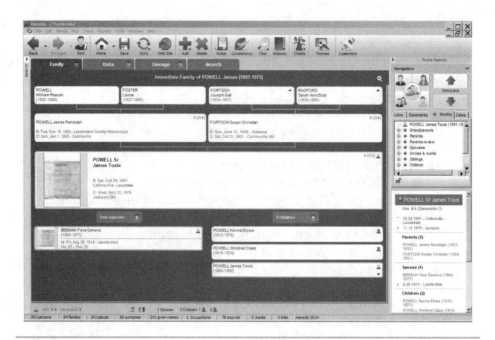

FIGURE 2-4. *Heredis has an Immediate Family tab that makes it easy to enter and modify data.*

The Migrations Map is fascinating: Taking the location data, it displays a family's movements on an interactive map, with numbered pins that display dates and events on mouse-over.

The Search Assistant shows the progress of the life a person, displays known or missing information, and highlights certain unexplored tracks. At a glance, you will know if a date or place is missing and what associated source, witnesses, media, or notes go with an event.

Finally, with this version, Heredis has launched an online presence to upload and backup your data, much along the lines of FamilySearch. You can search the trees uploaded there when you register for a free membership.

Consider the Surface Scratched

The short list presented thus far merely scratches the surface of available genealogy programs by presenting those that are arguably the most popular. For more options, consider these that are certified to work with the new LDS FamilySearch site:

- Ancestral Quest

- FamilyInsight

- Gaia Family Tree

- Get My Ancestors

- Legacy Family Tree 8

- MagiKey Family Tree

- Ordinance Tracker

Also, go to Cyndi's List (www.cyndislist.com/software.htm) and poke around a few websites. Go to local meetings of your genealogy club and ask for recommendations. Finally, use a search engine to find matches for "genealogy software" and your computer. Download some trial versions and check them out. Then you'll be ready to choose.

Smart Phones and Tablets

Handheld web-enabled devices, netbook computers, and cell phones with e-mail access are becoming the standard. They all can offer you convenience when traveling, but cost will be a big factor. Sometimes, you might have issues with connectivity, depending on your data plan, and for those with far-sightedness, those tiny screens can be hard to see. Still, you might find some of these useful.

Tablets

Tablet computers have thoroughly replaced the old personal digital assistants of old. From Asus to Google to Apple, every company you ever heard of, and several you have not, now have taken over the small digital world.

- **GedStar** for Android and iPad phones and tablets. The Windows version takes your data from Master Genealogist, Family Tree, RootsMagic or a GEDCOM and puts it on your smaller device or on an SD card to be inserted into your phone or tablet computer. This app has a nice interface. This program also lets you browse a GEDCOM (see the Glossary) and could be useful for trips to the library.

- **FamilyBee** for Android was favorably reviewed by Dick Eastman. It stores your data on an SD card, which your desktop computer can probably also read.

- **Ancestry.com**, **FamilySearch.com**, **MyHeritage.com**, and **Genealogy.com** all have a smart phone app as well as a tablet app. Genedroid is the app for Geni.com.

- **BillionGraves** is an app for tombstone/cemetery transcription projects. Take a picture, upload it to the website, and help preserve cemetery data.

Additional Programs

There are other programs that are not, strictly speaking, genealogy programs. These include databases, journaling programs, and other, more mundane software, such as word-processing programs, that can be used to make your quest for family history easier. You may want to consider any combination of these.

Add-On Programs

A subset of genealogy programs work with your main database program such as Legacy or RootsMagic. Some help you search, some help you organize, some help you notate. Some to consider are

- **Catch** is an app for keeping a diary of your research and posting it to the cloud with tags. It can be used for text, sound, and images, which all can be shared or protected by password as you choose.

- **Evernote** can be used much as Catch, with the added ability to save the picture of a piece of paper as a searchable PDF document. Think of it as photocopying to your computer. With Evernote, you can upload to the cloud or keep it only on your device. If you search for "using Evernote for genealogy," you will come up with several good articles on that topic by leading genealogists. The key is to use tags, not "notebooks," to organize your gleanings. Evernote has a free version and a paid version with more storage space on the cloud.

- **Clooz** is a $40 program to consolidate, index, analyze, and report document and image data. This Windows desktop program can help you gather, analyze, and validate clues and evidence about potential or suspected ancestors. It can export data to Legacy Family Tree software. At clooz.com, you can download a trial version.

- **GenSmarts** (www.gensmarts.com) analyzes the data you have and develops a profile of your ancestors based on where and when they lived. This $25 program uses artificial intelligence to analyze your existing genealogy file and give you research recommendations. GenSmarts reads popular genealogy software file formats directly; no need to create a GEDCOM.

Database CD-ROMs

You'll find that many records have been indexed and transcribed or scanned onto CD-ROMs. Some of these you can access at a local library; some you can order with software or by themselves; some are available from the Family History Centers. Census records available on CD-ROM include the U.S. federal census, various census records from Canada and the UK, Cherokee and African American census records, and a few local censuses. Cemetery records and death records from all over North America and the UK are available on CD-ROMs; so are parish records. Check out www.cyndislist.com/cd-roms.htm#Vendors for sources of these CD-ROMs.

Word-Processing Programs

Don't overlook the lowly word processor as one of your genealogy tools. You can use it for journaling your genealogy quest, creating custom write-ups of your results, and even creating a book. You can use a word processor to create and track your to-do lists, write letters for vital records, and more.

As with your genealogy program, you need a word processor that can handle all of your chores, yet isn't more trouble to use than it's worth.

Maps

Sooner or later in tracing your genealogy, you're going to need maps, and not just your handy 2014 road atlas. The boundary lines of cities, counties, states, and even countries have changed over the years; Kentucky used to be part of Virginia after all! A dictionary or index of place names is called a gazetteer. As I mentioned in Chapter 1, a hard copy is a handy thing to have, but you can use software and Internet versions, too.

E-mail

Reading mail is the biggest part of online life. Some of the best information, and even friendships, come through e-mail. Personally, I prefer to have all my e-mail in the cloud, and for that I use Gmail. But if you want to use Outlook, Thunderbird, or Eudora, they are all fine choices. Whichever way you go, use the features they all have to make your life easier.

Filters

A filter is an action you want the mail program to take when a message matches certain conditions. It can have your e-mail program reply to, copy, move, or destroy a message based on such things as the sender, the subject line, or the words found in the text. You can have the e-mail program do all that before you read your mail, or even before the e-mail is downloaded from the mail server. When you start getting involved in active mail lists, you'll want to sort your mail by geography, surname, and time period, at least. Most e-mail programs and sites also come with built-in detectors for the unsolicited advertising e-mail and scams that circulate regularly.

Audio Resources

The Internet has become a broadcast medium, and shows originating thousands of miles from you can stream right down to your computer over the Internet. To listen, you need a good media player, whether it is Microsoft's Windows Media Player, RealAudio, iTunes, or some other program. Most such programs have a free version and are usually easy to set up and use.

Viruses and Worms

No journey is without risk. Whenever you enter the wilds of cyberspace, that dreaded microorganism, the computer virus, might be lurking about. Not only that, but your activities could attract Trojan horses and worms, too, so keep a sharp eye out.

A virus is a program hidden on a disk or within a file that can damage your data or computer in some way. Some viruses simply display a message or a joke, while others can wipe out all the information you saved to the hard drive. Some simply reside and track your online activity; others hijack your computers' memory to be used by someone elsewhere. Both will really slow your computer down. Therefore, I strongly recommend that you inoculate your computer before using any mode of electronic travel.

AVG Anti-Virus FREE and Ad-Aware Free Antivirus+ shared *PC Magazine*'s Editors' Choice honors for the best free protection you can get.

Note

Even if you have virus-protection software, you need to take precautions. Make a backup of everything that is important to you—data, letters, or e-mails—and resave it no less than once a month. The virus-protection software may offer the ability to make a recovery disk; do so. This can save you much time and trouble later on down the line if your system needs to be restored.

Virus protection is good, but if you opt for a high-speed, continuous connection, such as digital subscriber line (DSL) or cable Internet, you also need a firewall to help protect you from hackers, Trojan horses, and worms. A firewall is a piece of software, hardware, or combination of both that forms an electronic boundary, preventing unauthorized access to a computer or network. It can also be a computer whose sole purpose is to act as a buffer between your main computer and the Internet. A firewall controls what goes out and what comes in according to how the user has it set up.

Examples of firewall programs are ZoneAlarm by Zone Labs, BlackICE Defender from NetworkICE, and Internet Security 2000 by Symantec Corp. A detailed description of how firewalls work can be found on Shields Up, a website devoted to broadband security created by programmer Steve Gibson, head of Gibson Research Corp. (www.grc.com) of Laguna Hills, California. Run the tests. You'll be surprised.

Wrapping Up

- You will probably wind up using both a desktop computer and some smaller device such as a laptop, tablet, or smart phone to run your computer software.

- You will need a good, reliable ISP and Wi-Fi capabilities.

- You will need a browser that can play podcasts, video files, and sound files and display most graphics files.

- A genealogy program that can run on all the devices you have is a good thing.

- Helper programs such as Evernote and Clooz can make research easier.

- Get a reliable, free virus and malware protection program.

- Ninite.com can help you download many of the programs you need with no malware, adware, or other software attached.

- Back. Up. Your. Data.

Chapter 3

Ethics, Privacy, and Law in Genealogy

Genealogy has a long history of legal and ethical concerns: the settling of estates, the eligibility of soccer players for national teams, even who rules a nation. The validation of genealogical information and the publishing of that information, online and otherwise, will also have legal and ethical ramifications. Therefore, ethics, privacy, and copyright are important to consider when you practice your genealogy.

Note

Disclaimer: I am not an attorney, and this chapter is not meant to be legal advice, but merely information.

Say, for example, you find an illegitimate birth, an ethnic surprise, or a convicted criminal in your family history. If the information is only one or two generations back, you perhaps would deal with these facts differently than if the events happened over 100 years ago.

You will have three basic issues to confront in genealogy: accuracy, privacy, and copyright. These issues are just as important in the "real world" as they are online. Happily, it isn't hard to be on the right side of all of these issues!

Note

Keep these three principles in mind:

1. Do not publish vital statistics about living persons because the data can be used in identity theft.
2. Do not use anything you find in a book, a magazine, GEDCOM, or online without proper attribution and permission. Facts are not copyrightable. The presentation and formatting of facts are copyrightable.
3. Be aware that not everyone in the family will be thrilled to see family skeletons published. In fact, you may find that some relatives have emotional reactions to what you find; be prepared.

Privacy

Many professional genealogists agree that simply publishing everything you find is not a good idea. What you find might not be accurate; it may be accurate but damaging; it may be accurate and not damaging, but surprising. Discretion, consideration, and tact can go a long way to avoiding trouble.

Judy G. Russell, JD, CG, CGL

Author of the blog, The Legal Genealogist (www.legalgenealogist.com/blog), Judy G. Russell is a genealogist and attorney. I asked her several questions about the legal and ethical aspects of genealogy.

When you find the family skeleton, what should you do?

"[That] depends on how far back it is in the branches of the family tree," Judy said. "While we are enjoined as ethical genealogists to be 'sensitive to the hurt that revelations of criminal, immoral, bizarre or irresponsible behavior may bring to family members' [quoting from National Genealogical Society, Genealogical Standards], we are also required as family historians to be faithful to the truth."

Judy said that her rule of thumb is that a skeleton in the closet of a living person must remain there, and a skeleton in the closet of a living person's parent(s) may remain there if disclosure will be humiliating or hurtful to the living person.

When someone begins genealogy, what are the privacy concerns?

"The biggest, most compelling concerns are the rights and interests of living people," Judy said. "We all have aspects of our lives that are within our personal zones of privacy, that we don't want spread around on the Internet, shared indiscriminately, or shared at all. A terrible illness, the tragic loss of a child, a misstep with the law—these private struggles are ours alone, to share or keep to ourselves as we choose. Genealogy is not an excuse to invade the privacy of others."

Judy cited the famous "The Right to Privacy" article in the Dec. 15, 1890 *Harvard Law Review* by Samuel Warren and Louis Brandeis, which said in part a right to privacy "implies the right not merely to prevent inaccurate portrayal of private life, but to prevent its being depicted at all." She also cited the Board for Certification of Genealogists, Code of Ethics and Conduct section that says, "I will keep confidential any personal or genealogical information given to me, unless I receive written consent to the contrary."

"Genealogical codes of ethics require us to respect the privacy of other living people at all times in all media, including what we may have thought was a private e-mail to a single individual," she added.

Given that, how much should you share of what you find?

Again referring to the National Genealogical Society, Genealogical Standards: Guidelines for Publishing Web Pages on the Internet, Judy pointed out that publishing your findings on the Web should be done carefully.

"Genealogists must also be careful not to copy or reproduce copyrighted materials and 'share' them on the Internet or elsewhere (even in e-mail). Some small copying may be allowed under the fair use principle, but wholesale copying is a violation of the author's copyright," Judy said. "Beyond those major concerns, I see no reason not to share my research with others, both family members and others. I may choose to delay sharing until an article I'm working on is published, or until after a particular lecture or presentation. But my purpose in doing genealogical research is to further my family history—and I can accomplish that best by working collaboratively with others."

What are some good sites to help a beginner understand copyright, ethics, and privacy in relation to genealogy?

"Hmmm... there's this blog called The Legal Genealogist that deals with a lot of these issues on a regular basis." Judy said. "And I do recommend reading her blog regularly. It is always insightful and interesting."

Judy also made the following recommendations:

- All of the National Genealogical Society standards and guidelines at its website are good resources (http://www.ngsgenealogy.org/cs/ngs_standards_and_guidelines).

- Cyndi's List has a category "Ethics & Etiquette: General Resources" at http://www.cyndislist.com/etiquette/general/.

- Cyndi's List, in the category "Copyright Issues", has a good overview of copyright law for genealogists, with many links to sites around the Web (http://www.cyndislist.com/copyrite .htm/).

- Elizabeth Shown Mills' discussion of the privacy issue at "§2.8. Privacy," in *Evidence Explained: Citing History Sources from Artifacts to Cyberspace* (2nd rev. ed.) (Baltimore, Maryland: Genealogical Publishing Co., 2012).

- International Association of Jewish Genealogical Societies, "Ethics for Jewish Genealogists," at http://www.iajgs.org/ethics.html.

- Kimberly Powell's "Dos and Don'ts of Online Genealogy" at http://www.netplaces.com/onlinegenealogy/putting-it-all-together/dosand-donts-of-online-genealogy.htm.

- The Board for Certification of Genealogists (BCG) Code of Ethics is subscribed to by all credentialed genealogists—CGs and AGs alike—and can be found online at http://www.bcgcertification .org/aboutbcg/code.html.

- U.S. Copyright Office website Circular 1: Copyright Basics can be found at http://www.copyright.gov/circs/circ01.pdf.

What are some legal issues to consider besides copyright?

"Website terms of use and plagiarism are major issues for genealogists above and beyond copyright," Judy said.

For terms of use, Judy said everyone should read Ed Bayley's "The Clicks That Bind: Ways Users 'Agree' to Online Terms of Service" at the Electronic Frontier Foundation. The PDF link is www.eff.org/files/eff-terms-of-service-whitepaper.pdf.

Judy said the best resource on plagiarism ever is Elizabeth Shown Mills' "QuickLesson 15: Plagiarism—Five 'Copywrongs' of Historical Writing," posted at Evidence Explained: Historical Analysis, Citation & Source Usage (http://tinyurl.com/atojr6w).

Can you be sued for finding an illegitimate birth, for example?

"You can't ever be sued for finding a fact in an historical record or through an interview or other investigative methods. Disclosing a fact not publicly known where it is certain to be humiliating to a living person may get you sued for invasion of privacy, but merely finding out that, for example, a birth was out of wedlock isn't actionable," she said.

Do you have an anecdote or success story to tell?

"You mean like the time I accidentally updated my personal website and didn't strip out the private notes section of my database program... and ended up with information on the Web that should never have been there?" Judy said. "It had a happy ending, since one piece of information that made it online ended up bringing a grandfather together with a granddaughter he had never met... but I am much, much more careful now when I update my website."

Gormley's View

"Genealogists are sharing, caring people, and most of us think nothing of handing over all of our genealogical data to distant cousins, even strangers," says Myra Vanderpool Gormley, Certified Genealogist (CG), editor of RootsWeb Review and author of the Ancestry Insider blog. "However, we should start thinking about the ramifications of our actions. The idea of sharing genealogical information is good, and technology has made it easy. However, technology is not exclusively a tool for honest people. If detailed personal information about you and your living relatives is on the Internet, crooks can and do find it, and some scam artist might use it to hoodwink your grandmother into giving out the secrets that will open her bank account. It has happened. If your bank or financial institution still uses your mother's maiden name for a password, change it," Gormley said.

Remember that your living relatives have the same rights to privacy that you do, and among these rights are:

- The right to be free of unreasonable and highly offensive intrusions into one's seclusion, including the right to be free of highly objectionable disclosure of private information in which the public has no legitimate interest

- Use of one's name or likeness by another only by consent

- Not being in false light in the public eye—the right to avoid false attributions of authorship or association

Publishing private genealogical information—and the important word here is *private*—about a living person without consent might involve any or all three aspects of their right to privacy. Publishing is more than just printed material or a traditional book. Publication includes websites, GEDCOMs, message boards, mailing lists, and even family group sheets or material that you might share with others via e-mail or traditional mail. They might be able to seek legal relief through a civil lawsuit. It is okay to collect genealogical information about your living relatives, but do not publish it in any form without written permission, Gormley said.

"We should exercise good manners and respect the privacy of our families—those generous relatives who have shared personal information with us or who shared with a cousin of a cousin," Gormley added. "Additionally, there is another and growing problem—identity theft. Why make it easy for cyberthieves to steal your or a loved one's identity? But, identify theft involves much more than just your name, address, or phone number. This idea that one's name, address, phone number, and vitals fall into the area of privacy laws is a common misconception by many people. In reality, the facts of your existence are a matter of public record in most instances. However, personal information, such as health issues, a child born out of wedlock, spouse abuse, how much money you have in the bank, etc.—those are things that are not general public knowledge, and these are personal things that if you publish them about your living relatives, there could be an invasion of privacy involved (but I'm not a lawyer)," Gormley says.

DearMYRTLE's View

DearMYRTLE (Pat Richley-Erickson) the daily genealogy columnist, says, "Fortunately, I know of only one person who has stated she is unwilling to share her compiled genealogy data and documentation with others because she plans to print a book. I suspect, though, that the individual in question most certainly benefited from previously compiled research in books, websites, and CD databases. It would be impossible to avoid the use of these items as clues leading to the discovery of original documents. For example, one would even have to consider a clerk of the court's marriage indexes as previously compiled research. Such an index is indeed one step removed from the original creation of marriage licenses and marriage returns."

In other words, all the data has been used before, or you would not be able to collect it in the first place. Still, Richley-Erickson said, one must always be sensitive to the feelings of others who might be affected by the data you publish.

Eastman's View

"The concept is simple, although it is far more complicated in execution. In short, ask yourself repeatedly: 'Is there anyone who will mind if I publish this information?' There are legal issues as well with living individuals and with publishing info about people within the past 72 years in the United States, 100 years in Canada and the UK," says Dick Eastman, editor and publisher of one of the most popular genealogy columns online. Eastman's genealogy tips have helped thousands of online genealogists over the last 15 years. His blog, Eastman's Genealogy Newsletter, has been a treasure trove of news and tips for years.

"Protecting the privacy of living individuals and the issue of whether or not to publish sensitive family information (such as a great-great-aunt's child born out of wedlock) are big concerns," Eastman says. "Those can become legal issues if a distant (or not-so-distant) relative takes exception to your publishing such information. Lawsuits have been launched because of these things."

Note

"When you post public messages (on message boards and mailing lists, for example) about your research, it is sufficient to say you are researching a Jones or a Cynthia Jones line. You don't have to reveal relationship by saying she is your mother or maternal grandmother. In the pursuit of our ancestors, let's not inadvertently hurt our living family members or ourselves. Think twice before you post or share any data about the living."
—Myra Vanderpool Gormley, CG

Copyright

A sad fact of Internet life is that some have come to believe that the entire Internet is "public domain"—that is, free for the taking. It just isn't so. Copyright applies equally to online material and offline material. The fact that any material is online changes nothing about its copyright or lack thereof. Copyright laws are not, however, the same all around the world, and that's where online copyright becomes complicated.

As a genealogist, you should educate yourself about copyright laws (not just U.S. copyright laws) and understand what "fair use" of another's work is and what is copyrightable in the first place. A good start is the publication "Copyright Basics" from the Library of Congress, available online at www.copyright.gov/circs/circ1.pdf and in hard copy.

Be aware that if you take copyrightable material without permission, you may be plagiarizing. In most instances, however, genealogists will share some or all of their material with you, if you ask first.

Copyright laws vary by country, but for most countries, the basic premises are the same:

- Facts and data cannot be copyrighted.

- Narration, compilations (that includes a genealogy database), and creative works can be copyrighted.

Some International Copyright Information Sites

- Australian Copyright Council: http://www.copyright.org.au/

- Canadian Intellectual Property site: http://www.cipo.ic.gc.ca/

- European Commission page on copyright: http://ec.europa .eu/internal_market/copyright/index_en.htm

- United Kingdom page on intellectual property: http://www .ipo.gov.uk/home.htm

- World Intellectual Property Organization site: http://www .wipo.int/clea/en/

- Nolo.com: http://www.nolo.com—click the Patents, Copyright & Art tab

Protecting Yourself

The other side of the coin, of course, is to decide how you want to protect yourself from plagiarism. The presentation of facts can be protected by copyright, but not the facts themselves. When you present data in your own distinctive format, such as a book, then that presentation of the material is protected by copyright, even though the facts are not. Still, when you put your work out there, expect others to use it.

Gormley says, "If you do not want to share your genealogical research, that is fine, but you cannot claim copyright to facts, and a great deal of 'online genealogy' is nothing more than compiled facts—although seldom verified or even referenced as to the actual source of the information. If you don't want to be 'ripped off'—and if by that you mean that you do not want others to use genealogical facts you have compiled—then don't share your genealogy with anyone: Put it in a vault."

Note

Just as bad as stealing another's work is posting your data with certain facts changed, such as a date, to "protect" your information. Posting what you know is not to be true does not advance the art and science of genealogy in any way. Don't ever do it.

"I wish I knew!" says Dick Eastman when asked how to protect data you have carefully collected. "There is no foolproof method [to avoid] being ripped off. Of course, you should always add copyright claims. But that only stops the honest people and maybe a few unknowledgeable ones who never thought about copyrights until they read your claim.

"I used to recommend technical solutions: I recommended Adobe Acrobat PDF files. However, a free program appeared that does a great job of converting PDF files back to useable text, so now even that recommendation has been weakened. I do not know of any other way." Eastman says there are no easy answers, only guidelines. "The person who is to publish the information needs to ask himself: 'Am I sure that I have a legal right to use this information?' If you have any doubts, don't publish! However, determining whether or not you do have a legal right to publish a piece of information can become very complex. I spent a lot of time discussing this with a lawyer who works for a Boston legal firm that specializes in intellectual properties issues. She is also an experienced genealogist and a member of the advisory board for a prestigious society. The more she talked, the more confused I became. At the end of our conversation, she said, 'Well, there really is no easy way,'" Eastman concluded.

However, complicated as it is, there are still steps you can take. You can (1) ask for permission to use data when you find it on someone else's site and (2) copyright your own formatting and presentation of that data. Use the above-mentioned "Copyright" section to find out how to do both.

Note

"In a perfect world (online or off) everyone would cite their sources properly and give credit to all who have shared research and information with them. Alas, there is no such place—never has been. Even basic good manners—such as saying 'thank you'—are rare. But the genealogist with good manners is far more likely to be rewarded with a wealth of material and help than those without."
—Myra Vanderpool Gormley, CG

Other Matters

Be prepared for relatives to be sensitive about certain family history, as my husband's grandfather was (see Chapter 1). A long thread on the Ancestry.com ethics discussion board described one researcher's problems in tracing her husband's line. Her in-laws became angry and insulting when asked a simple question about her husband's grandfather. She then researched discreetly, without asking her in-laws any more questions. When she came across a fact that may have been what upset her in-laws, she resolved to keep the data private.

In such a case, you may even want to put the information aside in something to be opened with your will and ask your descendants to add it to the family tree after everyone involved is gone.

Give Back

Finally, it is at least as good to give as to receive, and it is more ethical to give back to the genealogy community than to just take everything you find. Once you have some experience, you should consider contributing to the amount of good, accurate information available online. For example, on www.familysearchindexing.org, you can volunteer to be part of their indexing project. In the first quarter of 2007 alone, volunteers indexed nearly 30 million names by simply reading scanned documents and typing the names and page numbers. This was done by thousands of volunteers, some of whom can only spare one hour a month. But in that hour, you can probably index 50 or so names. Multiply that by the hundreds of thousands of people who use www .familysearch.org, and you can see what an impact that can make!

Similarly, most of the USGenWeb and international GenWeb sites are thrilled to have volunteers help them index and transcribe wills, deeds, letters, tax rolls, or any other primary source you can get your hand on. Again, give an hour a month, and you can be of great help to many other researchers! Check out www.usgenweb.org, drill down to the states and counties for which you have data, and contribute. Join a local historical or genealogical organization, and share your findings with the membership in their publications and online sites.

As an example of giving and receiving good genealogy karma, for years, my mother edited *Le Despencer*, the Spencer Historical and Genealogical Society (www.spencersociety.org/) newsletter, which ran articles such as transcribed original materials from letters and diaries and narratives about ancestors of the members. She indexed each volume herself, too. She learned a lot about our branch of Spencer ancestors, as well as lots of other branches in the process, while disseminating invaluable data.

NGS Standards

In the back of this book, you will find the standards for genealogy published by the National Genealogical Society (NGS). These Genealogical Standards and Guidelines are aimed at making the practice of genealogy clearer, better, and more understandable. While NGS is neither an accrediting nor an enforcement agency and will not keep track of whether you as an individual are following these standards, nevertheless, if you use the Standards and Guidelines in your personal pursuit of family history, then they have served their purpose.

Wrapping Up

- Ethics, privacy, and copyright are the three concerns with genealogy legalities.

- Do not publish anything about living people, on the Web or otherwise. This helps prevent someone from getting a name, birth date, and birth place to create a false identification or to steal an identity. On the other hand, do not try to protect privacy by publishing anything you know to be untrue. To do so will result in bad data becoming part of the Internet forever.

- Be sensitive about publishing information on those who have passed on. You may find it fascinating that your great-great-grandfather was illegitimate and a pirate; perhaps your cousins won't be so enthralled.

- Cite your sources, both to protect intellectual property rights and to leave a wide audit trail for future genealogists.

- Contribute to the collection of good, accurate data on the Internet by becoming involved with indexing, transcribing, and discussing original sources.

- Do your best to follow the standards and guidelines of the National Genealogical Society, and familiarize yourself with the codes of ethics professional genealogists use.

Part II

Using the Internet for Genealogy

Chapter 4

Genealogy Education

A lot of genealogy is learning by doing, but that's no reason to reinvent the wheel. Workshops, seminars, reading, and courses can help you start climbing that family tree efficiently and effectively.

"I always stress education, especially for those who are new to genealogy and think that everything is on the Internet," said Liz Kelley Kerstens, CG, CGL. She is the creator of the software program Clooz—the electronic filing cabinet for genealogical records, is managing editor of *NGS Magazine,* and authored the books *Plymouth's First Century: Innovators and Industry*, a photo history of Plymouth, Michigan; and *Plymouth in Vintage Postcards*, a postcard history of twentieth-century Plymouth. She is the executive director of the Plymouth Historical Museum and retired from the U.S. Marines as a major.

"I'm always telling people about the NGS courses and conferences because it's hard to learn in a vacuum. The courses and conferences fill your head with so many ideas that you have to take something away from them." Kerstens said that she herself, a genealogist of note, is currently pursuing a master's degree in history, pacing her studies around pursuing her own genealogy and work. She recommends the system of melding work, study, and research.

"Even one course can be overwhelming with my life's pace, but I finish them because I made a commitment," she said. "And when I'm taking a course, I try to give it as much attention as I can because, first, I'm paying a lot for graduate tuition, but also, the whole point of taking the courses is to learn. It's so much more fun to learn when you're not worrying about getting a fabulous job or the next promotion. I already have a fabulous job and can't think of anything I'd rather be doing (other than sleeping)!"

Teach Yourself, Be Taught, or Do Both

You have many options when it comes to learning about genealogy, and none are mutually exclusive. You can read books like this one, take college-level courses, read genealogy blogs and RSS (Really Simple Syndication) feeds, or read "how-to" articles on websites. You can learn about one aspect such as wills or land grants, or study to become a Certified Genealogist. You can go to a class or have a class come to you over the Internet. If you decide to go to a class, you can still sign up for it online, usually. Find what suits you best!

Books, magazines, and online articles, such as blogs and RSS feeds, are ways to teach yourself about genealogy. The advantage of this method is that you can choose to learn at your own pace and choose the topics according to your needs at the moment.

However, if you want to learn from someone else, you can find resources for that, too. Online courses allow you to learn at your own pace, create your own experience, and keep the rest of your life going. There are courses that you simply read; in other online courses, you interact with the instructor and/or other students. Sometimes you might attend a class by logging on to a live video broadcast, or "webinar."

This chapter will show you several online courses that are free; others may involve fees, but will also confer education credits of one sort or another.

"Offline" classes, seminars, and conferences are also worthwhile. Amateurs and professionals, beginners and experts, all benefit from them. Most conferences and seminars have tracks for the beginning, intermediate, and advanced levels. Plus, there is an indescribable joy in meeting new friends who share your passion (which many family members may not yet understand!).

Most of the time, if someone else is teaching you, fees are involved—sometimes modest and sometimes more substantial—but if you share travel and lodging with a genealogy buddy, it need not be prohibitively expensive. And often, with a little research, you can find good conferences and classes right in your own backyard!

Teaching Yourself: Columns, Podcasts, and Blogs

Here are some resources to help you continually hone your genealogy skills and knowledge. In general, these are like periodicals, though the distribution method changes:

- FamilySearch Learning Center has hundreds of training videos on topics from using the site to researching specific types of records.

- Elizabeth Shown Mills' website (http://www.evidenceexplained .com) and book (*Evidence Explained*) will help you navigate the ins and outs of documentation.

- The Ancestry.com Learning Center, as well as the blogs, Twitter, and Facebook accounts, offer daily tips and information.

- You can find study groups for many different genealogy topics, such as:

  - The NGSQ Articles Online Study Groups meet once a month to discuss past articles published in the *National Genealogical Society Quarterly* (NGSQ). When you sign up you will get some articles to read that will help you learn how to read published articles critically. You will also get the list of articles that will be reviewed for the entire year. Members of each group take turns leading the discussion.

  - ProGen Study Groups will help you learn about *Professional Genealogy: A Manual for Researchers, Writers, Editors, Lecturers and Librarians* (Genealogical Publishing Company, 2001), edited by Elizabeth Shown Mills.

- Search YouTube for genealogy.

- Virtual Association of Professional Genealogists Chapters: APG-Virtual, and APG-SL (Second Life).

- Ancestry Family History Wiki, by Kay Rudolph.

- And as Kay Rudolph says, "blogs, blogs, blogs, and blogs!"

  Speaking of blogs, let's look at some of the important ones for a genealogist to follow, no matter what your level of expertise.

DearMYRTLE

Pat Richley-Erickson has been helping folks do genealogy online and offline for nearly two decades. Her screen name, DearMYRTLE, comes from one of her great-grandmothers, and was her ID on AOL's genealogy forum. At DearMYRTLE.com, you will find links to her Genealogy Community on Google+, Feedly, Facebook, and Twitter, her Lessons, and more.

   Just one example is her web-based class on the book *Mastering Genealogical Proof* by Thomas W. Jones (National Genealogical

Society, 2013). Both the 2013 and the 2014 Study Group videos can be found on YouTube.

"RootsTech is reaching out to over 250 remote locations in multiple languages throughout the world," Pat Richley-Erickson said. "You will 'major' in the study of *Mastering Genealogical Proof* for the duration of this series. We're going to eat, sleep, and breathe this project until we get it down pat. There are some revolutionary thoughts in this book that will be a paradigm shift for even some experienced researchers. This DearMYRTLE's MGP Study Group is not sponsored by the author or publisher of Mastering Genealogical Proof. The 10-session series is designed for genealogy researchers to study Dr. Jones' ideas in a positive, collaborative, peer-group setting. These methodology ideals can be translated into any locality or ethnic group research a genealogist is likely to encounter."

Another fun way to learn random genealogy facts is to listen in on her weekly Mondays with MYRT on Google Hangouts. Each week, a panel of up to eight genealogists will discuss one or more topics making the news in genealogy. She announces how to attend each week on DearMYRTLE.com (see Figure 4-1). Mondays with MYRT happen noon Eastern Standard Time, 11:00 AM Central Standard Time, 10:00 AM Mountain Standard Time, and 9:00 AM Pacific Standard Time.

DearMYRTLE's daily genealogy blog has free news and tips, problem solving and other discussions, and much more. It's a must-read for any beginner. You can visit her site (www.DearMYRTLE.com) to subscribe by RSS feed and have her writing come to you.

Success Story: Using Message Boards Solves a Mystery

Betty Krohn took one of DearMYRTLE's classes on Internet genealogy research, where it was recommended that the students go to www.rootsweb.com and check out the message boards. Betty decided that her first task was to find information on Robert Suiters, Sr., an uncle of Betty's who had left Ohio in 1929 and lost touch with his family.

"The very first message to pop up when I entered the name of Suiters (my maiden name) was from a person who was looking for any family of Robert Suiters. Until that time, I had been unable to locate any trace of Robert Suiters. We knew he existed, but didn't know if he was still alive or where in the world he would be living. So you can imagine my excitement when I read that message," Betty said. "We learned that Robert had gone to Oklahoma, married, and had a son, Robert, Jr., but that marriage ended in divorce, and Robert, Sr. left again, leaving the son and never contacting him again."

Robert was alive, and he was soon on the phone with Betty's father. Through the message board, Betty was able to reunite much of the family.

—Betty Krohn

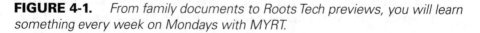

FIGURE 4-1. *From family documents to Roots Tech previews, you will learn something every week on Mondays with MYRT.*

Lisa Louise Cook's Genealogy Gems

This is both a podcast (audio only) and a YouTube channel (video and audio). Lisa's emphasis is imparting information in an efficient way. In the podcast and videos, she sifts through all the new technology and genealogy resources to bring you what she likes best in family history resources—the "genealogy gems." You go to the YouTube site to subscribe and get the videos, or watch old ones, and you use an iTunes account to subscribe to the free Genealogy Gems podcast at https://itunes.apple.com/podcast/genealogy-gems-podcast-lisa/id250987403?mt = 2.

> **Note**
>
> Institutes are week-long courses of study on a specific area, usually held at the same site every year, with class size ranging from 15 to 30 students, allowing more personalized instruction. Conference formats are usually speakers and panel discussions over a few days, where attendance for each session can be in the hundreds, and the site usually changes every year. Seminars are somewhere in between with regard to duration and group size.

Eastman's Online Genealogy Newsletter

Eastman's Online Genealogy Newsletter is one of the oldest and best sources of information for the amateur and professional genealogist alike.

The daily blog has interesting articles on new products, sites, and online resources, as well as discussions on techniques. Like DearMYRTLE's blog, the site allows comments by readers, which are sometimes even more interesting than the original article. The free blog will often have news updates, such as Ancestry.com's newest databases or the National Archives and Records Administration (NARA) newest workshop. The main value of the daily blog is that Dick is so good at keeping up with the latest news and releases. The "Plus Edition" has more detailed articles, most of all his thoughtful and honest reviews of sites and software. The "Plus Edition" is about $20 a year, or you can try it for three months for about $6.

Other Blogs and Feeds

It is completely possible to spend your entire day reading interesting, informative, and entertaining genealogy blogs. But if you did that, when would you do your genealogy? So, out of the hundreds of blogs and feeds out there, I'll point out the ones you should start with and let you explore further to discover others that fit your schedule and needs:

- **Ancestories** by Miriam J. Robbins is a wonderful collection of success and failure stories, interesting historical facts, and more. She also maintains Online Historical Directories and Online Historical Newspapers websites. In addition, she leads Scanfests, encouraging others to spend an afternoon scanning in original documents, photographs of ancestors, and even handwritten research notes to digital form. Find her at http://www .ancestories1.blogspot.com/.

- **We Tree** (http://www.wetree.blogspot.com) by Amy Coffin is subtitled "Adventures in Genealogy." Coffin says she is the fruit of a storied family tree. She has a Master of Library Science degree and a persistent streak. "Both have come in handy as I find more pieces to my family puzzle," she said. You can subscribe by RSS feed.

- **Ancestoring** (http://www.ancestoring.blogspot.com) is a site where professional genealogist Michele Simmons Lewis answers your research questions and provides helpful tips and advice to assist you in your family history adventure. This blog is geared toward the beginner to intermediate researcher.

- **Roots and Rambles** at http://www.rootsandrambles.blogspot .com/ is by Marian Pierre-Louis. She is a full-time House Historian and Professional Genealogist who focuses on New England research, as well as a producing the podcast Fieldstone Commons.

- **The Educated Genealogist** is the product of Sheri Fenley of Stockton, California, a professional genealogist who blogs about courses, seminars, books, and classes in genealogy, as well as news and technology, at http://www.sherifenley .blogspot.com/. She is director of the West region of the

Association of Professional Genealogists; is on the board of the California State Genealogical Alliance; and a member of the National Genealogical Society, International Society of Family History Writers and Editors, National Society of Daughters of the American Revolution, California Genealogical Society, San Joaquin Genealogical Society, and Global Alliance of Genealogy Professionals.

- **Eats Like A Human** (http://www.eatslikeahuman.blogspot .com) is the blog of a programmer who has worked with The Church of Jesus Christ of Latter-day Saints (LDS) and pursues genealogy with a software engineer's perspective. "Taking Genealogy to the Common Person" is the subtitle of his blog. He recently used Twitter to pose a genealogy question (how to find a death certificate in Kansas prior to 1911) and recorded all the responses, and how quickly they came in, on the blog.

- **FamilySearch Labs** at https://www.labs.familysearch.org/ chronicles the newest software for FamilySearch.org. Great for the geeky genealogist!

- **Random Genealogy** (http://www.randomgenealogy.com) picks up news stories involving genealogy that other blogs haven't seemed to mention.

- **Renee's Genealogy Blog** (http://www.rzamor1.blogspot.com) started in September 2005 and uses AtomFeed to syndicate it to readers. Renee started doing genealogy at 15, and is now the secretary for the Utah Valley PAF Users Group and a Family History Consultant at the Alpine Family History Center. Renee is an old hand at genealogy and generously shares her insights and news. Her blogs are thoughtful and eclectic. A good read!

- **Elyse's Genealogy Blog** by Elyse Doerflinger is a great discussion, exploration, and learn-by-doing exercise. The author is young, but wise in the way of online genealogy! She has been a speaker at many genealogy societies in Southern California and at Southern California Genealogy Society's Jamboree conference in 2010. She has also written for *Internet Genealogy Magazine*, *Family Chronicle*, and been featured in *Family Tree Magazine*. In addition, she works for the family tree building website WikiTree.

- **BlogFinder** at http://www.blogfinder.genealogue.com is a good way to keep on top of the newest blogs, but again, be careful not to let blogs substitute for genealogy! See Figure 4-2 for the "Who's Blogging Where" page of this site, which covers worldwide blogs, not just the United States. If you want to find a French genealogy blog, for example, this is the place to go!

Note

Bloggers use prompts and memes for posts, and it can be fascinating to compare what your favorite bloggers have to say about Wordless Wednesday, 99 Things Genealogy, or 52 Weeks of Family Traditions. Check out www.geneabloggers.com for links to some great ones!

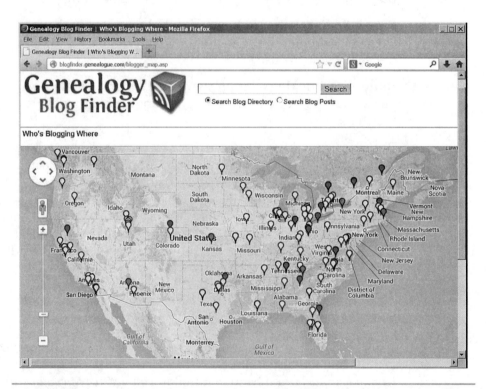

FIGURE 4-2. *BlogFinder helps you find blogs by topic and location.*

Online Courses

In some cases, you can have the education come to you—that is, learn by independent study. Genealogy societies and even universities have such courses, and in some cases, you can take the class over the Internet.

MOOCS

What is a MOOC? The most popular web definition is "a massive open online course [MOOC] is an online course aimed at unlimited participation and open access via the Web." Institutions from Yale to local community colleges are offering them.

For example, in September 2013, 23andMe, the leading personal genetics company, was working on a MOOC on human genetics to be called Tales from the Genome. And the online study groups mentioned earlier, while not conferring any continuing education units (CEUs) or college credit, can also be considered MOOCs.

For this category, check out https://familysearch.org/node/1171, in particular, an article titled "140 Free Online Genealogy Research Courses." That should get you started!

Note ——————————————————————————

A good listing of both resources and education in genealogy, and a site that was quite up-to-date as of this writing, is at www .academic-genealogy.com; look for the topics and regions you need.

Genealogy.com

Genealogy.com has several free, self-paced courses to help you get started in genealogy. Click Learning Center on the home page navigation bar to find them. The Learning Center has the following articles:

- Begin Your Research at Home

- What's in a Name?

- Collaborating with Others

- Finding Existing Research
- Outfitting Your Genealogy Toolkit

Brigham Young University

Brigham Young University (http://ce.byu.edu/is/site/courses/free
.cfm) has a series of free, self-paced online tutorials on family history
research. Among the courses are:

- Introduction to Family History Research
- Writing Family History
- Family Records
- Vital Records
- Military Records
- Courses on researching in France, Scandinavia, and Germany

National Institute for Genealogical Studies/University of Toronto

At www.genealogicalstudies.com, you can find The National Institute
for Genealogical Studies, which has joined forces with the University
of Toronto, Faculty of Information Studies, Professional Learning
Centre, to provide web-based courses for both family historians and
professional genealogists. Countries included are the United States,
Canada, England, Germany, Ireland, and Scotland. There are also
certificates in librarianship and general methodology.

Search College Sites for Other Courses

Use any major search engine to search "genealogy courses independent
study" or "genealogy courses distance learning," and you will come
up with many smaller colleges and institutions that offer at least a
course or two, and sometimes CEUs. Also, go to the site of the nearest
community college, junior college, or other higher-learning site and
simply search for "genealogy." Often, library science and information
science majors will include a course or two in genealogy.

Offline

Getting your genealogy education online is fun, but perhaps you would like some face-to-face (F2F) time with others who are learning too. In that case, you might investigate the following ideas for some educational opportunities in the real world.

Professional Organizations

Several institutions accredit the services of professional genealogists and researchers around the world. One of their primary goals is to establish a set of standards and a code of ethics for the members. Often, the accrediting body will offer courses, instruction, and testing. You don't have to be accredited to do family history research for hire, but it does offer clients assurance of a level of standards and professionalism that is accepted within the profession. Genealogy Pro (http://genealogypro.com/articles/organizations.html) has a list of several such organizations in English-speaking countries.

Genealogy Conferences and Cruises

The publishers of Wholly Genes software came up with the idea of a late-year educational cruise of the Eastern Caribbean with a series of speakers and workshops on genealogical research methods, tools, and technologies from some of the most popular speakers and authorities in those fields. Several genealogy companies jumped on the bandwagon, so to speak, and now conferences at sea are a regular event. Put "genealogy cruise" in your favorite search engine to find one, or go to www.cyndislist.com/travel/tours-and-cruises/.

National Genealogical Society

At www.ngsgenealogy.org, you can find many resources for online and offline learning. Courses they offer are shown at www.ngsgenealogy .org/cs/educational_courses.

American Genealogy   For many years, NGS has offered a home-study correspondence course entitled "American Genealogy: A Basic Course." The NGS recommends that you take the online introductory course first and then move on to the home-study course, which covers some of the same topics in more depth and includes many more besides. Those who successfully complete the online introductory course will receive a discount coupon that can be applied toward the home-study course. Check the NGS website for the current fees.

The 16 lessons are "hands on" and require trips to libraries, courthouses, and other sites, as well as the ability to write well about your research. The NGS website, however, has online resources to help you with this. Most people take 18 months to complete the course, although extensions are granted.

Brigham Young University Center for Family History and Genealogy

The Center for Family History and Genealogy supports the Family History (Genealogy) students at Brigham Young University. At http://familyhistory.byu.edu, you can find information on:

- Family History (Genealogy) Major
- Family History (Genealogy) Minor
- Family History Certificate
- Map for Majors
- Family History Internships

University of Washington Genealogy and Family History Certificate

A nine-month evening certificate program for teachers, librarians, amateur researchers, and others interested in researching their families, this on-campus program is described at www.pce.uw.edu/certificates/genealogy-family-history.html. Participants develop a completed family history project as part of classes that meet one evening per week on the University of Washington campus in Seattle.

Through lectures, discussions, readings, and field trips, students learn how to use the resources and methods necessary to develop a family history and to examine such topics as the migration of ethnic groups, population shifts, and the differences in urban and rural lifestyles. Students have access to the resources of the University of Washington libraries while enrolled. Participants receive nine CEUs and a certificate when they complete the program. Check the website for fees.

Genealogy Events

Finally, you can learn about genealogy at events such as seminars, workshops, and even ocean cruises! You can search for them on the following websites:

- About.com Genealogy Conferences (http://www.genealogy .about.com/cs/conferences)

- Cyndi's List (http://www.cyndislist.com/events.htm)

- Genealogy Events Web Ring (http://hub.familynhome.org/ hub/gencon)

Federation of Genealogical Societies Conferences

The Federation of Genealogical Societies (www.fgs.org/) holds a national conference each year for genealogists of all levels of experience. The conferences spotlight management workshops for genealogy organizations, genealogical lectures by nationally recognized speakers and regional experts, and exhibitors with genealogical materials and supplies. Check the website for fees, which historically have been under $200.

National Institute on Genealogical Research

Information on this venerable genealogy institute can be found at www.rootsweb.com/~natgenin. The National Institute on Genealogical Research started in 1950 and is sponsored by the American University, the American Society of Genealogists, the National Archives, and the Maryland Hall of Records. The National Archives provides strong support, including meeting space. The cost for this week-long event is usually around $350.

The institute's program takes an in-depth look at federal records of genealogical value located primarily in the Washington, D.C. area. The program is for experienced researchers (genealogists, historians, librarians, and archivists) and is not an introductory course in genealogy.

Institute on Genealogy and Historical Research

Held at Samford University (Birmingham, Alabama) every June, this five-day event is for intermediate to advanced genealogists. It is academically and professionally oriented, and is cosponsored by the Board for Certification of Genealogists. Small classes are held during the day. Each evening of the institute features a dinner with a speaker as well. Details and registration information can be found at www4.samford.edu/schools/ighr/. Check the website (see Figure 4-3) for fees, which historically have been under $400.

The Salt Lake Institute of Genealogy

Held at the Family History Library in Salt Lake City, Utah, by the Utah Genealogical Society, this is a week-long, hands-on event, usually held

FIGURE 4-3. *The IGHR in Birmingham, Alabama, is an intensive five-day event.*

early in the year. Check the Utah Genealogical Association website at www.infouga.org for fees, which historically have been under $400. In 2010, attendees could choose from 12 different courses of lectures, including topics on American, Canadian, and German research.

Regional and Local Workshops and Seminars

Many state historical societies hold seminars. Simply use your favorite search engine to search for your state genealogical society and "conference."

Finding a local class, seminar, workshop, or other event near you is the best way to start. Query a search engine for "genealogy" and the name of the town you live in or will be visiting. Also, check Cyndi's List page (www.cyndislist.com/events.htm), Dick Eastman's weekly newsletter, and DearMYRTLE's sites often for announcements.

Success Story: Learning to Plat at a Conference

Ann Lusk, attending a beginning genealogy course in her hometown of Huntsville, Alabama, learned about platting deeds. To plat a deed, you draw a picture of a piece of land from the description on the deed. Taking what she learned from the class, Ann worked with two Tennessee deeds, described in metes and bounds, a method that notes adjoining land. By platting two deeds for land owned by men with her husband's surname, cutting them out, and laying them on the table together, she saw the two pieces fit together "like hand and glove." This helped her show that the two men were father and son, and from that she could look for the original family plat. This information not only helped her Daughters of the American Revolution (DAR) application, it also qualified her for the First Families of Tennessee (www.east-tennessee-history.org/index.cfm/m/52).

—Ann Lusk

Wrapping Up

- You can learn about genealogy at all levels, online and offline, and both venues are enjoyable.

- Taking beginners' courses can save you some time and effort in your research.

- Seminars, conferences, institutes, and courses are a good way to meet other genealogists and expand your skills.

- Local, regional, and national programs give you a wide choice of how to learn about genealogy.

Chapter 5

Revving Up
Search Engines

As I write this book, I am pointing you to the best genealogical resources on the Internet as I know them. I am aware that you may find some of the links are broken. By the time you read this, untold numbers of sites may have been created, or deleted, or changed from wonderful to not-so-much, and vice versa. Keeping track of all this is made much easier by search engines and portals. Search engines and portals offer ways to send changes and news stories that match certain keywords to you via e-mail or push technology, and I will show you how to take advantage of that.

Certainly, as a genealogist, you've experienced the thrill of discovering things for yourself—it can be quite a kick to find a website or blog none of your friends know about. To do this, you need a way to find genealogical resources on the Internet on your own. That's where search sites come in.

Defining Terms

A *search engine* is an all-purpose label used to describe anything that will let you search for terms within a group of data. That data could be on a single site or on billions of pages on the Internet, or on some subset in between the two. Just about anything that lets you search can be called a search engine, but some other terms are more accurate for specific sites.

A *spider* is a program that looks for information on the Internet, creates a database of what it finds, and lets you use a search engine on that database to find specific information. As noted, this can mean billions of pages or only the pages on one site.

> **Note**
>
> If you are interested in search engines, how they work, and how they compare to one another, check out Search Engine Watch (www.searchenginewatch.com).

A search site might claim to search "the whole Web," but, in reality, most probably cover only about 15 percent of the Web at any given time. This is because pages quickly appear and disappear on the Web. That's why you might want to use several different search sites when you are searching for specific information or for general types of sites. Or, you might want to try one of the many meta-search engines that try several search sites at once. You can also use Google Earth to plot your ancestors' land holdings or see where a town used to be.

A search site called a *directory* or a catalog uses a search engine to let you hunt through an edited list of Internet sites for specific information. The value of these sites is that in a directory or catalog, websites are sorted, categorized, and sometimes rated. Most often, the directory is included in a portal, which pulls together searches of news, information, text, pictures, and whatever into one page, which you can modify to your liking.

Then there are *portals*. Yahoo! (www.yahoo.com) was one of the first catalogs or directories established online; it is also a good example of a portal that offers other services, such as chat, news, forums, RSS readers, and more. A portal is a little bit of everything: a search engine for the Web at large, a catalog of sites the owners recommend, and usually a group of other features, including stock prices, web-based e-mail, shopping, and so on. Excite, AOL, Google, MSN, and news sites such as CNN and MSNBC all have portals you can customize to some extent.

A *meta-search engine* submits your query to several different search sites, portals, and catalogs at the same time. You might get more results, and you will usually be able to compare how each one responded to the query. These searches may take longer, however, and getting millions of results is almost more trouble than getting one. There are genealogy-specific meta-search engines, and you will find information on some of them later in this chapter. Examples of general meta-search sites are Lycos, Dogpile, and Metacrawler. You can also check out the page www.dmoz.org/Computers/Internet/Searching/Multi-Search (see Figure 5-1) for a list of many different meta-search engines.

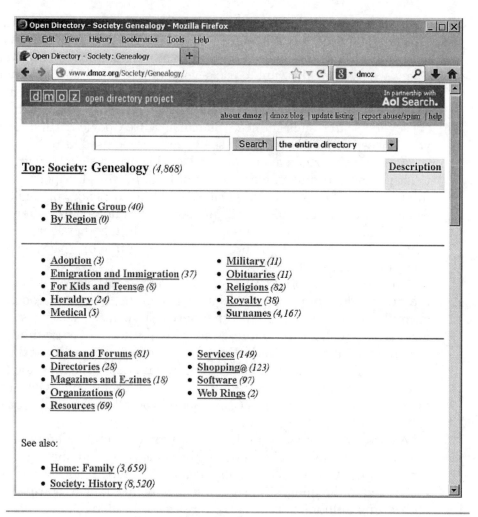

FIGURE 5-1. *DMOZ, The Open Directory Project, has an edited list of meta-search engines.*

Searching with Savoir Faire

Searching can be as easy as typing "Powell Genealogy" and clicking the search button. Two problems: (1) you may get so many hits that you feel you are drinking from a fire hose; and (2) the top ones will be very common, popular sites you have already heard of.

It doesn't have to be that way. You can make the spiders boogie if you just sing the right tune. Thankfully, search algorithms (the language of the spiders) have come a long way since the days when search engines could not tell the difference between a blind Venetian and a Venetian blind!

Here are some general search tips:

- Choose your search terms carefully, and use phrases or several words that are relevant to your search. Typing "Spencer genealogy Ohio" will narrow a search quite well.

- Use quotes to search for a specific order of words. Searching on the phrase "Spencer family history" (without quotation marks) will match all pages that have any of those three words included somewhere on the page, in any order, and not necessarily adjacent to each other. Searching the phrase "Spencer family history" (with quotation marks) will return only those pages that have those three words together.

- The more specific you are, the better. Searching for Irish genealogy databases will give you fewer, but closer, matches than searching for Irish genealogy.

- Use plus and minus signs in your searches. A word preceded by a plus sign (+) must appear on the page to be considered a match. A word preceded by a minus sign (–) must not appear on the page to be considered a match. No spaces can be between the plus and minus signs and the words they apply to. For example:

```
+Spencer -royal genealogy
```

  Entering the above code would ask the search engine to find pages that contain the word "Spencer" but not the word "royal," with the word "genealogy" preferred, but optional. Most search engines would get some Spencer genealogy pages but leave out those that include Lady Diana, Princess of Wales. More about this type of search can be found in the following section about Boolean searches.

Every now and then, search for "geneology" instead of "genealogy." You will be amazed at how many pages out there use this misspelling in their titles and body text!

Another tip: Look carefully at the results page of whatever search engine you use. You may find links to limit or sort the searches by date, length of the page, language, and other parameters.

> ### Note
> Narrow your search if you get too many matches. Sometimes, the search engine results page will have an input box to allow you to search for new terms specifically among the first results. This might mean adding terms or deleting terms and then running the search again just on the results from the first search.

Using Boolean Terms

Searching the Internet is no simple matter. With literally billions of sites, some of them with millions of documents, and more words than you can imagine, finding exactly the right needle in all that hay can be daunting. The key, of course, is crafting a precise query.

Boolean operators are handy tools for honing your searches. Named after George Boole, the nineteenth-century mathematician who dreamed up symbolic logic, Boolean operators represent the relationships among items using terms such as OR, AND, and NOT. When applied to information retrieval, they can expand or narrow a search to uncover as many citations, or hits, as you want.

The Boolean OR

When you search for two or more terms joined with an OR operator, you receive hits that contain any one of your terms. Therefore, the query:

```
Powell OR genealogy
```

will retrieve documents containing "Powell" or "genealogy," but not necessarily both. Note that nearly all search pages default to OR—that is, they assume you want any page with any one or more of your terms in it.

You can see it makes good sense to use OR when you search for synonyms or closely related terms. For example, if you're looking for variations on a name, search for:

`SPENCER SPENCE SPENSER`

The average search engine will assume the OR operator and find any page with any one or more of those terms. However, the average search engine will also sort the results such that the pages with the most relevance appear at the top, using all your search terms to score that relevance.

The Boolean AND

In the Boolean boogie, joining search terms with AND means that all terms must be found in a document, but not necessarily together. The query:

`George AND Washington`

will result in a list of documents that have both the names "George" and "Washington" somewhere within them. Use AND when you have dissimilar terms and need to narrow a search. Usually, to use AND in a search, you type a plus sign (+) or put the term AND between the words and enclose everything within parentheses, like so:

`(Spencer AND genealogy)`

The Boolean NOT

When you use NOT, search results must exclude certain terms. Many search engines don't have this functionality. Often, when you can use it, the syntax is to put a minus sign (–) in front of the unwanted term. The query:

`Powell NOT Colin`

will return all citations containing the name "Powell," but none including "Colin," regardless of whether "Powell" is there. Use NOT when you want to exclude possible second meanings. "Banks" can be found on genealogy surname pages as well as on pages associated with finance or with rivers. Searching for:

```
banks AND genealogy NOT river
```

or

```
banks +genealogy -river
```

increases the chance of finding documents relating to the surname Banks (the people, not riversides). In some search engines, the minus sign often takes the place of NOT.

Note ────────────────────────────────

Remember, a simple AND doesn't guarantee that the words will be next to each other. Your search for George AND Washington could turn up documents about George Benson and Grover Washington! To be sure you get the exact name you want, use the quotation marks.

The fun part is combining Boolean operators to create a precise search. Let's say you want to find documents about the city of Dallas, Texas. If you simply search for "Dallas," you could get copious hits about Dallas County in Alabama (county seat: Selma), which might not be the Dallas you want. To avoid that, you would use AND, NOT, and OR in this fashion:

```
(Dallas AND Texas) NOT (Selma OR Alabama)
(Powell AND genealogy) NOT (Colin AND "SECRETARY OF STATE")
```

Note that parentheses groups the search terms together.

Beyond AND/OR/NOT

Some search engines enable you to fine-tune a search further. The WITH operator, for example, searches for terms that are much nearer to each other. How "near" is defined depends on the engine.

Some search engines would look at "George WITH Washington" and deliver documents only containing the words "George Washington" next to each other. Others might consider words in the same sentence or paragraph to be near enough. This makes a difference if there might be an intervening (middle) name involved in your search.

You can also sometimes use a question mark or an asterisk to find many different variants of a word. Check the search engine's help files to see if it uses wildcards or word stemming (for finding all variations of a word, such as ancestry, ancestral, ancestor, and ancestors).

Using these techniques, you can search the Web much more efficiently, finding just the right document on George Washington Carver or a genealogy site on the right set of Powells. Learn the steps to the Boolean boogie, and you'll soon be web dancing wherever you please!

Some Google-Specific Tips

Google has some Boolean "operators" that can help you limit the results as well:

- `filetype` Finds a result in a certain file type, such as PDF format. This also works for other file types, such as .doc, .jpg, .ppt, and so on.

- `site:` or `-site:` With this operator, you can find results *only* from the specified site, or with the - sign you can exclude results from a certain site.

- `~` Use the tilde to search for synonyms of your terms.

- `. .` Use two periods to find a range (for example, 1800..1802).

- `*` The asterisk is a wildcard, and can be used for whole words or parts of words. For example, you can put in "`a * is as good as a *`".

- `related` This term followed by the website address will bring up similar pages. If you find a website you like, try using `related:[insert URL]` to locate comparable websites.

Google also has specialized searches that can be powerful. Book Search will look only at online books uploaded to Google Books. Image Search can look for faces, colors, and sizes. Map Search can look for "`cemetery 35801`" or any other geographical term.

> **Note**
>
> Syntax does not matter with operators. `filetype:` and `site:` can be used together in any order, for example.

Search Sites

The Web has an embarrassment of riches, some of which are more useful to genealogists than others. The following is a representative list of genealogy-related catalogs, portals, and search engines.

Ancestral Findings

At www.ancestralfindings.com, you will find a free surname database, which is useful for the beginner, but the real value of this site is that volunteers will search indexes of public records, published genealogies, abstracts, and books for you. Some lookups involve a charge, but many are free, and every week one or more of the paid resources are featured as free lookups. Here is how to do it: Choose a category. Click one of the titles within that category to request a lookup (only one per day). Databases are labeled "FREE" Lookup or "PAID" Lookup. First, you will see an automated message letting you know the request is entered, and later you will get the results. As it is all-volunteer, it can take up to a week, but you will also be entered in the weekly Free Genealogy Resource Drawing.

Linkpendium

Linkpendium is a wonderful search site, brought to you by Karen Isaacson and Brian (Wolf) Leverich. This hugely useful site is a catalog of links to U.S. genealogy information, records, pages, and sources, organized by geography. You can search by a surname and get links within every state, or you can start your search in a specific state or specific county. Links to obituaries, cemetery lists, wills, biographies, and more will be the result.

A quote from the site: "Linkpendium's goal is to index every genealogy, geneology, :) family history, family tree, surname, vital records, biography, or otherwise genealogically-related site on the Internet."

The site's creators are part of online genealogy history, being two founders of the venerable and still indispensable RootsWeb genealogical community/information/data/search site. RootsWeb started as a few pages that a bunch of genealogists who worked together created to help each other. For more than a decade, RootsWeb was *the* starting place for online genealogy.

Access Genealogy

At this site, www.accessgenealogy.com, you can read and search for many different types of records for genealogy research, including newspapers and periodicals; emigration and immigration forms; census reports; voting records; and archives from libraries, cemeteries, churches, and courts (see Figure 5-2). The site is also widely known for Native American data.

Ancestor Hunt

With this meta-search site (www.ancestorhunt.com), you can search for ancestors and locate surnames in some of the best and largest databases of genealogy records online. The site has unique searches, such as the Surname Search Portal and the Obituary Search Portal, both of which search several sites at once.

Two of the exceptional pages are Genealogical Prison Records and Past Sheriffs of the United States. You will find these, along with many other search engines and free genealogy resources, in the Genealogy Search Engines And Contents menu, which is located on each page.

One of the most popular sections is the Bible Records Transcriptions. These family bibles are completely indexed by surname, with over 200 pages of transcriptions and scanned images. This site is one to bookmark!

Biography Guide

Was any ancestor of yours a member of Congress? Search for biographies of members by last name, first name, position, and state at this site: http://bioguide.congress.gov/biosearch/biosearch.asp. If your ancestors are in the database, this fascinating site can add a new dimension to your family history.

FIGURE 5-2.   *Access Genealogy is a family history meta-search site with quite a bit of Native American data.*

Cyndi's List

The site www.cyndislist.com catalogs about a quarter-million genealogy websites. You will find links to the genealogy sites and sites that simply would help a genealogist. This is the first place many new online genealogists visit. The links are categorized and organized, and there's also a search box for finding the subjects you want quickly. Cyndi Howells works on the list every day, updating, deleting, and adding sites. Each new or updated link will have a small "new" or "updated" graphic next to it for 30 days.

The main index is updated each time activity occurs on Cyndi's List. Check the date under each category heading to determine when the last update was made for that category. The date is also updated at the bottom of each category page.

Free Genealogy Search Help for Google

This free site (www.genealogy-search-help.com/) is designed to help you use Google for genealogy-specific searches. It will create a series of different searches using Google's advanced features that will likely improve your results.

The site has a small family tree as a form for you to fill in with an ancestor, and this site will set up the best searches for you, based on what you enter. If you don't know an ancestor's parents but know one of the ancestor's children, use the child's name for the First Name and Last Name fields (and spouse, birth, and death) and then enter the ancestor as the Father or Mother. This gives more information for building a search.

It's quick and easy and gives good results.

GenGateway

Another version of a catalog of websites organized into categories for genealogists is www.gengateway.com by Steve Lacy. It has daily updates, so you can find newer genealogy sites and data online under the "New Genealogy" link. Another section is Genealogy Help, a collection to links to help when you hit a brick wall in your research. What I like about this site is that Lacy strives for uniqueness in content and presentation. Choose the category you want to search, such as surname or obituary, and you'll get well-sorted results.

To navigate the site, use one of the many useful gateways listed in the navigation bar on the left of the home page. If you're new to the site, first try the Beginners Gateway or the Search Pages.

RootsWeb Search Thingy

This is one of the first genealogy search sites I ever used on the Web, and I still go to it often. Go to www.rootsweb.com, click Searches, and click Search Thingy. Then put in your search terms. The meta-search goes through all RootsWeb pages and databases. The disadvantage to

Search Thingy is that OR is the only Boolean operator you can use, so a search for James Reason Powell will return any page with any one of those terms.

Obituary Search Pages

Several pages enable you to search recent and older obituaries:

- Free Obituary Searches (http://www.obituary-searches.com) lists several different pages for death notice searches around the world, mostly contemporary, but some historical.

- Legacy.com (http://www.legacy.com/Obituaries.asp) has a box on the home page to search contemporary obituaries.

- Obituary Links (http://www.obitlinkspage.com) searches cemetery records, obituaries, and other pages from sites such as Ancestry.com, RootsWeb, and so on. This is a meta-search engine that focuses on death records.

- Origins.net (http://www.origins.net) is a fee-based genealogy search site; you can try a sample search for free. Users pay a license fee for use of the Origin Search software at $5 for 24 hours or $15 for 14 days. Origins.net provides access to databases of genealogical data for online family history research in the United Kingdom, Canada, Australia, New Zealand, and the United States.

White Page Directories

So far, you've looked at search engines and directories for finding a website. But what if you need to find lost living relatives? Or what if you want to write to people with the same surnames you're researching? In that case, you need people search engines, called White Page directories. Like the White Pages of your phone book, these directories specialize in finding people, not pages. In fact, all the search engine sites mentioned previously have White Page directories.

The AT&T site (www.att.com/directory) has an excellent set of directories for people and businesses, with a reverse phone number lookup (put in the phone number; get the name). It's basically a White Pages for the whole United States. AT&T now also owns Switchboard (www.switchboard.com). It's free, and it lists the e-mail addresses and telephone numbers of millions of people and businesses, taken from public records. It's also a website catalog. If you register as a user (it's free), you can ensure that your listing is not only accurate, but also has only the information you want it to reveal.

Wrapping Up

- Learn to use Boolean search terms to target your web searches.

- Use genealogy-specific sites to search for surnames and localities.

- Use general search sites and catalogs that gather news and links about genealogy.

- Use White Pages search sites to find living people.

Chapter 6

Talk to Me: Twitter, Skype, IM, and Google

At times, you might want to talk to a fellow genealogist to resolve problems you're encountering in your research. The online world can help you there too, with more ways than you can shake a stick at. Twitter, Voice over Internet Protocol (VoIP) and video chat programs, and instant messaging can all help you make personal connections with other genealogists.

When you send messages, pictures, and videos to a public online site such as Twitter, that has been called "microblogging"—a web blog in tiny snippets. When you exchange voice, video, or text messages with just one person, that comes under the blanket of instant messaging.

Twitter

Twitter has become a phenomenon as well as an Internet application. Twitter is free, and it combines social networking with blogging on a very small scale. With it, you can send and receive messages, links, and more.

When you send something on Twitter, it is called a tweet. A tweet is a message of no more than 140 characters on your Twitter profile page delivered to your followers, who are people who have subscribed to your tweets. Tweets can also be links to pictures, sound files, or videos.

You can choose who will see your tweets, or open it up to the world (the latter is the default). You can send and receive tweets via the Twitter website, Short Message Service (SMS) on your smart phone, or external applications.

Note

While Twitter itself costs nothing to use, accessing it through your smart phone's SMS (text messages) could rack up fees from your phone service provider, as each tweet will be a text message.

That 140-character limit also spurred usage of URL-shortening services such as tinyurl, bit.ly, and tr.im, where you can shorten a long address to just a few characters.

Since Jack Dorsey created it in 2006, millions of people have started using Twitter. Alexa web traffic analysis ranks Twitter as

FIGURE 6-1. *Genealogy tweeting is very popular.*

one of the 50 most popular websites in the world. And of course, genealogists are among them (see Figure 6-1).

An example:

```
ACoffin @epcrowe I use Twitter to share #genealogy news, hi-lite
blog posts and ask reference-type questions.
ACoffin @epcrowe I also use Twitter as a #genealogy news feed of
sorts. If it happens, someone will post it here, asap.
```

Your eyes are glazing over. I can see it. Okay, let's unpack this.

Note

A really good explanation of how Twitter works is at www .momthisishowtwitterworks.com/. I highly recommend it.

Replies and Mentions

Once you sign up for Twitter (a simple process, but it requires a valid e-mail address), you can have the program search your AOL, Google, or Yahoo! address books under "Find People." Everyone has a "handle," or user name, often some short version of a real name or a company.

An *@reply* is a message sent from one person to another, although everyone who follows them can see it. You should put the "@username" at the beginning of the message. When a message begins with @username, the Twitter software considers it a public *reply*. You do not have to be following someone to reply to that person, and all your replies and mentions are shown in the @username tab in your home page sidebar.

Note

A tweet that begins with @username is a reply, and a tweet with @username anywhere else in the message is considered a mention. Both kinds of messages will be collected to your sidebar and are public. A tweet that starts with the single letter D will be sent directly and privately. A tweet that starts with @someone will be public and show up as a mention. Also, you can send a private reply by starting the message with a D and a space, then the username to whom you are replying, then you are sending a private message. You can only send a direct message to a person who follows you. When you receive a direct message, it goes to your direct message inbox, which you access through the Direct Message tab in the sidebar in your home page. You can set your e-mail preferences to get an e-mail from Twitter when you get a direct message.

Hashtags

With all those millions of users tweeting 24 hours a day, seven days a week, how on earth do you find the messages that might interest you? Hashtags: using an octothorpe (#) to tag a message's topic.

The Twitter community created hashtags because the Twitter software had no easy way to sort out the tweets by category or add extra

Success Story: Amy Coffin Uses Twitter for Genealogy

Amy Coffin, MLIS, is a genealogy and records research librarian, blogger, and researcher (http://amycoffin.com) who uses Twitter daily.

"I use Twitter mainly as a news aggregator," she said. "I seek out the genealogy-related people and vendors I want to follow, and they are the only ones who show up in my Twitter stream. Twitter gets a bad rap from those who have never used it or don't see its value. I tell people Twitter is like television. There's a lot of junk on Twitter, just like there's a lot of junk on television. The key is finding what you want to see and blocking out everything else. There is useful genealogy information to be had on Twitter—you just need to set your account up so it comes to you."

She also uses it for live reporting just as people in many fields do. For example, conference attendees send live tweets right from the conference, allowing discussion about the event between those who are attending and those who are not.

"Usually before a conference, a dedicated 'hashtag' is established and everyone attending or talking about the conference uses that hashtag in their tweets. This makes them more searchable and distributes the information better. For example, I'm attending the Southern California Genealogy Jamboree where the hashtag will be #scgs14. If you search Twitter using "#scgs14" during that time, you will see all the tweets about the conference," she said.

It also serves as her "mini-reference desk," she said. She uses her Twitter account to ask questions of other genealogists and librarians that she follows.

"Once, I had a distant cousin tell me that our great-great-grandfather was given acknowledgement in a book of an award-winning author. Could this be true? I sent a request to all my librarian Twitter followers and had my answer in minutes," Amy said.

Other uses Amy has found: publicity for her blog entries and friendship.

"I've become friends with many of my Twitter followers. It's always exciting to meet them for the first time at genealogy events," she said.

data with that 140-character limit. Hashtags have the octothorpe "hash" or "pound" symbol (#) preceding the tag—for example, #genealogy, #FamilyHistory, #DNA, or #ancestry. While the hashtags can occur anywhere in the tweet, often, you will find them at the end.

These hashtags are not an official element of Twitter, but they have become standard practice. You can see in Twitter Search that hashtag terms are often in trending topics.

Using Hashtags

If you add a hashtag to your tweet and you have a public account, anyone who does a search for that hashtag can find your tweet. There are no formal rules for hashtags, except never use one for spamming. Nevertheless, even though any word with a # in front could be considered a hashtag keyword, some are more commonly used.

It is a good idea to use them sparingly and always relevantly. A maximum of three hashtags to a message is considered good form.

As they have become accepted, you can now search for hashtags not only in Twitter, but also in Google and other search engines. If you search for #FamilyHistory and come up with good results, you can click "Save This Search" and have a link to all recent tweets with that hashtag. You can also create an RSS feed of your favorite searches, again with a single click.

But notice above the "any other keyword." If you search on anything—your surname, a noun, even a verb—you're likely to find tweets that match. The hashtag will help you filter out messages from someone *named* Powell from messages *about* a Powell.

You can also create lists of Twitter users to follow, which is another way to quickly categorize the tweet feed. Twitter lists are groups of people whose tweets you want to stay current on. If want to see the tweets of someone without adding that person to your follow inventory, lists let you to do that.

The Twitter software allows you to build lists several ways. Usually, you start one by clicking Lists and then New. You can also make the list public (everyone can see it) or private (only you can see it). At this writing, you are limited to 1,000 lists per account, which should do. However, some public lists are very useful, and you don't have to reinvent the wheel. Check out these lists:

```
twitter.com/TamuraJones/lists/geneawavers
twitter.com/AncestryDetect/lists/genealogy
twitter.com/BBPetura/lists/genealogy-family-history3
twitter.com/EnduringLifecom/lists/genealogist
twitter.com/OnlineGenGuy/lists/genealogy-tweets
twitter.com/TamuraJones/lists/genealogists@hikari17/
genealogysocieties
```

With public lists like these, you can start following several genealogists with a click and avoid building a list of 166 different accounts all by yourself. On the other hand, you can add people who tweet (including yourself!) to a list from most screens on Twitter. Just look for the "Lists" button.

On your Twitter home page, find the Lists link, which will bring up your lists page. On this lists page, you can do list maintenance, such as editing the list name and deleting the list from your profile. Following a list looks just like following any other Twitter user. Go to the list page and click Follow underneath the name of the list you want to read. You can quickly view your subscribed lists, as well as lists that you created yourself, on the sidebar. You can always remove yourself from a list by blocking its creator.

As of this writing, some 30 applications are available in various smart phone and tablet platforms for using Twitter, including the one from Twitter itself. These programs range in price from free to about $20, but my favorite at the moment is the free application called Twitterrific.

VoIP and Video Chat

When you use your web camera, a microphone, and maybe even earphones to communicate with others, you are probably using VoIP to video chat. There are many ways to do this: Google Plus, Facebook, Microsoft Cloud, and Skype just to name a few. How can a genealogist use these programs? Well, talking to distant relatives for free is one way. Recording video journals of your research is another. Most often, they are used to conduct online meetings, seminars (webinars), and chats. DearMYRTLE's Mondays with Myrt are an example of a way to use Google Hangouts, as in Figure 6-2.

An additional use: instant messaging. Most of these programs can communicate in text messages, send files, and do all the other tasks an instant messaging program such as AIM or Windows Messenger can do. And many of them have versions for laptops, tablets, and smart phones as well.

Google

Google + gets a lot of snarky putdowns online, but there is no doubt that Google Hangouts and On Air are growing in popularity.

FIGURE 6-2. *Mondays with Myrt is one way to learn about genealogy using video, in this case Google Hangouts On Air.*

Google products you can use include audio/video/text programs for communication over the Internet using VoIP. Google Hangouts and On Air can be saved and posted to YouTube, so it has proven very popular with online genealogists like DearMYRTLE. It is also high definition, which many other programs such as Skype are not.

Skype

Skype is available for systems running Linux, Linux-based Maemo, Mac OS X (Intel and PC), iPhone OS (iPhone and iPod Touch), Microsoft Windows (2000, XP, Vista, Windows Mobile), and even gaming systems from Sony and Xbox. There is a pay version that lets you call any phone number, whether on Skype or not, but most people use the free version, even though you can only use it to communicate with other Skype users. With some helper programs like Wiretap Studio and Pamela, you can also record and post Skype calls. However, on some platforms, Skype is not as high definition as is Google Hangouts.

Facebook, Yahoo! et al

Instant messaging programs such as AOL Instant Message (AIM), Yahoo!, and so on now integrate with social networking sites such as Facebook, Twitter, and others. Furthermore, Facebook itself now has a video message function as well as the IM function.

Similarly, Windows Live Messenger is now integrated with Skype as well as with the Windows cloud apps such as mail and document storage.

All of these can be used to chat live or delayed delivery, both with text and with audio/visual messages. Again, the main use for a genealogist for these is to connect with relatives, share research and lookups, and attend virtual gatherings of different groups.

Instant Messaging

IM has been around for 20 years, thanks in large part to America Online's Instant Messenger program, known to users as AIM, and MSN Messenger, Yahoo! Chat, and other similar programs. In this form of messaging, a select list of people (from two to a whole "room") exchange typed messages in real time.

The other most common chat program is a Java-based chat that shows in your web browser. As long as you have the latest version of Java on your computer, nothing else is needed to participate. Different programs enable you to have one-on-one or multiperson conversations with people. Some require you to sign on to a chat server, where the program you use doesn't matter. Others only let you chat with people using the same program and who have allowed you to put them on their "buddy list." The former lets you connect with more people; the latter gives you more security. A few will let you do both.

Success Story: GenPals Solves a Mystery

Charlene Hazzard and Mary Martha Von Ville McGrath solved a mystery through GenPals. Though the group disappeared when GeoCities died, the example is still a good one of online collaboration.

"When new to the Internet, I found a message on Guenther/Ginther/Gunter/Gunther (from Charlene Hazzard), and when I finally figured out how to write a message, got an answer from her. She had my line into what is now a different country in Europe and had it back two generations from there!" Mary Martha had a town name of Herstom in Germany. Charlene knew that this was the common nickname for Herbitzheim, which is now in France. Charlene had communicated directly with the Herbitzheim (aka Herstom) town historian until he died in 2000. "I had only a nickname for the town of origin, and Charlene explained the real name of the town. By the way, her message was from 1999, and she is the only one who had info from Europe," said Mary Martha. "What an answer to a 30-year-old prayer. Thank you, God!"

Success Story: Where's Amos?

I wandered into Uncle Hiram's Chat Cabins at www.bhocutt .com. I thought it best to familiarize myself with my new "digs" before the following night's grand opening and my hosting debut. Thinking I'd be alone to try this and that, I was surprised to find three chatters in a deep genealogical discussion. They told me that DearMYRTLE's newsletter had guided them to this corner of cyberspace. I could tell by their conversation that they were veterans in the field, but I pressed on and asked if there was anything I could do to help them with their research. One chatter stepped forward and presented his brick wall. The ancestor's name was Amos HURLBUT. He had recently found him in the 1870 census in Iowa and was looking for his parents. The census told him that he was born in New York and was 36 years old. He already knew that Amos and wife Sarah POTTER were married in New York and that Sarah was from Franklin County, New York. He ended by telling me that Marvin HURLBUT was also found in the same part of Iowa as Amos and may be related. Eager to please, especially on my first "unofficial" day, I told him I would look to my resources and see what I could find. I always feel it best to start with the facts, so I pulled up the 1870 census to see what the chatter saw. I easily found Amos in the Iowa 1860 and 1870 census, and I saw the Marvin HURLBUT he was speaking about. But this didn't get me any closer to Amos's parents. I thought, hmmm, if Sarah was from Franklin County, New York, maybe Amos was as well. So I decided to search the 1850 census with Soundex for HURLBUTs in that county, but all matches came up empty. Not an Amos to be found. I turned to other facts in the case. Who was this Marvin fella? I decided to search for his name to see what I could find. To my surprise, Iowa cemetery records showed a Marvin HURLBUT born in 1826 in Onondaga County, New York. This seemed to match the age of the Marvin previously found on the census. My next thought: If Marvin was born in 1826, he just might be a head of household in 1850. A search produced a Marvin HERLBUT in Chautauqua County, New York, matching the age and wife of the Marvin I'd been seeking. Marvin seemed to be found, but where's Amos? Assuming Marvin was related and that families moved in packs, I decided to give a look in 1850 for other HURLBUTs in Clymer, Chautauqua County, New York. And it was there in the index where I found Daniel HERLBUT. When I viewed the census for Daniel, I let out a yell, for there was a son named Amos at home at the age of 17. Perfect match! I could have ended there, but my curiosity took over. I then found Daniel in the same town in the 1840 census. Then I found a Daniel in 1830 in Onondaga County (yes, the same county in which Marvin was born). Although I have a strong feeling, I cannot prove that Amos and Marvin are related or that Marvin is Daniel's son. But the information I found on Marvin led me to find Amos. It just goes to show you that any piece of information found can be vital to your research.

—GenHostMike

Note

As with any online genealogy topic, search your favorite portal (Google, Yahoo!, MSN, Excite, etc.) for "genealogy chat" (or "geneology chat"), and see what comes up!

Reach Out and Touch the World!

To me, what is exciting about all these different programs and formats is that they are all becoming interconnected. Your entry into AIM can be mirrored to your Twitter account; your Twitter tweets can show up on your Facebook page, and on and on.

As Amy Coffin pointed out, you can spend all day shooting questions, links, observations, and files to other genealogists and getting them back. You start typing messages with your buddy in Omaha on Twitter, and then your son at college calls you on Skype, and then your sister-in-law hails you on Google Talk, and suddenly you discover the day has slipped by. All forms of chat are this addictive. Beware!

Wrapping Up

- Internet messaging can take many forms and help you connect with other genealogists.

- Twitter is a form of "microblogging" that can help you keep up to date with the news in genealogy.

- Video chatting programs take instant messaging into audio and video as well as text formats.

- Instant messaging (e.g., AIM, ICQ, and Windows Live) is the most common form of chat and the simplest to use.

- All these forms are becoming more and more connected and usable on many platforms.

- All chat forms can be addictive—handle with care!

Chapter 7

**Fun with E-mail:
Mail Lists,
Newsletters,
and More**

Y̶ou can have more genealogy pen pals than you ever dreamed up using mail lists and forums dedicated to genealogy. Like chat and messaging, it can be addictive: You can spend all your day reading and replying to genealogy mail!

Electronic mail (e-mail) lists are discussion groups based on e-mail messages. All subscribers can send and receive e-mail from the list. Messages sent to the mailing list get forwarded to everyone who subscribes to it. No message is private when posted to the list, even though you will receive them with your e-mail program just as you do private messages. Replies to messages from the list get sent as well, where they are forwarded to all participants. These are often mirrored to sites such as RootsWeb or Ancestry, where forums of messages still reside.

Mailing lists can be completely automated, with a program taking care of subscribing people to the list, forwarding messages, removing people from the list, and sending your chosen lists to your e-mail box. Or, real people can get into the loop, handling any and all of the mailing list functions that programs can do. Either way, if it is a mirrored list, to read the messages on sites such as RootsWeb or Ancestry.com, you have to log in with your user name and password and then go to the forum of interest.

Such "moderated" mailing lists can take two forms: They might have restricted memberships, where you need to be approved to subscribe, or a moderator (or moderators) might let anyone join but will review each incoming message before it is distributed, preventing inappropriate material from getting on to the list.

Forums are message-based systems where the messages are held on a website, waiting for you to come read them. Most forums are divided into topics, which are general categories of messages. Topics are usually locations, surnames, and general genealogy issues. Within the topics are more specific messages called threads.

Forums may have an option to e-mail you a notice when a message is posted. Others may have the option to e-mail you all new messages one by one or in a collection called a digest, which makes them like a mailing list to the user. Certain forums are moderated; most genealogy ones are.

Many mailing lists and forums focus specifically on genealogy. In addition, many more lists and forums, although not specifically for genealogists, cover topics of interest to genealogists, such as ethnic groups, historic events (e.g., the Civil War), or research techniques.

Mailing Lists

With a decent mail program, participating in mailing lists is easy. You simply have to figure out how to subscribe, manage, and unsubscribe to a list. Often, the instructions are included in the mailing list's home page.

Subscribing to Mailing Lists

Say you want to know more about genealogy in the DNA for a certain surname. Sure enough, mail lists exist for that. Searching for POWELL DNA MAILING LIST in Google, you find the RootsWeb page with details on the list. The following shows typical information for such a list:

```
POWELL-DNA-L
lists2
Topic: The POWELL-DNA mailing list is for the discussion and
sharing of information regarding DNA projects for the Powell
surname and variations (e.g., Howell, Pauwel, Pauwels, Pouel,
Powel, Powells, Powels). Additional information can be found on
the Powell Surname DNA Project website below:
There is a Web page for the POWELL-DNA mailing list at www
.flash.net/~parino/powell-surname-dna-project.htm.
For questions about this list, contact the list administrator at
POWELL-DNA-admin@rootsweb.com.
Subscribing. Clicking on one of the shortcut links below should
work, but if your browser doesn't understand them, try these
manual instructions: to join POWELL-DNA-L, send mail to POWELL-
DNA-L-request@rootsweb.com with the single word subscribe in
the message subject and body. To join POWELL-DNA-D, do the same
thing with POWELL-DNA-D-request@rootsweb.com.
Subscribe to POWELL-DNA-L
Subscribe to POWELL-DNA-D (digest)
Unsubscribing. To leave POWELL-DNA-L, send mail to POWELL-DNA-
L-request@rootsweb.com with the single word unsubscribe in the
message subject and body. To leave POWELL-DNA-D, do the same
thing with POWELL-DNA-D-request@rootsweb.com.
```

```
Unsubscribe from POWELL-DNA-L
Unsubscribe from POWELL-DNA-D (digest)
Archives. You can search the archives for a specific message
or browse them, going from one message to another. Some list
archives are not available; if there is a link here to an
archive but the link doesn't work, it probably just means that
no messages have been posted to that list yet.
Search the POWELL-DNA archives
Browse the POWELL-DNA archives
```

Now you know how to subscribe. Because you are sending this message as a command to a mailing list program, it's best to put "END" on the line below "subscribe." That way, should your automatic signature slip in, it will be ignored by the list program. If you do not do this, it's very likely that you will get a message back describing all the different ways the program does not understand what you sent.

You will receive a welcome message, which you should save to a text or document file. It will tell you how to manage your subscription to get off the list, suspend it temporarily, and prevent your own messages to the list from coming to you from the server.

An important point to note in the listing: Most mailing lists have two e-mail addresses. You use one address to subscribe or change how you use the mailing list and another to post messages to the other people on the mailing list. Some mailing lists might have a third address to use for certain administrative chores, such as reporting some violation of the list's rules to the moderator. One of the most common and annoying mistakes one sees on mailing lists is when someone posts "unsubscribe" to the address for posting messages instead of to the same address used to subscribe. Some folks simply refuse to look at the directions and continue to post "unsubscribe" messages to the message address over and over until someone flames them. Don't be one of these people.

Note that in some mailing list programs, you can send a command—who or reveal—to find out who is subscribed to a certain list. To prevent your address from being listed in the who command, you often have to send a specific command to the list server. The welcome message will tell you how, but it's usually the command conceal.

Success Story: Board Leads to Reunion

The most meaningful success I have had was because of posting to boards. I found an aunt I never knew I had. Got to go meet her. She lives about 40 miles from me. I was adopted, so finding a biological relative was great. It was from an old posting, so keep posting everywhere. You never know when you will see results!

—*G.F.S. Tupper, host of Maine Genealogy Chat, Beginners Chat, and Beyond Beginners Chat on AOL*

There are other mailing lists besides the ones at RootsWeb (although you do need to check out both www.rootsweb.ancestry .com/∼maillist and www.lists.rootsweb.ancestry.com)—for example, Yahoo! Groups.

If you go to http://groups.yahoo.com and search for "Genealogy", you will find discussion groups on Ethnic Origin, Location, General, Lineages and Surnames, Royal Genealogies, and Software, and all discussions can be e-mailed to you just as the mailing list mentioned previously can. The difference is that you have to be a registered user on Yahoo! (which is free). Other than that, you set whether you want each individual posting or a digest format with the whole day or week in one message.

Forums You Might Explore

Forums are message exchanges on a website or portal. They are usually just like mailing lists, except the messages stay on one site instead of being delivered to your e-mail box. However, there are exceptions: Some forums do have an e-mail option so that messages on topics you choose are e-mailed to you. In that case, a forum will look just like a mailing list to you. You can visit the forum often to see if there are new messages, but people just take advantage of the notification option.

You can specify that you want to know when someone posts to the "SPENCER" board, for example, and an e-mail message will be sent to you when that happens. Sometimes the actual message will also be delivered to you.

Forums

Genealogy forums abound on the Internet. Genealogy.com has 14,000; RootsWeb.ancestry.com has 161,000 message boards. The best way to find what you want is to use a search engine for the topics.

For example, let's assume I would like to discuss Powells in South Carolina. In Bing, I could search for "Powell South Carolina genealogy forum". That gets millions of hits, the top ones from

Success Story: The Web Helps Mobility-Challenged Genealogist

Being mobility challenged and on a very limited income, I have to depend mostly on the Internet at this time for my genealogy work, and I've had some success. I had a query on an Irsch surname board for my great-grandfather and the fact he had married a Pitts in Noxubee, Mississippi, in 1860. I just happened to decide to go to the Pitts surname board and posted the same query for a Lucretia Emmaline Pitts, who had married a Frank Irsch. I received a tentative confirmation from someone whose great-grandfather had a sister who had married an Irsch about that time. A few back-and-forths later, we thought we might have a connection; I asked if she had ever heard the names Aunt Em and Uncle Henry Hill. I had heard my grandmother speak of them, but didn't know if they were blood relatives. We both knew we had established the connection. "Aunt Em" was the sister of her great-great-great-grandfather, Lafayette Newton Pitts, and another sister, Lucretia, had married Frank Irsch. Their father's name was James W. Pitts, and their mother's name was Mary. We still haven't discovered her maiden name. She had a picture of some of the Irsch family that Lizzie Eaton-Bennett had identified for them as her brother and family and Grandma Pitts. She wasn't sure if the older woman was her Grandma Pitts, but she didn't think so. Lizzie Eaton-Bennett was my grandmother, and if she identified the older woman as Grandma Pitts, it would have been her grandmother, Mary ?-? Pitts. I remember my mother telling me of Aunt Annie Irsch and Grandma Pitts sending Christmas gifts when she was little. Now we proudly know we have a picture of our shared great-great-great-grandmother. We are working on other shared lines, but I would call this a wonderful tale of success from the Internet!

—*Louise McDonald*

GenForum.com, Genealogy.com, Genealogy.about.com, and Ancestry.RootsWeb.com.

All these forums will also have search functions, so I can click a link and then start searching for my ancestors among the messages.

Another good technique is to use a search engine to search for the name, date, and place you are looking for. This will result in hits from both forum and mailing list archives. Or visit some of the top sites listed in Chapter 20 and search those forums. Finally, search the portals mentioned in previous chapters. Here is a short sampling:

- **JewishGen (http://www.jewishgen.org/JewishGen/ DiscussionGroup.htm)**   The Jewish Genealogy site hosts two or three dozen groups based on geography, projects of the site, and other interests.

- **Yahoo! (http://groups.yahoo.com)**   Yahoo! has thousands of discussion groups based on surnames, geography, and ethnicity. Some are public, which means anyone can post to them, and some require you to sign up before you can post to them. Go to the Yahoo! Groups page, and search for "genealogy" and/or the surnames you need.

- **GenForum (http://www.genforum.genealogy.com)** Genealogy.com's discussion groups are lively and searchable by keyword.

- **Genealogy Register (http://www.genealogyregister.com)** This site lists links to personal family histories, and features message boards for discussion.

- **Family Tree Circles (http://www.familytreecircles.com)** Here you can post your research information and connect with other Family Tree researchers.

- **Wikitree G2G (http://www.wikitree.com/g2g)**   Wikitree.com has a forum where you can post general genealogy questions and learn more about how to use Wikitree. The site can be searched by keyword, and you can elect to have an e-mail sent to you when a question is answered. See Figure 7-1.

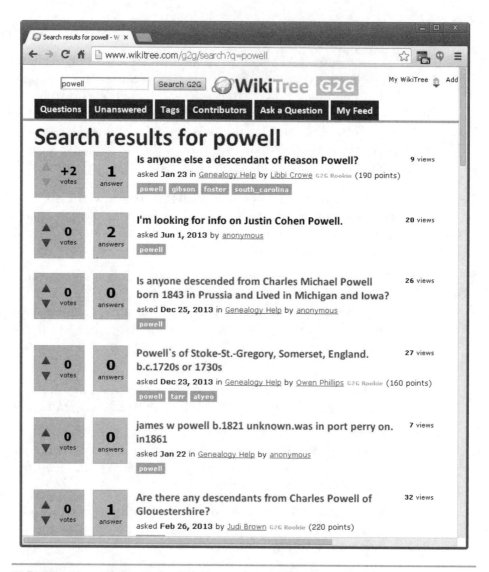

FIGURE 7-1. *The Wikitree G2G forum is a good place to ask about genealogy, place queries, or learn to use the site.*

Finding More Mailing Lists and Forums

Even though it may seem like we've covered more mailing lists than you can shake a stick at, many more exist. To find more, first check out the RootsWeb website for their ever-growing list. If you point your web browser to www.rootsweb.org/∼maillist, you'll have access to the hundreds of mailing lists hosted by RootsWeb.

Another site that keeps a list of discussion boards is Genealogy Today. To find some forums, lists, and boards, go to www.genealogytoday.com/genealogy/city/genforum.html.

For years, the best categorized and detailed list has been the one maintained by John P. Fuller. He died in 2009, and Linda Lambert and Megan Zurawicz are carrying on the list in his memory at www.rootsweb.com/∼jfuller/gen_mail.html (see Figure 7-2).

Cyndi's List (www.cyndislist.com/magazine.htm) is always a good site to visit to keep up on the latest in mailing lists and newsletters.

Wrapping Up

- E-mail discussion lists bring other genealogists right to your e-mail inbox. When you subscribe to a mailing list, always save the reply message, which usually has the "unsubscribe" instructions as well as the rules of the list.

- Forums are usually associated with websites. You can go to the site to read the latest messages or have them e-mailed to you, so that it is as easy as a mailing list.

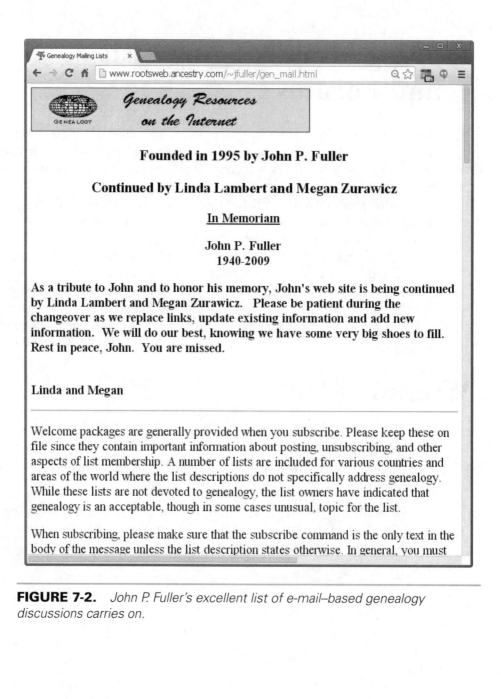

FIGURE 7-2. *John P. Fuller's excellent list of e-mail–based genealogy discussions carries on.*

Chapter 8

Social Networking

Social networks are the most popular way to contact other folks on the Web these days. You can keep up with genealogists all over the world with social network services. Using these tools, you can have conversations involving video and sound, read up on the latest news, make new friends, and have fun generally. Oh, and by the way, get some genealogy done!

"Social networks have expanded in all directions, and it's often difficult to wrap your head around the size and the scope of all these possibilities," said Amy Coffin, a professional genealogist, librarian, and blogger. "Genealogists who are just beginning to discover all that is available online should pick one or two social networking tools and learn to use them for the benefit of family history research."

As of January 2014, one site that measures popularity by number of users, number of posts, and number of responses had this ranking of social network sites:

1. Facebook
2. Twitter
3. LinkedIn
4. Google +
5. Pinterest
6. Tumblr
7. Flickr
8. VK
9. Instagram
10. MySpace
11. Tagged
12. MeetUp
13. Ning
14. MeetMe
15. ClassMates

Now, you probably could find a genealogist or two on each and every one of them, but the first five plus MeetUp are the most popular with the family historians I know.

Almost any social media network you choose will have a web-based presence that you can access with your desktop browser as well as apps for portable devices such as smart phones and tablet computers. Most of the time, signup and setup are more easily accomplished on the desktop than on an app, so all these descriptions will assume you are using your desktop computer.

A Few Definitions

Some academics define social networking sites as having three common elements: a member profile on a web-accessible page, a user-defined list of contacts, and interaction between members of different contact lists with user-defined degrees of access. As you can see, this definition would have fit Prodigy, AOL, MSN Network, and CompuServe in the early days of this century, except for the web access part. CompuServe and Prodigy are long gone, while AOL and MSN have morphed into portals, leaving room for these new and interesting "social networking sites" to pop up.

While social networking sites vary in the tools and functionality they provide, usually, where the old "online services" had forums, the newer social networking sites have a way for you to search based on common interest, connect with people, and exchange public or private messages. However, it is not as easy as it used to be. In the old days, you only had to sign on to CompuServe, input the GO word "genealogy," and wind up someplace where that is all that's going on. Now, you have to work at it, but you can build your own filters to keep things manageable. So let's look at how to use these tools for genealogy.

Social Networking 101

Most hobbyist genealogists belong to one or more of the very general ones, like Facebook. As that is the one I use most often, I'll take you through using Facebook to contact other genealogists. Once you know how to use one of them, the rest are fairly easy to use. Signing up for Facebook can be very simple: your real name (or company name) and a valid e-mail address.

Now that you have yourself set up, you can begin to search for friends, blogs, and applications to make Facebook useful for your genealogy. The easiest way to do this is to allow Facebook to search your contacts on Google, AOL, Yahoo!, or whatever you use. Then you can choose to send people e-mail announcements that you are now on Facebook.

But Facebook has pages for more than individual people. You can find groups, companies, products, and organizations using keywords. At the top left of the Facebook page is the search box. Type in **genealogy**. You will see a page similar to the one in Figure 8-1.

Just as you can for Twitter, you can create a list of people that follow an interest. On Facebook, you will see a toolbar down the left side. Click Interests and you will see an option to create a list. When you do, you can choose among your Facebook friends and "liked" pages to see a newsfeed that has only those postings. Or, you could choose to follow the posts of someone else's list, just as on Twitter.

The genealogy exchanges and information on Facebook are fun, but often, feeds will scroll by before you see them. Unlike Twitter, you cannot search the recent history of Facebook for posts that mention genealogy. The closest you can come is an Interest list like the one mentioned earlier. For this reason, it is hard to post a query about a specific genealogy problem and get a response until you have several friends yourself. You can, however, send private messages to, say, West Kentucky Genealogy or the Allen County Genealogy Center, and perhaps get a response.

Facebook does have a video chat feature like the two services mentioned later, but the interface at this writing is clunky and hard to use. It will probably improve in the future to be more like Google Hangouts, which is described later.

Another big drawback to Facebook is that the postings can be thinly disguised advertising, requests to play silly games, or outright political shill. You can block such posts, but you have to be diligent to stay ahead of Facebook's "intelligence" software that throws such postings at you. It is easier to simply glance and scroll past them.

Still, just reading the posts from genealogists, the National Archives, libraries, and more can be addicting! There is value to Facebook.

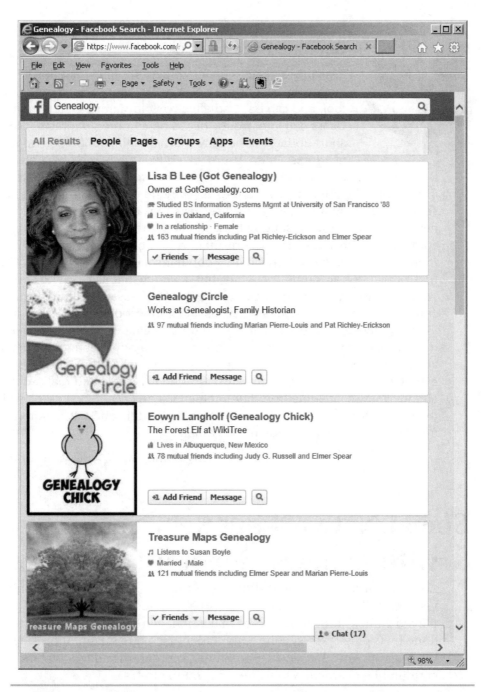

FIGURE 8-1. *Search for genealogy in Facebook, and you will find not only people, but also groups and companies with "genealogy" in their profile.*

Success Story: Facebook Connections Become Face to Face

"Facebook used to be for college students, but that's no longer the case. Now it's a mainstream social networking tool, and can be used effectively for family history purposes. Users can join groups based on common interests, provide short updates about any topic, and link to 'friends' to form networks. Often, users' extended family members are also on Facebook, and you can use the site as a way to collect family history information. Beginners may want to ask a friend or family member to help set up an account and learn the ropes. Facebook can be overwhelming until new users learn how to set up filters and limit the amount of information coming in at the same time. The result is worth it, however, as many friends can be made with this highly popular social networking tool. "I've had a Facebook account for a while, but never used it as a way to connect with genealogists until 2008. Using Facebook's message feature, I started contacting other Texas genealogists asking if they would be my friend. Many agreed and we got to know each other online. Fast-forward several months later, and I made plans to attend a genealogy meeting three hours away. Since I was new to the group, I expected to sit in the back watching everyone else chat. Imagine my surprise when I arrived and realized that I already knew six people from our interactions on Facebook. I didn't sit in the back of the room. In fact, I sat right in the middle and talked with all my friends like we'd always known each other."

—Amy Coffin, MLIS, APG, amycoffin.com

Social Networking Services with Avatars: Second Life

Long ago in the early days of online services (circa 1985), one could visit virtual "rooms." In these rooms people held conversations, played games, and "traveled" to make-believe realms. It was all done by typing text, so you really had to use your imagination. At the beginning of this century, many chat programs added avatars, cartoon-like characters to represent you to others.

Now, games, meetings, conversations, and more are possible with sound, animation, music, joint web browsing, and more. One such service is Second Life. The software is free, and most of the use of Second Life is too. You can, if you want, spend real money on virtual goods and a premium account, but you don't have to.

Note

Second Life is feature rich and resource greedy. Before you download the software, read the system requirements. Second Life is not compatible with dial-up Internet, satellite Internet, and some wireless Internet services. It may not run on graphics cards other than the ones listed on the webpage. You should have an earphone/microphone headset to fully enjoy the voice chat. When traffic gets heavy, say over two million connections, you may find yourself losing your connection repeatedly.

Go to www.secondlife.com and download the free software. Signing up is as simple as creating a handle, entering a real e-mail address, and confirming the e-mail address. Once registered, you can fill out a profile that has some details of your life in the real world, or not. As in Facebook, this Second Life profile is most useful if you include your genealogy interests so that others will see your entry when they search for "genealogy."

Your avatar can walk, talk, touch and carry things, and change clothing (the genealogists do have costume parties from time to time), as well as sit, fly, and teleport. The software shows you the steps for modifying hairstyles and adding clothing to your preferences.

But you can skip all that, take an avatar as created by the software, and go find others to talk to and interact with—others who share your love for climbing family trees. DearMYRTLE, otherwise known as Pat Richley Erickson, recommends genealogists join in on Second Life's genealogy discussions in real time and mingle with family historians at all levels of expertise. To find any genealogy-related area, use the Search button (see Figure 8-2). Click an entry in the list, read about it, and click the Teleport button to take your avatar there.

I suggest you start with Just Genealogy.

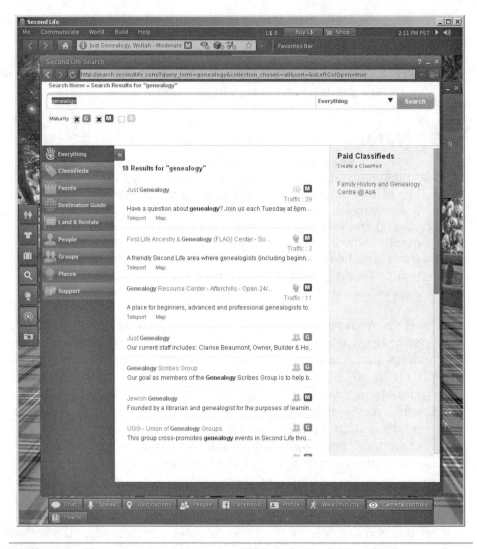

FIGURE 8-2.   *Use Search to find genealogy venues, people, and groups in Second Life.*

Just Genealogy

This is an area of Second Life where the scene is a castle and surrounding venues. All these computer graphics are designed to make Just Genealogy in Second Life a place to learn how to do family history research effectively.

Coming to Terms with Second Life

Second Life has its own jargon. Terms you will see include:

- **Avatar** The virtual reality personage (cartoon character) you create for yourself after signing up for a free account with Second Life.

- **RL** Real life.

- **SL** Second Life.

- **In-world** Signed on to SL, or online with the software.

- **SL time** U.S. Pacific Time (Universal Time –7 in Daylight Saving Time or –8 in Standard as appropriate for the time of year).

- **Voice chat** Turn on your computer speakers to listen to the discussion in-world. If you have a microphone (best with a headset), you may contribute to the conversation verbally. Those without microphones may pose questions by typing in the SL screen, just as in any chat.

- **Teleporting** Using the Second Life command to put your avatar in a different scene.

- **Gestures** Commands to have your avatar laugh, wave, pick up an object, and so on.

When visiting Just Genealogy, you'll see the avatar Clarise Beaumont (who is Pat Richley-Erickson). This avatar develops the schedule of events and coordinates with other genealogy groups in Second Life. Clarise and others host a weekly genealogy chat each Tuesday at 7:00 p.m. "SL time" (which is the same as U.S. Pacific Time, Daylight Savings when applicable). But the Just Genealogy castle isn't empty the rest of the week. All along the walls of the castle and environs, you will see placards, tartans, and other objects. They are not just decorations; they are clickable links to useful and important genealogy places on the Web—blogs, podcasts, database sites, maps, how-to info, mailing lists, message boards, etc.

The Main Event: Live Chats with Sound and Animation

The chats are the big draw. Though any chat group can be small, usually no more than 20 or so visitors, in general, the participation is active and lively. Sometimes chats can garner up to 80 different visitors. Attendance largely depends on the topic of the week. One time the topic was using "eyewitness reports" to document the life and times of an ancestor. During this chat:

- One person read a letter from his World War I ancestor using the voice function so others could hear.

- A French-Canadian genealogist described an "eyewitness" report he found in a 1587 document, which he was able to post on the chat. He had digitized the document while on his annual research trip to France.

One person read over the voice chat from *The Civil War Love Letter Quilt* by Rosemary Young (Krause Publications, 2007), a part of David Coon's letter home to his wife, Mary, describing camp conditions on March 11, 1864, for the New York 36th Regiment of the Union Army. That is just a small sampling; much more was accomplished that night! Many other social network services with avatars are popping up on the Internet, and you may eventually want to explore them too. However, Second Life is one where genealogy has established a firm beachhead and is creating new communities regularly.

Google+

Google+ is newer than Facebook or Second Life, and has not gotten the media love of the other two. This can be an advantage. It is much easier to sift through the postings to find the items and people of interest, Google+ doesn't throw so many advertising posts in your face, and it is very user friendly.

Google+ requires you to have a Google account. This is as easy as Yahoo!, AOL, Facebook, and other social networking sites. All that is required is name, e-mail address, and, optionally, wireless phone number if you want a way for them to send you a text when you forget your password. Once you do that, you also have a Google Mail (Gmail) account and a Google calendar. All the Google apps are quite useful and available with a single click from the Google Chrome browser's apps grid at the top of the browser window.

> **Note**
>
> As mentioned in Chapter 4, you can find a Google Calendar for online genealogy seminars at http://blog.geneawebinars.com/p/calendar.html. With one click, that can be added to your Google calendar.

Profile

The next step is to fill out your Google + profile. Of course, you can put in just as much or as little personal information as you'd like to share. One convention among genealogists is to include the surnames and the localities you research in either the Introduction section or under the Other Names section. In the Introduction section, you can use text editing, such as bold, italic, underlined, a bulleted or numbered list, and even a link. In Other Names, your entries will be plain text, but you can list as many lines as you like. You can see in Figure 8-3 that I not only entered my maiden and pen names, but I also listed parents', grandparents', and great-grandparents, surnames and the states where those occur.

You want to set up your profile first so that when you ask people to connect with Google + they can easily see you are not a spammer. It will also help if you allow Google access to your address book so that people you already know can be among those you ask to be in your circles.

Circles

On Google +, the people you are connected with ("follow") are in your circles. Circles are categories you define and only you see. Aunt Martha will not know whether she is in your circle called "Family" or in the circle called "Fruitcakes." All she will know is that you added her to your circles.

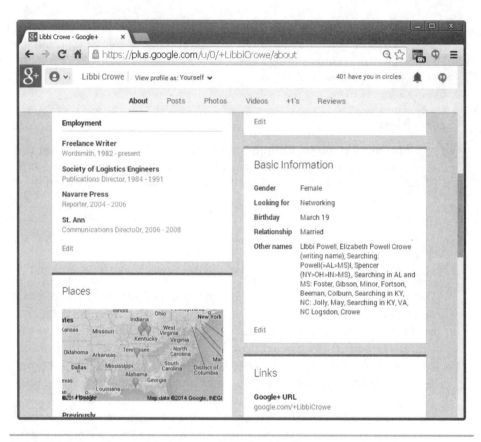

FIGURE 8-3. *In completing your Google+ profile, you can include the surnames you research in either your Introduction or under Other Names as I have done here.*

The default circle is called Following; however, you can define as many circles as you want by whatever names you like. The posts from all the people you follow will appear in your Stream, the opening page of Google+. With one click, you can restrict the Stream to show one particular circle you defined. That way, you can see only posts from your Genealogy Circle or read only posts from your Quilting Circle.

You can follow an account even if that account does not follow you back; this is one big difference between Google+ and the other two social networks covered in this chapter. Another is that you can easily search posts by keyword, so if you are looking for posts and discussions of wills or land grants, it is quite easy on Google+.

How do you find people to follow? As mentioned before, if you upload your Outlook or other e-mail address database to Gmail, Google+ can search for matches with those already on the service. You can also use the Google+ search bar for topics and names to find people to follow. Others who use Google+ may find you in their searches and ask you to follow them. Finally, once you have followed a few people, Google+ will start making suggestions.

Pages and Communities

In addition to individual people, you can follow pages or communities. A page is the account for an organization, brand, product, destination, and/or project. You can create your own page to display your family history discoveries, for example.

Communities on Google+ are equivalent to the groups on Facebook: one post going to several people or the entire Stream with posting privileges limited to the members of the community. You can find both Google+ pages and communities when you use the search bar.

Stream

The Stream is the display of posts by those you follow. The posts on Google+ may be short text-only entries like tweets, or may be longer with pictures, embedded video, or links. You can express approval for a post by clicking the 1+ button on the lower left of each post, much as you "like" a post on Facebook.

Use the search bar at the top of the Stream display to search for "Genealogy." You can filter the results by Everything, People and Pages, Communities, Posts, or Photos. Whichever filter you choose from the top, you can also filter those results by "Best Of" or "Most Recent." What appears in the search will include both those you follow and those you do not.

Note

Remember that Google also owns YouTube and Blogger; searching those for "genealogy" is an interesting exercise as well!

Hangouts

While you are on Google+, you may notice tucked up in the right side of the toolbar what looks like a quotation mark. This is the link to Google Hangouts and Google Hangouts On Air. These are live video chats, as described in Chapter 6. Just like the Stream, you can search for Hangouts about genealogy. A Hangout On Air is public by default. A Hangout is usually private by default, open only to those invited. Let me elaborate a little on that.

Hangout On Air is a live broadcast on your Google+ account, YouTube channel, and anywhere else you want to put the link. When you host a Hangout On Air, you can have an unlimited number of attendees, but only up to 10 can actively participate with camera and microphone at a time. Everyone who clicks the link can view and send text comments to the host. Most of the time, a Hangout On Air is an event, announced in advance and publicized to some extent. Hangouts On Air are recorded, and you can download that recording for editing and later uploading to YouTube or any other video sharing site, or let it be uploaded to your YouTube channel automatically as is.

A Hangout, on the other hand, is more private by default and, in practice, more spontaneous. All viewers are able to comment and watch the Hangout, but viewing live in real time and participating is by invitation only. Google+ shows who on your Follow list is online right now when you click that quotation mark, and you can invite them to Hangout. Or, you can tell your cousin to log onto Google+ at a certain time and date so that you can initiate a Hangout.

Note

You can make a Hangout On Air private instead of public by beginning the Hangout On Air on the YouTube page instead of from the Google+ page. In setting up the Hangout On Air from YouTube, choose Private if you do not want comments, or choose Unlisted if you want participants to comment.

As a genealogist, you will want to use Hangouts and Hangouts On Air often. The Association for Professional Genealogists has one chapter that meets only by Hangouts.

Success Story: Mondays with Myrt Finds Hessians!

It was a typical Mondays with Myrt Hangout On Air on March 18, 2013. During all Myrt's Hangout On Air sessions, both the video and the typed comments are saved. You can go to http://plus.google.com/+PatRichleyErickson/posts/UPSGKeNGxpL and read how in the original Hangout On Air comments, Heather Wilkinson Rojo mentioned a great site for researching Hessian ancestors. At the end of the session, Heather mentioned to Pat that she was going to go research her Hessians. Within a week, Pat was able to post the following:

> This just in via e-mail/iPad from Heather: "We were just on the 3rd floor of the FHL. We found 20 volumes of the journal of the Johannesburg Schwalm Historical Society. Not only did we find my Hessian and his regimental history, and other previously unknown tidbits of his story, but I found an entire article on the Anton Shoop mentioned by one of your listeners in the comments during the webcast.
>
> We happened to be sitting with Russ Worthington. He gave me the name of your "Shoop" descendant. I've photographed the chapter to mail to her later.
>
> I thought you'd get a kick out of hearing this little adventure!
>
> —Heather Rojo

Many online genealogy seminars use Hangouts On Air; some genealogy clubs use Hangouts On Air for board meetings before the regular meetings; families can hold confabs during the holidays using Hangouts. Imagine using Hangouts to record an oral history with your grandparents to save for future generations. The genealogy applications are endless!

MeetUp

MeetUp.com is a different type of online social network. The point of MeetUp is to arrange face-to-face meetings in the real world. If you go to the site, you can sign in easily with your Facebook account. MeetUp reads your location from that and shows you the meetings in your area. You can search for genealogy MeetUps and see registered MeetUps from all over the world.

Uses for genealogy include local clubs and association meetings in the city where you live or to which you intend to travel, and finding other genealogists in your area to create a meeting if none exists. I briefly had regular MeetUps with two other genealogists at our local library to help each other tackle some brick walls.

Wrapping Up

- Social networking services help you collaborate with other genealogists.

- You can do it by text (the old-fashioned way) or with varying degrees of text, sound, video, animation, and pictures.

- Facebook has several genealogists, and is a convenient way to keep up with the latest in genealogy.

- Second Life is a multimedia social networking experience, with many genealogy lectures and chats happening regularly.

- Google+ is popular with genealogists precisely because the rest of the world has not discovered it yet.

- MeetUp can help you connect with genealogists in real life.

Chapter 9

Blogging Your Genealogy: Sites, Software, and More

ousin Bait. That's what Amy Coffin, MLIS and genealogy blogger at WeTree.blogspot.com, calls her blog posts (see Figure 9-1). If you want to cast your nets for possible connections in your genealogy, a regular blog is a great way to do it. It's also an excellent place to share your research problems and genealogy happy-dance moments to other genealogists around the world. Blogs can truly be one of the most important tools for your genealogy research!

Bill West, whose blog West in New England is at http://westinnewengland.blogspot.com, said, "I've had a quite a few cousin contacts through my blog, mostly from my dad's side of the family. The most dramatic one for me, though, was the one with the cousin from my mom's paternal side. Her parents divorced when she was a child back in the 1930s, and there was no contact with his family that I know of after I was born. Then one of my cousins found my blog and contacted me. We've exchanged phone calls and pictures, and I met with another cousin for lunch."

FIGURE 9-1. *Amy Coffin of We Tree Blog writes to attract more cousins.*

Caroline Marshall Pointer said, "I've had lots of them on my blog Family Stories (http:// yourfamilystory-cmpointer.blogspot.com) and then I incorporate them into my blogging, which leads to more success stories. And then I share some blogging with cousin bait tips on BloggingGenealogy.com (www.blogginggenealogy.com/blog .html)."

Amy Coffin said, "I started this blog (1) so I could talk about genealogy without bugging my nongenealogy family and (2) to get my ancestral names out there online, in the chance that someone would be searching for the same names and stumble on my blog. This has happened many times; I just don't always write about it.

"The best success story had to do with my great-grandmother Getrude Baerecke. I knew all about her, but nothing about her ancestors. The situation remained unchanged for months until one day a woman read my blog and e-mailed me saying she had been researching the Baerecke line. She knew everything about the Baerecke family, except for a woman named Gertrude who was an elusive mystery to her. Would I happen to have any information on Gertrude? Right there, the puzzle pieces fit together.

"I really, really, really believe blogs are one of the easiest, cheapest, and most successful ways to advance personal genealogy research. I believe in this tool so much that I came up with 52 ideas (one for each week), which I share freely on my website."

So, are you ready to jump on the blog bandwagon?

Blogging Guidelines

Your blog must have a purpose: to give, share, and relate. The more you do these things, the more you will receive in return. This is much easier than you think!

Your blog will be a dynamic webpage that you can easily change daily, or more than once a day if you wish. Remember, web search spiders love "fresh" content and take note whenever a page changes. So when you blog, you become very findable on the Web! When you create a blog and often mention the surnames you are searching, then you will pop up in the search engines. A visitor may find something on your blog that is of help or has something that helps you, and there you have online genealogy at its best!

> ## Note
>
> A dictionary definition for *blog* is "a website that contains an online personal journal with reflections, comments, and often hyperlinks provided by the writer; *also* the contents of such a site." The verb "to blog" means to make entries in such a journal. The etymology is short for "web log," and it first started appearing around 1999. One who writes a blog is a blogger. The gerund is blogging.

How to Blog Effectively

Writing a blog is not any harder than any other writing, and no easier! But writing for the Web is a little different than writing a book or a magazine article.

When you write for the Web, you must picture your reader leaning forward, ready to click away from here as quickly as interest flags. When reading a book or a magazine, the reader tends to be more relaxed and usually has set aside this time to be reading. Reading something on the Web usually has to do with accomplishing something else, and doing it while in some sort of office chair, or at the least while holding a smart phone. Not relaxed, in other words. Your genealogy blog has to capture the eyeballs and hold them to the end, or the mouse clicks them away like the heels of Dorothy's ruby slippers. But though that makes it sound like work, it can also be very rewarding.

As Robert Ragan of Treasure Maps Genealogy (http://amberskyline .com.treasuremaps) puts it, a blog gets your genealogy done.

When you blog, you are giving back to the world of online genealogy, and that helps keep you motivated to find even more. Remember what goes around comes around! If you address your readers and use the first person sparingly, that keeps your blog from being self-centered blather. That way, you are focusing outward, not inward, and drawing the reader in. You can encourage readers to leave comments, ask questions, offer suggestions, and contribute information by holding back some of your information, indicating you have more to share.

Here is a quick list of writing tips:

- **Be passionate**   If today's topic is your personal genealogy, let your excitement show. If it's a friend's genealogy success you are writing about, convey that sense of joy.

- **Be informal**   Write your blog exactly as you would talk to a friend. In fact, that's what you are doing: telling all your web friends what is new about your search for family history.

- **Breezy is good, but long-winded is not**   Draft a post, read it over. Look for repeating yourself, wandering off topic, or using needless adjectives. Also give up clichés, unless you are using them as irony.

- **Spell check**   Most of the blogging sites and software (see the Note) have a spell check. Or, write it in your word processor first, spell check, and then paste into your blog software. Learn to love www.dictionary.com. I do!

- **Pay attention to layout**   Line breaks, subheads, boldface, and italics can help you express yourself. Bulleted lists catch the eye and make the reader feel efficient.

- Occasionally, go with a narrative or a picture so that your blog doesn't look the same every day, making the reader feel like they have read it already.

- Every entry should have a good headline and descriptive tags. Draw those readers in with creative teasers, helping them know what to expect from your posts. This can be as fun as finding a female ancestor!

Software and Services for Blogging

Blogging platforms are as plentiful as mosquitoes in a swamp. Give several a try, but you will find these three at the top of most "Best Blogging" lists:

- **Blogger** (http://www.blogger.com), from Google, is one of the oldest and most stable of the free online blog services. Blogger's best feature is how easy it is to set up and use; you can have your blog up in 15 minutes or less, regardless of your experience level. With drag-and-drop template editing, dynamic updating, geotagging for location-based blogging, and easy publication from editing tools like Google Docs, Microsoft Word, and Windows Live Writer, it is the blogging tool of choice for all the genealogists quoted earlier.

- **WordPress** (http://www.wordpress.org) is a free blogging tool and weblog platform. It is also a wonderful site for learning about blogging because they have tutorials for every aspect of the subject. Even if you go with another platform, look at WordPress's how-tos—they will help. I have been using WordPress for several years.

- **Tumblr** (http://www.tumblr.com) is very popular with under-30 web users. It is a microblogging site. You get more characters than Twitter, but not so many as with Blogger and WordPress. Images, links to video, and the like are possible, and you can customize the look; in addition, you can write your Tumblr post in no time. It's a good way to dip your toe into the blogging ocean.

Note

Choose one platform and stick with it. If you jump from platform to platform more than once, it will confuse the search engine spiders and make it hard for them to find your current site. If you decide to switch, download all your posts from the old one and put them on the new one. Yes, that is just as tedious as it sounds, but it will be better in the end.

Success Story: Another Jones Surprise, or Why Genealogists Should Blog

We Tree Adventures in Genealogy. Monday, August 3, 2009, by Amy Coffin, MLIS Texas, United States. Reprinted with permission.

In my last entry about Keeping Up With The Joneses, I shared that I was learning about my Jones line. I discovered that they spent some time in Cooke County, Texas, but that I had yet not found the time to learn about the area and its genealogy resources.

In the comments section of that blog post, one of my friends and faithful readers, who also happens to be a very smart librarian, shared with me a link for a Jones Cemetery and asked if these were my Jones folks. They were!

Many of the names in the cemetery are familiar. Duckett and Bostick stand out. Probably anyone from Asheville, North Carolina, has a connection. However, what stood out on that page was a grave marker transcription for:

> JONES, Harriet Elizabeth 8 Oct 1859 - 18 Aug 1861 dau of R. M. and
> Sarah Neilson Jones note: no longer found

This entry got me excited because R. M. and Sarah are my great-great-great-grandparents. Harriet was a child I did not know of! My great-great-grandfather, Frank Wiley Jones, had another sister! I went to enter her name in my files and I stopped...

She was born on the same day as my great-great-grandfather. He was a twin.

The only evidence I had that Harriet even existed came from the Jones Cemetery transcription webpage. I've yet to find them in the 1860 census. I'm wondering if they were en route from North Carolina to Texas then.

The only reason I now know about it is because I blogged about my Jones line and someone took the time to comment and share what she knew.

This is why all genealogists should blog. We are not islands. So many other folks out there have information to share. You don't have to be an expert writer. Just get your surnames out there. You'll be surprised at what you find... or who finds you.

Time and Circumstance

This may all seem very time consuming, and getting set up can take you the better part of a day as you define for yourself your blog's focus, theme, design, and permanent home. But after that, it really only takes a little bit of each day, or week, or month, as you decide, to keep it up to date and fresh.

Here are just a few ideas to get your genealogy muse working:

- Manic Monday (things about genealogy that drive you crazy)

- Tombstone Tuesday (pictures or descriptions of interesting, unusual, or pertinent tombstones)

- Wordless Wednesday (usually pictures, sometimes a link, sometimes a map)

- Thursday Treasures (heirlooms and their stories)

- Follow Friday (blogs you follow and why)

- Surname Saturday (highlight a surname you are pursuing, where and when)

- Night Moves (genealogy you found late at night on the Internet!)

Many more blogging prompt ideas can be found at http://geneabloggers.com/daily-blogging-prompts. There you will find at least six ideas for any day of the week!

Wrapping Up

- Blogging is free, fun, and easy to set up.

- Sharing your genealogy on a blog can garner responses from others searching your surnames.

- You need only spend a few minutes a day keeping your blog current.

- Blog entries are best when they are casual in tone, have enough information to intrigue the reader, and are tagged to help web engine spiders find them.

- Idea prompts can help you get started and keep going.

Chapter 10

DNA Genealogy

The most important advance in genealogy in the last 20 years after the Internet is DNA genealogy. Many different companies and websites can help you pursue this aspect of family history. However, this field has jargon and terms that can make your head spin, so let's look at that part first.

DNA (deoxyribonucleic acid) is a nucleic acid molecule. It makes up the chromosomes that contain genes. Genes determine the hereditary characteristics that pass from one generation to the next. You have seen television shows where DNA solved crimes; now it is being used to solve genealogy!

As far as chromosomes go, you will remember from high school biology that girls have XX and boys have XY. That Y-chromosome changes (mutates) very slowly because the majority of the Y-chromosome DNA does not mix (recombine). The Y-chromosome is passed down the male line from father to son, just as surnames are in Western societies, so using the Y-chromosome for genealogy can tell you a lot about common male ancestors. Using the mitochondrial DNA (mtDNA) can trace female ancestry the same way.

So you can get tests on YDNA for male ancestors and mtDNA for female ones. But that is not all. You can also get autosomal DNA, which tests for all the other chromosomes besides the ones that make you a boy or a girl.

With DNA testing, you can find out if two people are descended from a common ancestor, if you are related to another group of people with the same surname, whether the paper trail you are following is accurate, and get clues to what regions of the globe your ancestors came from.

Note

Remember the discussion about surprises from Chapter 3. The DNA test may find a "Non Paternal Event." This is often expressed as NPE, and it means the test found a difference between the tested Y-chromosome and the surname. This could be because of a formal or informal adoption, a "wrong side of the blanket" event, a child using a nonfather surname (mother's maiden name or stepfather's name), the use of an alias, or an intentional change of surname. If this contradicts the paper trail, remember—family is more than biology sometimes.

The test results will be full of jargon, which I will try to describe a little bit here.

An *allele,* or *marker,* refers to at least one (maybe two or more) alternative forms of a gene arising by mutation found at the same place on a chromosome. It is one way to tell two people are related.

A *haplogroup* is a broader indicator. It is more about ancient ancestral groups, stretching back to prehistory, and is a way to map the migration of human beings all over the globe.

It's easiest to explain by example. Anthony Moore, a genetics graduate student at Duke University, did a 23andMe DNA test, partially out of professional curiosity and partially because the family knew very little about their genealogy. The test had some surprises, he said.

"The percentage of European admixture was higher than I would have guessed," Anthony said. "Also, now I can pinpoint that my mom's family likely hails from Southeastern Africa, which I did not know before. It identified distant cousins (fifth and sixth cousins) I could contact. I declined, though if they had identified as closer familial relationships, I would have been tempted."

DNA Overview

Judy Russell is a genealogist with a law degree who writes the blog The Legal Genealogist. She blogs to help folks understand the often mysterious and even unfathomable legal concepts and terminology that are crucial to pursuing family history. She also covers DNA genealogy, especially her own successes and challenges with it. Judy holds a bachelor's degree in journalism and political science from George Washington University in Washington, D.C. and a law degree from Rutgers School of Law – Newark.

Judy said in her opinion is it never too early to begin your DNA genealogy, and indeed, should become as standard a practice as searching for wills and deeds.

"It's only part of the plan; it can only work when it's used with the usual paper-trail genealogical research and is never done instead of the paper-trail work. But it's [a] part that can steer you in the right direction from the outset," Judy said.

Just for an example, Judy said one of her ancestors was constantly in trouble with the law—so much that she suspected he might have changed his name in trying to stay one step ahead of the law. One simple YDNA test for a direct male line ancestor told her the ancestor did indeed keep his surname through it all. But if he had changed it and she had no DNA test, she might have spent years chasing the wrong bloodline.

There are limits to what the DNA tests can do, however. For example, more than five generations back, autosomal DNA tests may not prove what you need to know. With the autosomal DNA, your chances of making a match decrease with every generation. For a second cousin—that is, you two have a common great-grandparent—it is very accurate. Results are about 90 percent accurate at the third cousin level, about 50 percent accurate at the fourth cousin level, 10 percent accurate at the fifth cousin level, and less than 2 percent accurate beyond that. The autosomal DNA does recombine, or change, with generations. All of this is well described on Judy's blog or at the wiki of the International Society of Genetic Genealogists (ISOGG).

However, as noted, the YDNA and mtDNA (tracing the mother's line) are for markers that do not change much, that do not recombine or mutate very often. These markers can often remain valid back for hundreds if not thousands of years.

Judy pointed out that a DNA test can confirm or disprove a surname, or a direct paternal (YDNA) or direct maternal (mtDNA) link. It can confirm a link to a cousin via autosomal DNA, but it cannot disprove it. It can determine that two people are related.

"It can't tell you *how* two people are related," Judy said. "A 67-for-67 YDNA match could be uncle-nephew, or father-son, or paternal cousins, or some other relationship. Autosomal DNA can't even tell me for sure that I'm not related to someone else; it can only tell me that I don't share enough DNA with another person to be confirmed."

Judy said to her, the best aspect of DNA genealogy is how it can show you what the paper trail cannot, but the biggest shortcoming is the lack of definition on how people are related.

Judy's Success Story

"I've confirmed a circumstantial case as to the identity of one set of third great-grandparents through autosomal testing. My second great-grandmother was married before 1850, so she was never on the census by name in her parents' household. There is no birth, marriage, or death record to be found and no will identifying her as a child of this couple. But the DNA evidence is compelling," Judy said. The story, which was detailed in *National Genealogical Society Magazine,* October-December 2011, is summed up here.

Martin Baker (1797-1868) and Elizabeth Baker (1797-1854), buried in the Baker Cemetery in Parker County, Texas, were the brick wall in Judy's case. Although the family had confidence Martin was a son of Revolutionary War soldier David Bake, Elizabeth was a mystery. Lots of census and bible records seemed to match up. Yet, one census record gave Elizabeth's birthplace as Kentucky, instead of North Carolina, and a published report had Elizabeth Buchanan married to someone other than Martin Baker.

Well, YDNA and mtDNA can't solve this sort of problem, as no unbroken line, male or female, could be shown in the paper trail. But autosomal DNA testing appeared.

Unlike YDNA and mtDNA, autosomal DNA "frees us from the tyranny of direct gender lines," according to Megan Smolenyak Smolenyak in the article Judy wrote. Using DNA in chromosomes that are not gender specific allowed a comparison of a maternal uncle to a documented descendant of William and Elizabeth Buchanan.

"We have no other potential lines in common with the Buchanan descendant, and we match... We now know we are Buchanans," Judy said.

The other big drawback, according to Judy: "I keep paying for DNA tests for cousins who match everybody else in my family but don't share enough DNA in common to match me! (That needs a smiley face emoticon.)" She also said the percentages you are given about nationalities—say, for example, 75 percent British and 25 percent Italian—are better for cocktail party fodder than genealogy data.

Online DNA Sites

Of course, this twenty-first-century tool is all over the Web. Here are few places to start:

- The ISOGG, mentioned earlier, is at http://www.isogg.org/. Here you can find a place to study, discuss, and participate in many online DNA genealogy subjects.

- The National Genealogical Society has a free, self-paced course at http://www.ngsgenealogy.org/cs/genetic_genealogy.

- DNA Gedcom (http://www.dnagedcom.com/) is especially useful for adoptees, but anyone with a DNA test result can use their tools to compare and contrast your data with others. It has a very simple way to upload your 23andMe file, and several good documents explaining DNA genealogy.

- As of this writing, most of the major online genealogy sites such as Wikitree allow you to upload DNA results. So do the major genealogy software packages.

- Steve Morse has tried to demystify DNA genealogy at http://www.stevemorse.org/genetealogy/dna.htm.

- Genetealogy.com is a portal for DNA genealogy, forums, discussion groups, and surname groups.

So many companies now test and so many people have now participated that the databases of surnames is overwhelming. Still, if you search for the surname you are researching plus "DNA genealogy," you will probably come up with a good site like the one in Figure 10-1. This is the Powell Surname DNA Project. All the participants have taken the test from FamilyTree DNA and are comparing results to find cousins. You can see in the second line that George Washington Powell is one of the ancestors identified in the tests; he is a son of my William Reason Powell, so I am definitely joining this group!

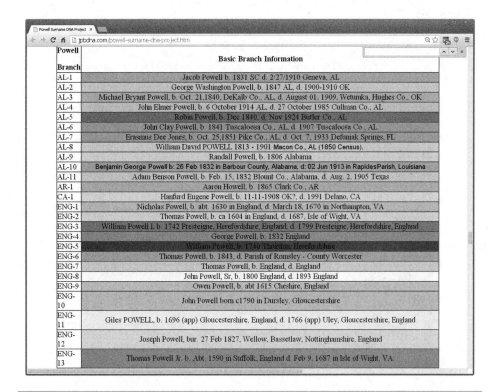

FIGURE 10-1.   *Surname-specific DNA sites and projects are appearing on the Web.*

Wrapping Up

- DNA genealogy is becoming a common way to search family history.

- Tests include YDNA for male lines, mtDNA for female lines, and autosomal DNA for broader groups.

- DNA genealogy can help you break down brick walls.

Part III

The Nitty Gritty: Places to Find Names, Dates, and Places

Chapter 11

Vital Records and Historical Documents

Vital records are the foundation and building blocks of your family history research. These are the records of life: birth, marriage, and death. At the very least, for everyone you find in your ancestry, you need the time and place of the birth, marriage (if applicable), and death. But genealogy can also be about family history: What were the times like? What important historical events affected your ancestor?

Other important records are naturalization, census records, and land ownership. Other milestones in life can also be included in your genealogy data: baptism, bar/bat mitzvah, graduation, divorce, and so on. More and more, you can find at least clues to these records online; in some cases, you can get digitized versions of the records themselves. Historical documents, such as censuses, diaries, wills, court cases, and government publications, can put flesh on the bones of our ancestors, at least in our imaginations, when they mention individuals.

Such records are usually stored in some form at archives and libraries. In this chapter, you'll learn that some things can be found online, while others can be ordered online, and still others you have to visit in person or ask for by mail, but you might be able to print the form you need from an Internet site.

Among the best of the online sites maintained by the U.S. federal government are the Library of Congress (LOC) and the National Archives and Records Administration (NARA). Both the LOC and NARA sites have been revamped recently, with links to genealogy guides, tips, and resources gathered together for easy access. You'll find these sites useful to help you decide what to ask for by mail or if you should visit in person.

Note

You'll eventually want to visit a NARA branch or the LOC in person because, although many resources are online, not every book or document is available that way. Also, NARA sites have free access to many of the online genealogy services that are available only by subscription to individuals.

Other important federal records online are the Bureau of Land Management records of original land grants and patents, immigration records, and naturalization records. Some states and counties also have certain vital records and censuses—sometimes online and sometimes just the contact information for ordering a copy.

This chapter gives you a short overview of what's where and how to access the resources of these sites. Most of the examples I give pertain to finding American records; however, vital records are available in many countries, and Chapter 15 will deal with that.

Vital Records

In the United States, most birth, adoption, death, divorce, and marriage records will be at the state level, although some counties may also have copies. Usually, you have to write to the organization that has the records and enclose a check to get a certified copy. You need to have a date and a place to go with a name in order to find where an ancestor's vital records are. In rare cases, you can find the actual document online, unless it is more than a century old and some volunteer group has scanned or transcribed it to be uploaded to the Internet. Furthermore, as discussed in Chapter 1, many professional genealogists insist on a certified copy, if not the original document itself, for proof of genealogy.

To get a certified copy of any of these records, write or go to the vital statistics office in the state or area where the event occurred. Addresses and fees are often found online at the state's website. Usually, a fee for each document will cover copying and mailing. Each time you request a record, include a check or money order payable to the correct office and in the correct amount for the number of copies requested; sometimes, a credit card will be accepted. Don't send cash.

When you find information on an office, a phone number is usually included. Before you send off your request, be sure to call to verify that the rates haven't changed. Also, in many cases, you can find an online page with the address for obtaining current information, and sometimes you can even order the records online by credit card. Often, you will have to include something like a photocopy of your driver's license as well.

Other steps to take:

- Type or print all names and addresses in the letter.

- Be very specific about what you are asking for.

- Be sure to include the payment.

The National Center for Health Statistics has list of where to write for U.S. records at www.cdc.gov/nchs/w2w.htm. That is usually a good place to start. Also, if you know the state where your ancestor was born or died, search for "vital records" and that state in any search engine. The same is true outside of the United States.

These national sources are great for twentieth-century records. However, if you need information on earlier centuries, city, regional, and local archives may be your best bet. Use your favorite search engine to look for the term "vital records" and the geographical area you need. In Figure 11-1, you can see where I found Bedfordshire/Luton, UK, and searched for Gerard Spencer, Stotfold. The site's

FIGURE 11-1. *Using Bedfordshire's Archive search, I found a 1581 record of an ancestor.*

URL is www.bedfordshire.gov.uk/CommunityAndLiving/
ArchivesAndRecordOffice/.

> **Note**
>
> When requesting information, use the proper form and don't
> include your whole genealogy; simply include the pertinent data
> for the record you want. County clerks aren't going to read through
> a long narrative to find out what they need to do.

In another example, in the state of Tennessee, many vital records, such as births, deaths, and marriages, were not recorded by the state before 1908. Four cities—Chattanooga, Knoxville, Nashville, and Memphis—did keep local records that are now available through the Tennessee State Library and Archives. Searches of these records can be requested by mail if you know the year of the event (birth, death, etc.). The website for the Memphis Public Library has an online index to Memphis death records that covers the years 1848–1945 at www.history .memphislibrary.org. You can get land grant records, too. The fees for these services range from $5 to $20. Go to the Tennessee State Archives site (www.tennessee.gov/tsla/index.htm) for the forms and links.

Tennessee is quite typical: Before Social Security, many states did not keep birth and death records, but localities might have. When Social Security was enacted, many people born in the late nineteenth century had to request a birth certificate be created for them; marriage records in some states were also lax until Social Security. In these cases, you must ask for a delayed certificate, that is, one that was created at the request of the person involved after the fact.

Library of Congress

The mission of the Library of Congress (www.loc.gov) is to "make its resources available and useful to the Congress and the American people and to sustain and preserve a universal collection of knowledge and creativity for future generations." Today, the LOC has amassed more than 100 million items and become one of the world's leading cultural institutions. The Library of Congress site gives online access to a small portion of the holdings.

Note

You need to download and read the PDF file titled "Genealogical Research at the Library of Congress" at www.loc.gov/rr/genealogy/bib_guid/research.pdf.

The LOC Local History and Genealogy website has four sections that are of particular use to genealogists (see Figure 11-2). The Local History and Genealogy Reading Room page (www.loc.gov/rr/genealogy) has information on how to prepare for a visit to the reading room. It describes what the room holds and allows you to search the card catalog of holdings. You can search these by subject, author, and other criteria.

An important link from this page is to the search hints. As you can imagine, in a catalog of over 100 million items, finding your particular needle is possible, but tricky. Happily, the LOC catalog uses Boolean terms. Search syntax for keyword searching in the Library of Congress online catalog is similar to that of some Internet search engines—use double quotes for phrase searches and type Boolean operators in uppercase. For example, to get an exact phrase in the subject field, you can enter "Spencer family" or "Madison County Alabama." Do note, however, that the subject field may have county both spelled out and abbreviated as "co." so search on both. You can search for specific states' military pensions (military pensions Ohio), specific countries (Heraldry Ireland) and specific record types (Wills Madison County Alabama). You can search for specific books, too, by putting the title in quotation marks and the author after the connector AND.

Many items do not circulate; however, an interlibrary loan may be possible. For libraries in the United States, the Library of Congress serves as a source for material not available through local, state, or regional libraries. A book circulated this way must be used on the premises of the borrowing library; it becomes a temporary reference for that library's collection for up to 60 days. Requests are accepted from academic, public, and special libraries that make their own material available through participation in an interlibrary loan system. Participation is usually indicated by membership in one of the major U.S. bibliographic networks (for example the Online Computer Library Center or OCLC) or by a listing in the American

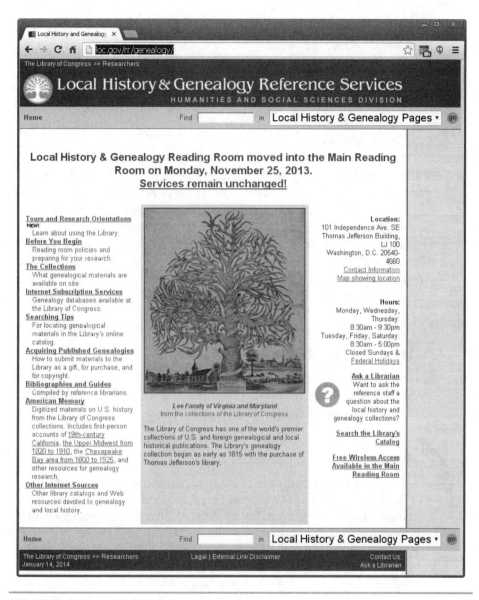

FIGURE 11-2. *The Library of Congress has a guide to using the resources there.*

Library Directory (Bowker) or the Directory of Special Libraries and Information Centers (Gale). So if you find an item that you feel may help your genealogy search, check with your local public library to see if they can participate. You will need the LOC call number (the

LOC does not use the Dewey Decimal System), author, title, and date of publication.

American Memory

This section contains documents, photographs, movies, and sound recordings that tell some of America's story. The direct link is www.memory.loc.gov.

On the American Memory home page, you can click Collection Finder to explore other primary source material. The collections are grouped by subject, then time, then place, and then library division. You can also browse by format if you want a sound file or picture. Each collection has its own distinct character and subject matter, as well as narrative information to describe the content of the collection. Whereas searching all the collections at once could leave items of interest to you "buried" in a long list, visiting a collection's home page and reading the descriptive information about the collection can give you more direction in finding what you want.

American Treasures

This section of the site is of interest more for the wonderful historical artifacts found there than for any specific genealogy information. The direct link is www.loc.gov/exhibits/treasures.

Note

If you're researching African-American roots, you'll want to look at the African-American Odyssey page at www.memory .loc.gov/ammem/aaohtml/aohome.html. This exhibition examines the African-American quest for full citizenship and contains primary source material, as well as links to other African-American materials at the LOC.

Using the Library of Congress

Click Using The Library of Congress on the home page, and you can click your way through an excellent tutorial on the ins and outs of researching the library in person. If you need to make a trip to the LOC, reading this section first can save you some time and frustration.

The Library Today

This link from the home page tells you about new exhibits, collections, and events at the LOC and its website. Visit it at least once a week because anything new posted to the website will be announced here. The direct link is www.loc.gov/today/.

Research Tools

The Research Tools page at www.lcweb.loc.gov/rr/tools.html takes you to a large set of useful links of interest for researchers, both on the LOC site and on other websites. These include desk references you can use on the Web, the LOC card catalog of all materials (including those not online), and special databases.

The Vietnam Era Prisoner of War/Missing in Action and Task Force Russia Databases at http://lcweb2.loc.gov/pow/powhome.html are examples of databases. This URL takes you to a page that gives you access to a massive database of over 137,000 records pertaining to U.S. military personnel.

National Archives and Records Administration

The Library of Congress and the National Archives and Records Administration together are a treasure trove for the family historian. However, using these resources can also be like a snipe hunt! Unlike a library, where you walk up to the card catalog computer, type a subject, find the Dewey Decimal System number, walk to the shelf, and get the book, the archive is organized by government agency. Furthermore, what you find in that catalog at the archives may be a book, a manuscript, or a government whitepaper. This complexity means that first-time archive users often need help.

At the NARA, whether online or in person, you can get that help. At many national archives, that is not the case. For example, Britain's Public Record Office has rows of volumes listing the contents of files for the Admiralty, the Foreign Office, and Scotland Yard, but the polite archivist there will simply point you to the right shelf. France's Archives Nationales and Germany's Bundesarchiv operate the same way. Though the NARA has a long tradition of helping researchers one on one, that may not be the case for long if funding woes continue.

Freedman's Bureau

Archivist of the United States Allen Weinstein announced in early 2007 that the National Archives completed the five-year project to preserve and microfilm the field office records of the Bureau of Refugees, Freedmen, and Abandoned Lands (the Freedmen's Bureau). Now the LOC has 1,000 rolls of microfilm reproducing over 1 million Bureau field office records from the former Confederate states, the border states, and the District of Columbia. All of the microfilm series of the field office records are available for research free of charge at the National Archives Building in Washington, D.C., and at the National Archives' 13 regional archives nationwide.

Following the Civil War, the Freedmen's Bureau helped former slaves make the transition from slavery to freedom by issuing food and clothing, operating hospitals and refugee camps, establishing schools, helping legalize marriages, supervising labor agreements, and working with African-American soldiers and sailors and their heirs to secure back pay, bounty payments, and pensions. The records created during the course of these activities are a rich source of documentation of the African-American experience in late-nineteenth-century America, and are essential for the study of African-American genealogy and Southern social history.

Note

Included in these extraordinary records are registers that give the names, ages, and former occupations of freedmen, as well as names and residences of former owners. For some states, there are marriage registers that provide the names, addresses, and ages of husbands and wives and their children. There are also census lists, detailed labor and apprenticeship agreements, complaint registers, rosters with personal data about Black veterans (including company and regiment), and a host of documentation concerning the social and economic conditions of the Black family. These are available for $65 per roll for domestic orders and $68 per roll for foreign orders—details on how to order are on the website.

Also, don't miss the section of American Memory that is devoted to African-American research. It has several pages describing how to research African-American and Native American genealogy in the NARA site (see Figure 11-3) that may help you. It's at www.archives.gov/research/african-americans/index.html.

FIGURE 11-3. *The African-American Research page on the NARA site may help you.*

Other NARA Areas to Explore

You can click the Research Room link in the navigation bar to the left of the home page and go to Genealogy from there, or you can go straight to www.archives.gov/research/genealogy. Here you'll find information for beginners, such as the About Genealogy Research page and a list of research topics in genealogy with links to NARA resources that deal with them. Also, the website has pages to help with Chinese, Hispanic, Japanese-American, Native American, and Other Ethnic Groups/Nationalities, as well as African-American genealogy.

More advanced genealogists will want to read about the census catalogs, the online catalogs, Soundex indexing, and the latest additions to the collection. All genealogists should read the frequently asked questions (FAQs) file and the latest list of genealogy workshops. After touring this general help area, you're ready to tackle the specific resources on the NARA site.

Access to Archival Databases

You can search various subsets of the NARA holdings from their web databases, starting at http://aad.archives.gov/aad. The Access to Archival Databases (AAD) is a searchable set of records preserved permanently in the NARA. These records identify specific persons, geographic areas, organizations, and dates over a wide variety of civilian and military data, and have many genealogical, social, political, and economic research uses. Among the most popular of these databases are:

- World War II Army Enlistment Records

- Records of Prime Contracts Awarded by the Military Services and Agencies

- Records on Trading of Securities by Corporate Insiders

- World War II Army Enlistment Records

- Records About the Proposed Sale of Unregistered Securities by Individuals

- Data Files Relating to the Immigration of Germans to the United States

- Central Foreign Policy Files

OPA

The Online Public Access (OPA) portal replaced the Archival Research Catalog (ARC) in 2013. Online Public Access searches all webpages on Archives.gov and returns the websites' pages, plus catalog records, biographies, and histories from the ARC. Among the results will be electronic records that are available in OPA for viewing and/or downloading. The results will have a line that reads something like, "Includes 18 file(s) described in the catalog." Any of the hits with electronic records available online will appear in the "Online Holdings" grouping of search results.

Part of what is so wonderful about this updated catalog is the quick access to specific collections, such as the Guion-Miller Roll Index and the Index to the Final Rolls (Dawes)—two censuses of Native American populations from the 1800s and early 1900s—the World War II Army and Army Air Force Casualty List, and the World War II Navy, Marine, and Coast Guard Casualty List.

ALIC

The Archives Library Information Center (ALIC) is for professionals such as NARA staff and librarians nationwide. Its website is www .archives.gov/research/alic.

ALIC provides access to information on American history and government, archival administration, information management, and government documents to NARA staff, archives- and records-management professionals, and the general public.

On the ALIC page, you'll see links to quick searches of the book catalog, NARA publications on research, and special collections. Under Reference At Your Desk, you'll see a list of topics, including Genealogy and History. The former has general links to NARA pages already covered in this chapter, as well as links to other websites that can help with genealogy. The latter does the same for general history sites.

Microfilms

From the NARA Genealogy page, you can click Search Microfilm Catalogs. The catalogs list the various microfilms you can purchase, rent, or view onsite from NARA. These 3,400 microfilms can be searched by keyword, microfilm ID, record group number, and/ or NARA location. Most of NARA's microfilm lists and descriptive pamphlets are not online. By searching for microfilm publications in the Microfilm Publications Catalog, however, you will be able to find out if a roll list or descriptive pamphlet is available. You will need to contact one of the NARA locations listed in the Viewing Location field(s) of the microfilm publication description to find out how to get a copy of the descriptive pamphlet or roll list.

Of particular interest is the Genealogical and Biographical Research catalog. This edited list of NARA microfilm publications is at www.archives.gov/publications/microfilm-catalogs/biographical/index.html. It lists the land records, tax records, court records (including naturalization!), and war records available on microfilm.

Federal Register Publications

The *Federal Register* (www.archives.gov/federal-register) is a legal newspaper published every business day by NARA. It contains federal agency regulations; proposed rules and notices; and executive orders, proclamations, and other presidential documents. NARA's Office of the Federal Register prepares the *Federal Register* for publication in partnership with the Government Printing Office (GPO), which distributes it in paper form, on microfiche, and on the World Wide Web.

Prologue

The quarterly NARA magazine *Prologue* has a webpage you can link to from the NARA home page, or you can go directly to www.archives .gov/publications/prologue. Special issues, such as the 1997 "Federal Records in African-American Research," may be posted almost in their entirety, but usually, a regular issue has one or two features on the website, plus the regular column "Genealogy Notes." A list of previous columns can be found in the navigation bar from the Prologue page. This site is worth bookmarking.

Note

Much of what is available on the LOC and NARA sites would be most helpful for intermediate to advanced genealogists. The best way to use these sites is to have a specific research goal in mind, such as a person's military record or a name in a Work Projects Administration (WPA) oral history from the 1930s. The beginner will find the schedules of workshops on the NARA site and the how-to articles on the LOC site helpful, as well as the schedule of NARA workshops and seminars around the country.

Government Land Office

I just "glowed" when I found this resource, the Government Land Office (GLO) site. You can search for and view online original land grants and patents between 1820 and 1928, and order copies from the site.

Land Patent Searches

Go to www.glorecords.blm.gov, and click Search Land Patents in the navigation bar. Type the state and name you are looking for, and you'll get a list of matching records. For individual records, you can see a summary, the legal land description, and the document image. Not all states are available now, but the BLO is working hard to include them.

> **Note**
>
> Land patents document the transfer of land ownership from the federal government to individuals. These land patent records include the information recorded when ownership was transferred.

You can also obtain a certified copy of a record you find. In addition, you will find a link to a glossary page with details on what the search fields mean. This site does not cover the 13 colonies, their territories, and a few other states, although the site does have resource links for most states. This is because in the early years of the United States, the Congress of the Confederation declared it would sell or grant the unclaimed lands in "the West" (that is, what is now Alabama, Michigan, parts of Minnesota, Mississippi, Illinois, Indiana, Ohio, and Wisconsin). The United States could then sell this unclaimed land to raise money for the Treasury. In turn, the United States gave up its claims to any land within the boundaries of the original colonies.

When you are researching these records, please remember that things were hardly organized in the first 50 years of our nation. Click the FAQ link for some good tips on what to look for. Here's a good example of the kind of help you'll find in the GLO FAQ:

Q. What is the Mississippi/Alabama and Florida/Alabama "Crossover?"
A. The St. Stephens Meridian and Huntsville Meridian surveys cross into both Mississippi and Alabama, creating situations where the land offices in St. Stephens and Huntsville, Alabama, and in Columbus, Mississippi,

sold lands in both states. We suggest that anyone researching that area take a look at the databases for both states. The original state line between Alabama and Florida did not close against the Tallahassee Meridian survey (which covered all of Florida), but rather against the earlier St. Stephens Meridian survey in south Alabama. The state line was later resurveyed, creating a situation where some Tallahassee Meridian lands fell across the border into Alabama. We suggest that anyone researching that area take a look at the databases for both states.

One of the best resources on this site is the database of survey plats, searchable maps of the original townships. This means that if you have a land grant that gives the boundaries, you will be able to get a small map showing the land. The drawings were created to represent survey lines, boundaries, descriptions, parcels, and subdivisions mentioned in every federal land patent.

With the online shopping cart, you may request certified copies of land patents, either electronically or through the mail. Hard copy will be on a letter-sized sheet of paper (8.5 × 11 inches) of your preference (plain bond or parchment paper).

Census Records

Census records are available in a variety of forms, both online and offline. Census Links is a site with many different country censuses. As you can see in Figure 11-4, www.censuslinks.com has transcriptions of censuses, such as "Roll of Emigrants That Have Been Sent to the Colony of Liberia, Western Africa, by the American Colonization Society and Its Auxiliaries, to September, 1843" and "Ecclesiastical Census of Revilla (Mexico) 1780."

Another good source is the Archives of Canada. The first census in Canada was in 1666 by Intendant Jean Talon, who listed 3,215 inhabitants. Talon is considered the "father" of modern census-taking in Canada. Regular censuses did not begin in Canada until 1841, however. Several Canadian censuses are searchable online at www .archives.ca.

Use your favorite search engine to search for "census" and the country you are looking in to find other census resources. For example, Brazil's census information has an English page at www1 .ibge.gov.br/english/default.php.

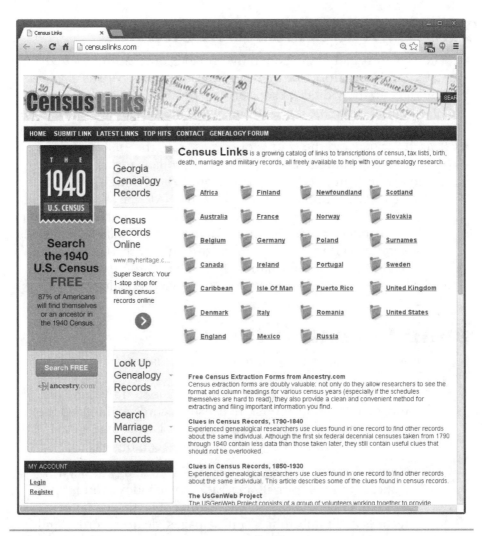

FIGURE 11-4. *Census Links is a good starting place for international census searches.*

Note

A fire in 1921 destroyed many of the original records of the 1890 census in Washington, D.C. An account of this incident is on the NARA site at www.archives.gov/research/census/1890/1890.html.

The U.S. Census Bureau

The U.S. Census Bureau generally provides only summary and statistical information for the first 72 years after a census is taken. The data on individuals is kept private until then. That means the 1930 census is the most recent one available for public use. The only services the Census Bureau provides related to genealogy are the Age Search Service and the counts of names from the 1990 census.

The Census Bureau does not have old census forms available. Copies of decennial census forms from 1790 through 1930 are available on microfilm, for research at the NARA in Washington, D.C., at ARCs, and at select Federal Depository Libraries throughout the United States. In addition, these records are available at various other libraries and research facilities throughout the United States. Additional important information at the Census Bureau site is their FAQ at http://www.census.gov/history/www/genealogy/.

Some Census Sites

Other census sites that are more local in nature include:

- The Ayrshire Free Census Project aims to transcribe all nineteenth-century Ayrshire census records and upload them to a free-to-view online database. This is part of the FreeCEN: UK Census Online Project at www.freecen.org.uk/.

- Massac County, Illinois History and Genealogy at www .genealogytrails.com/ill/massac/censusindex.html is an ongoing project to transcribe records of births, cemetery records and tombstones, census pages, death records, land grants, marriages, obituaries, biographies, and wills for this specific area.

- 1920 Yavapai County, Arizona Census Index at www.sharlot .org/archives/gene/census/index.html is a local project. The Sharlot Hall Museum in Prescott, Arizona, has posted transcriptions of the 1870, 1880, 1900, and 1920 Yavapai County census indexes. Genealogists can search the 1870, 1880, and 1900 census indexes for names and partial names and also get page numbers.

- African-American Census Schedule at www.afrigeneas.com/ aacensus/ is a volunteer project to transcribe pre-1870 census schedules.

- Transcriptions of censuses around the world are at the USGenWeb project at www.us-census.org. Click Census Surname Search from the USGenWeb home page, and then use the form to search all the census records or to narrow your search by state or year. And consider volunteering, as the work is far from complete!

- The 1940 Census is free at www.archives.com/1940-census. Earlier census lookups are part of the paid area.

State and Local Sources

Besides the U.S. federal census, some state and local governments took censuses for tax purposes. Such states include Illinois, Iowa, Kansas, Massachusetts, Michigan, Minnesota, New Jersey, New York, and Wisconsin, to name a few.

You can often trace the migration of families in America when state census records are used with other records, such as the federal census after 1850; family bibles; death certificates; church, marriage, military, probate, and land records; and other American genealogical sources. A major reference source is *State Census Records* by Ann S. Lainhart (Genealogical Publishing Company, 1992); also check FamilySearch or the catalog of a library under your state of interest and then under the headings "Census Indexes" and "Census."

Search the Internet to see if state and local censuses have been indexed. See especially the AIS Census Indexes at Ancestry.com (searching Ancestry's indexes is free; seeing the original record is for paying subscribers only).

State Archives and Libraries

Many state archives and libraries have vital records and census information. For example, www.nysl.nysed.gov/genealogy/vitrec.htm is a guide to getting genealogical records from the state of New York. The Alabama Archives has a list of available census information from the state's early years at www.archives.state.al.us/referenc/census .html. Search for the state you need, along with "census" or "archives," to find such sources.

Other Sources

Sometimes you can't find a birth, marriage, or death record in the "official" sources. In these cases, you can look in county and city court records, newspapers, cemetery and funeral home records, and local libraries. These sources can give you clues to parentage, marriages, and burials, which can help you discover where the records may be located—or that the records were destroyed in some way. Some other sources—both official and private—are working to make documents available online.

Success Story: Stepping Back Through the Censuses

The Internet is one of the few spaces in genealogy that is friendly to people not running Windows, so instead of using CD-ROMs, I subscribe to Images Online at Ancestry.com for easy access to the handwritten census pages. Reading originals instead of relying on transcribers and indexers was part of my success in finding my great-great-grandparents. Tracking my family back through ten-year steps is what worked for me. I had inherited a genealogical chart of my male Downs/Downes line in Connecticut, showing the names of the wives but nothing else about them. So I knew only that my great-grandmother was supposed to be a Charlotte Smith. First, the 1900 census showed my grandfather living with a Charlotte Thompson, described as "Mother" and shown as being born in 1849. The step back to 1890 had to be skipped, of course, because of the destruction of those records. Then the 1880 census showed my grandfather at the age of five living in Oxford, Connecticut, with a Jane M. Burnett, who called him her grandson. This allowed me to leapfrog over the puzzle of my great-grandmother Charlotte and jump directly into the puzzle of my great-great-grandmother Jane. I reasoned that for Charlotte to have been a Smith, it was necessary for this Jane M. Burnett also to have been a Smith when Charlotte was born, so I went to the 1850 census in search of Jane M. Smith.

The 1850 schedules list everybody by name, but the index lists mostly heads of household—meaning that almost all wives and children are invisible until you read the original pages. After spending two months following the wrong Jane M. Smith with no baby Charlotte, I abandoned the index and started wading through every name in Oxford and then in the surrounding towns. In 1860 Naugatuck, I found a Jane M. Smith whose age fit that of Jane M. Burnett, but still no Charlotte. Tracking that family back into the 1850 census, I couldn't find them in Naugatuck or in Oxford, but I did find them next door in Middlebury. And there, finally, was one-year-old Charlotte along with Jane and—for the first time with certainty—my great-great-grandfather David S. Smith. Since then, the census has helped me to solve many parts of the puzzle. The next steps—back to 1840 and beyond—will be much more difficult because those earlier schedules do not list names of family members except for the head of household, but I am very happy with my success so far.

—Alan Downes

Obituaries and SSDI

The Social Security Death Index (SSDI) is an invaluable tool for twentieth-century family history. However, in accordance with legal regulations, the SSDI will not be updated with names and death dates until a person has been dead three years. This is because claiming that the use of the SSDI led to identity theft (while offering no proof of that claim), Congress curtailed access to the SSDI and exempted its information from the Freedom of Information Act in late 2013. Unless genealogists protest loudly and long enough to have this repealed, the SSDI will now not have the latest data.

Sometimes you can find good clues to vital statistics in obituaries, although one must be cautious. My own parents' published obituaries had minor errors because the family was not thinking clearly at the funeral home. I suspect that is the case with many death notices. Still, the parents and progeny of the deceased were correct, even if some other particulars were not.

Go to Cyndi's List and look at the Deaths page (www.cyndislist .com/deaths.htm) for a good collection of sites that specialize in obituaries.

Once you have a place and year of death from an obituary, if your ancestor died in the twentieth century, you should look at the SSDI as a more reliable source for data. This is public record, and you can search it for free at http://searches.rootsweb.ancestry.com/ssdi.html. The results will give you the official birth date, death date, where the Social Security number was issued (usually the place of residence at the time), and where the last payment was made (usually the place of death at the time). With this information, you can use the state's vital statistics department to get a copy of birth and death certificates, which are primary sources.

Other sites with SSDI lookup are:

- FamilySearch SSDI Search is at http://www.familysearch.org/search/collection/1202535.

- Genealogy.com (home of Family Tree Maker) offers the SSDI for free, but only as part of their Internet Family Finder search. The advantage is searching many resources at once, but the disadvantage is the overabundance of results to weed through. You also can't search without the last name.

- GenealogyBank.com (access is free at many libraries) has over 84 million records updated weekly, which makes it quite a good source for recent deaths.

- Mocavo has a free SSDI search at http://www.mocavo.com/Social-Security-Death-Index/246389.

- You can search the SSDI in one step at http://www.stevemorse.org/ssdi/ssdi.html. Steve Morse has created a practical search form that augments the search logic of many of the free SSDI search engines on the Web. You can choose which of several SSDI databases to search. This is one of the easiest SSDI search interfaces available and a favorite of mine.

- Railroad Retirement Board at http://www.rrb.gov/mep/genealogy.asp is the place to look if your ancestor worked for a railroad company and was covered by the Railroad Retirement Act after 1936.

Interment.net

This is another volunteer site full of free uploaded burial records (www.interment.net). Volunteers transcribe and upload records of every bit of data they can find from a local cemetery. The records include the official name of the cemetery; the location of the cemetery (town, county, state, country, etc.), including the street address of the cemetery or driving directions; the date the transcription was compiled and how (tombstone inscriptions, sexton records, previous transcriptions); how complete the list is; and the names of the compilers. As of this writing, almost 4 million records were available for searching or browsing.

You can also subscribe to a newsfeed of all new transcriptions published on Interment.net daily and of the Cemetery Blog news and articles from the weekly web log of the site.

Fold3

Fold3 digitizes military historical documents, and works in partnership with NARA. The name comes from the way the flag is folded at military funerals. Here, you will find millions of images of original source documents, many of which have never been available online before. Hundreds of the documents are free, and if you find something you have background information on, you can comment on and annotate it. You can also create your own story page, pulling images from the collection to it.

Launched in January 2007, it has added about 2,000,000 items a month, most of them handwritten. You can browse or use a search box (you can do a Boolean search) to find military records, naturalization records, and more. As of this writing, only U.S. documents are being scanned and indexed, but Justin Schroepfer of Fold3 said that soon, more countries will be included. American Milestone Documents, Project Blue Book, Pennsylvania Archives documents from 1664–1880, and all indexed information and previews of all of the images are free. You are also invited to scan and upload your own historical documents, whether they are photographs, diaries, bible records, and so on. Access to other documents is by subscription.

Some of the free pieces of information include:

- The Ratified Amendments XI–XXVII of the U.S. Constitution

- Copybooks of George Washington's Correspondence with Secretaries of State, 1789–1796

- Naturalization Petitions of the U.S. District Court for the District of Maryland, 1906–1930

- Naturalization Petitions for the Middle District of Pennsylvania, 1906–1930

- Naturalization Petitions for the Eastern District of Louisiana, New Orleans Division, 1838–1861

- Presidential Photos of Coolidge, Eisenhower, Truman, and Roosevelt

- World War II Japanese Photos

- The Case File of the *United States v. The Amistad,* 1841

Online Searches

The UK 1901 census is available for searching online at www .1901censusonline.com/. This site had a disastrous beginning: When it first went online, it had over a million hits in the first hours, the server crashed, and it was months before it was back up. They finally got it all on servers able to handle the traffic, and now several UK censuses are available besides 1901: 1891, 1871, 1861, 1851, and 1841 census records and Birth, Marriage and Death (BMD) indexes. The censuses, like U.S. censuses, ask different questions for different censuses, such as occupation and place of birth. Other records are available, too, as this list shows:

- **Address search**   Find out who lived in your house in 1901.

- **Place search**   Look at who was in which enumeration district in 1901.

- **Institution search**   See who lived in hospitals, barracks, orphanages, etc., in 1901.

- **Vessel search**   Locate a naval or merchant vessel in the 1901 census.

- **Reference number**   Use this search if you know the National Archives census.

Like Ancestry.com and Genealogy.com, you can search the indexes for free, but looking at the actual record costs a fee. Unlike Ancestry.com and Genealogy.com, you can pay per record, put your subscription on hold, and buy a set of voucher lookups. Viewing transcribed data costs 50 credits for an individual and then 50 credits for a list of all other people in that person's household. Viewing a digital image of the census page costs 75 credits.

Transcriptions

As mentioned earlier, www.censuslinks.com is one way to find census transcriptions from around the world. Also check Cyndi's List at www.cyndislist.com/census.htm.

CDs and Microfilms

Several vendors provide CD-ROMs and microfilm of census records—sometimes images of the actual census form and sometimes transcriptions. Your local library, LDS Family History Center, or genealogy club may have copies of these microfilms and/or CD-ROMs with census images.

Bible Records Online

Bible Records Online (www.biblerecords.com) is a site dedicated to transcribing and digitizing the contents of records inside family bibles and in other important documents from as early as the 1500s through today. Often, these were the only written records of births, marriages, and deaths of a family, but they are usually inaccessible except to the person who owns them.

At www.biblerecords.com, you can browse or search by surname. The results will be a transcribed page. To submit your own family bible records, go to www.biblerecords.com/submit.html. Tracy St. Claire, the site's administrator, has a standard format for the transcriptions to make them easy to read and compare. If you can submit a scan of the original, that is wonderful, but she will take a transcription alone. The site also has a forum and a place for scans of photographs or other items people typically slip into the family bible as keepsakes.

Wrapping Up

- Vital statistics are the milestones of life: birth, marriage, sometimes divorce, and death.

- Most states have good vital statistics starting from 1938 (the beginning of Social Security). Prior to that, you may have to get creative, looking at obituaries, census records, family bible sites, and other sites.

- The Library of Congress and National Archives and Records Administration have several resources, guides, and databases to help genealogists.

- Many sites have transcribed and scanned original documents, indexed for searching by surname: bibles, cemetery records, and so on. Some are free and some are subscription based.

Chapter 12

The Church of Jesus Christ of Latter-day Saints: FamilySearch.org

FamilySearch.org is the online genealogy site of the Church of Jesus Christ of Latter-day Saints (LDS). You are probably aware that the members of LDS search their ancestry because of the church doctrine that marriage and families continue beyond this life if families are sealed together in the LDS rites. You can learn more about this at www.mormon.org/values/family-history. FamilySearch .org is one way they do that.

FamilySearch.org has undergone significant upgrades and redesign since the last version of this book. The site has new ways to find, record, and share your family history on FamilySearch.org. Searching uploaded family trees allows you to find data and collaborate with others. You can add photos and stories of ancestors and view your ancestry in an interactive fan chart, which can show you where your next searches should be. You can also now get live free help either through chat or the telephone help line.

FamilySearch.org Tour

The FamilySearch.org site (see Figure 12-1) has several tools, databases, and documents to help you with family history. Go to FamilySearch.org and register with a user name and password. If you have a GEDCOM, you can upload your own data to start your tree, or you can type all your genealogy into their user-friendly form online and save it that way.

The opening page has these links: Fan Chart (also a link to Puzzilla, which will be covered later in the chapter), Photos, Family Tree, Search, Indexing, and Family Booklet.

- **Fan Chart** This shows you an interactive graphic of your tree on FamilySearch.org. Each person is a clickable link to a page with the data you input, the historical records attached to it, the latest changes you have made, and any multimedia.

- **Photos** This is a link to the multimedia aspects of your tree. You can add not only photos, but also stories, scans of original documents, a list of the tagged people in your photos, and people in your tree that are tagged in other photos that have been uploaded. Once you leave the opening page, all this multimedia will be under the Memories link.

FIGURE 12-1. *The redesigned FamilySearch.org has links to the various site sections.*

- **Family Tree**   This is a link to your genealogy as input or an uploaded file.

- **Search**   This is the link to the records, genealogies, Family History Library Catalog, and the FamilySearch.org wiki, which explains and expounds on FamilySearch features and resources.

- **Indexing**   This is a link to the software to download if you want to volunteer to expand the records available on FamilySearch.org. Projects include civil records, church records, and more.

   Search and Family Tree are the links you will use the most, so let's look at those.

Search

Search has been redesigned and consolidated. Records will search birth marriage, death, probate, land, and military records, as well as IGI (International Genealogical Index) extracted records. Trees will include the old uploaded Ancestral File genealogies. Catalog, of course, is the Family History Library and Centers card catalog. Books will search over 100,000 digitized genealogy and Family History publications from the archives of Family History libraries around the world. Wiki searches the FamilySearch wiki. This is a user-written collection of more than 60,000 pages about records, localities, subjects, and methods that can help you find your ancestors. It's the how-to wiki by users for users.

Records

The new search includes several different databases and records. Among them are:

- The **IGI** is a database of over 400 million names extracted between 1973 and 2008 from public records by volunteers and also contributed to by LDS members. There are duplications, and some entries were indexed, while others were not. Other limitations include that burials and death records were not indexed, unless they apply to children who died before the age of eight, but illegitimate infants who died young were not indexed. Furthermore, some of the data were censored because

FamilySearch does not have permission to publish them online; such entries are still available on microfiche and CD-ROM versions of the IGI. Still, IGI is a good resource for clues.

- The **SSDI** is included in the searches as well. As noted in Chapter 11, Congress passed restrictions on access to the most recent three years' records of the Social Security Death Index (SSDI). The older records are still part of the searched databases at FamilySearch.org and can help you find people who died after 1938. You will find that some sites charge you for this search, but on FamilySearch, it is free. Under Search | Genealogies, you can also search the trees of all other FamilySearch.org users, the old Ancestral File and Pedigree Resource files, and other user submissions.

- **Ancestral File** is a collection of databases uploaded with Personal Ancestral File (PAF). As mentioned in Chapter 2, the PAF software is no longer supported, but the uploaded data is still on the site. The **Pedigree Resource File (PRF)** is a searchable database of submissions from FamilySearch.org users.

In addition to these, the search includes indexed public, church, and fraternal records. It really is an amazing collection.

Trees

Personal genealogy databases are called trees in FamilySearch.org. My tree is shown in Figure 12-2 in Fan Chart view. This view makes it easy to see where I need to put in more data. However, it only shows direct lineage; for example, all my grandfather's siblings are not shown.

Other views include Portrait, which shows any pictures you have uploaded, and Traditional, which contains boxes and lines with names and dates. The Traditional view gives one more piece of information: the FamilySearch.org record number. Someone else who is descended from William Reason Powell, for example, will have entered him into FamilySearch.org as well. That entry will have a different number. If you use the Search for Duplicates Number feature, you can find other entries in family trees that might be the same as yours. If so, you can merge the two into one record. Furthermore, you can search all

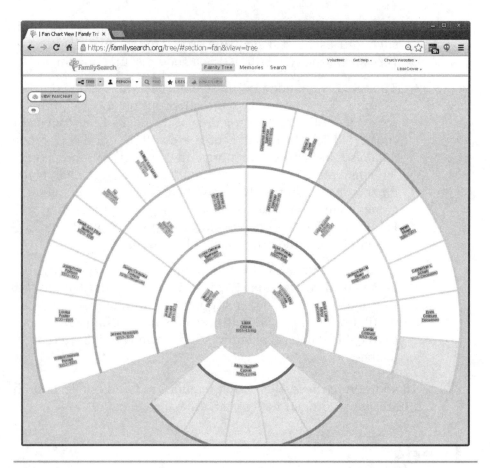

FIGURE 12-2. *Fan charts can be viewed and printed in the Family Tree tab of FamilySearch.org.*

family trees for your ancestor's assigned number to see if he appears elsewhere. Finally, if you find a person in a record that you want to add to your trees, you can search by that number to see if you already have them.

As with most online genealogy sites, you can upload a GEDCOM of your genealogy, or as noted in Chapter 2, several genealogy software packages are able to connect directly with FamilySearch.org and input the data online as you enter it on your desktop computer. But let's say you are starting from scratch and will enter each family member one at a time.

As you enter each name, starting with yourself, you can enter sources for the information, or once you have the name, at least one date, and a place for that entry, you can click Search. This will first search the records section, but with a click, you can also search each section.

Now in the 1910 census I find my great-grandfather at age 56, my great-grandmother at age 51, my grandfather at age 18, and my grandfather's siblings at ages 15, 12, and 8. Attaching the census record to J. Toxie Powell (my grandfather) and his parents is easy because they are already in my tree. Adding the other people is a little trickier. I have to keep my family tree open in one tab (or window if that is easier for you) and the census record in another. In the Family Tree tab, I click Add Person, type in **Renie Powell** (one of the sisters), and put in what data are available from the census record: female, parents, estimated birth year. Once I click Save, FamilySearch.org first checks that I have not already entered her. If not, then she is assigned a number in my tree. However, it will also search other trees to see if someone else is also searching this family, and if there is a match, offer to merge.

Once people are entered, I can go back to the census record and attach it as a source to each person. I can note in the entry that the census is why I think this is an accurate entry (besides the fact that my grandfather told me of them when he was alive). You have to be very careful, however. Because I have three generations of James Powells and the display truncates names, it was easy to accidentally put my grandmother as spouse to my great-grandfather instead of to my grandfather. Fixing that was not easy or intuitive at all.

Also, someone else's trees had the same people, but with mistakes on the births. After the search for duplicates, I had a chance to tell those users how I would change those entries and why and let them decide whether to accept that.

Note

When you find an online family tree, remember it is inspiration, not gospel. Another volunteer uploaded that data, so ask for permission before you use it, and check the original sources yourself.

Puzzilla

Puzzilla.org is a third-party site connected to FamilySearch that I found very helpful. At Puzzilla, you log in with your FamilySearch account. Give it a few seconds to load your genealogy information into a diagram that looks like a wire schematic (see Figure 12-3). You are at the center at first. Hover over a dot, and it will show you the vital statistics for that relative. Click a relative, and that person's descendants are drawn. Clicking a descendant's data balloon will take you back to the FamilySearch default search. For example, find an ancestor with large gaps between children, search on one of the parents, and you may find a child or widowhood you didn't know about before. Or you may find that you have data that are not yet attached to that person and you need to add them to your tree. While in Puzzilla, you can change the number of generations shown, change the root person to a specific FamilyTree ID number, and

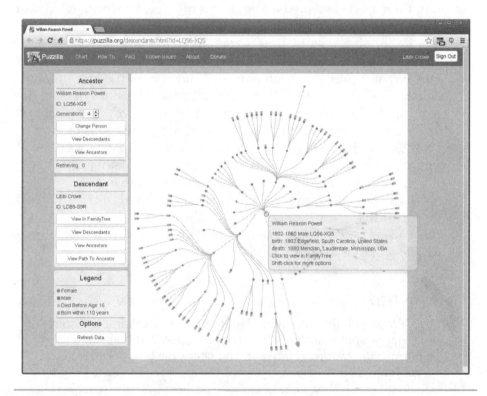

FIGURE 12-3. *Puzzilla helps you visualize your FamilySearch.org tree and search for more data.*

select View Path To Ancestor/Descendant for a direct line view. As you complete each of these changes, records are retrieved from FamilyTree one family at a time, which is time consuming, so you have to be patient. The "Retrieving" count in the control panel shows how many requests are still waiting for a response from FamilyTree. New requests wait until prior requests have finished.

Once Puzzilla sends you to search in FamilySearch, look on the right side for Research Help and click Search Records. This searches for historical records for that descendant and takes you to the Search Results page. Tune your searches by varying the search parameters.

Compare the descendant's details in FamilyTree to the records in the Search Results page. If they match, you have found historical record information about the descendant. Add the new record to your sources, and add spouse, children, and parents to the descendant in FamilyTree.

Success Story: FamilySearch Proves a Family Legend

I had the names of my great-grandfather, his two brothers, and both parents—along with the name of the little town they were born and raised in Wales. For three years, I searched for evidence of the parents who were presumably named Hugh Jones and Mary Ellen Williams. The information was furnished by their grandson.

In the quest to acquire as much evidence as possible on every person in my line, I ran a query on the LDS site. Some of this information was transcription, and some was by submission of family group sheets (without source citations). I was fortunate to find what could potentially be my great-grandfather's christening record as a transcribed set of bishop's records for the parish. Correct place, correct year, but wrong parent names—or so I thought. I was able to run a query using the parents' names only so that I could find all birth records in that county where these two names appeared as mother and father. Sure enough, each of the other two boys and a bonus daughter appeared. The parents were Moses Jones and Elizabeth Jones.

Subsequent research further supports the information. In fact, both died before the grandson informant was even born! Perhaps he mistook an "adopted" set of grandparents as his own... who knows? Three years of trying was blown away by five minutes' worth of Internet research. Now, I use the Internet for a large portion of my research.

—*Heather Jones DeGeorge*

FamilySearch Indexing

This is where you can give back to the world of online genealogy. Using this software, you can extract family history information from digital images of historical documents to create indexes that assist everyone in finding their ancestors. This could be census pages, church records, vital statistics records, and so on. It is fun, interesting, and one way to give back to the genealogy community at large.

Get Help

Tucked way up in the top-right corner is a small link: Get Help. It has a drop-down menu, or you can go straight to the page at FamilySearch .org/ask. From the drop-down menu, you can call or chat with staff members, learn how to visit the Family History Library, or send a message.

    The other links can take you to pages for help with products, how to get started, videos on how to use FamilySearch.org, and the wiki with how-to articles. It is under the Learning Center link where you will find the excellent research guides on how to search places, subjects, and so on.

Note

Need to know where your local Family History Center is? Check the phone book under "Churches—LDS," or go to www .familysearch.org/locations and search by typing in the city you want.

A Visit to a Family History Center

Family History Centers (FHCs) are to genealogists what candy stores are to kids. There are big ones and little ones, elaborate set-ups and simple ones. But they all have something to help your search, and going to one is usually a treat.

    The best way to find a Family History Center near you is to look in the White Pages of the phone book for the nearest Church of Jesus Christ of Latter-day Saints. Call them and find out where the nearest

FHC is and the hours. Honestly, because the hours vary so much from place to place, the best time to call is Sunday morning around 10:00 A.M. Everyone's at church then!

If you call any other time, give the staffers lots of rings to answer the phones, which might be on the other side of the church from the FHC. Another easy way: Use the Search box on the FamilySearch.org main page. Scroll about halfway down the page, and you'll see a box to input your ZIP code. For a more detailed search, go to www.familysearch.org/Eng/default.asp.

Note

Some FHC directors insist that if you use a disk to take home information, you buy one from the FHC. This is to prevent accidentally introducing a virus into the system. Similarly, while Wi-Fi may be available in a certain FHC, if your laptop has a virus, you will be asked to take out your connection card.

All FHCs are branches of the main LDS Family History Library in Salt Lake City. The typical FHC has a few rooms at the local Mormon Church, with anywhere from one to ten computers; a similar number of microfilm and microfiche readers; and a collection of atlases, manuals, and how-to genealogy books. The FHC in my neighborhood in Navarre, Florida, is small and cozy. Others in bigger towns are larger and more elaborate. All of them have materials and expertise you can tap into when you visit.

Wrapping Up

- The LDS Church is the largest online resource for genealogy.

- The newly revised site has several formerly separate databases under one search.

- User genealogies are now more interactive than before.

- The Indexing program has projects you can search and help index.

- Family History Centers are where you can view microfiches and microfilms of actual records, as well as order copies of records. Most FHCs also have Internet access, including access to subscription online databases.

Chapter 13

Ellis Island Online: The American Family Immigration History Center

A re you one of the 40 percent of Americans who can trace an ancestor to the immigration center at Ellis Island? If so, you definitely want to check out Ellis Island Online at www.ellisisland .org (see Figure 13-1).

The secret to success is searching this or any other ships' list database is to have at least some data at hand. You should have

FIGURE 13-1. *Immigration records from 1892 to 1924 are available at www.ellisisland.org.*

a guess as to when the immigrant arrived. Sometimes, you can find this on a death record as "how long in the United States," or whatever country you are searching. Sometimes, you can find this data, or enough to make a good guess, in census records or naturalization papers. Other clues that help are approximate age, occupation, and birth location. It also would help to know with whom the passenger might have traveled. Relatives for sure, but also friends or employers might give you a clue as to where to look.

The opening page of the site has a link called Genealogy. It will lead you to the Genealogy Learning Center with these links.

Genealogy Getting Started Tips

This section for beginners to family history research serves as an online "Genealogy 101" to guide you through the basic steps. This step-by-step approach will help you to grasp quickly the key concepts of all levels of genealogy research.

Genealogy Charts and Forms

The section has several different downloadable documents for you to print, copy, and share freely with others as you organize your family data. These include multigeneration pedigree charts, family group sheets, and other documents in PDF format, and should be accessible by most computers. You have to print them out to fill them out.

Locating a Genealogy Society

Any aspect of genealogy research has a corresponding genealogy society: surname, geographic area, historical, ethnic heritage, and family societies have been the foundation of American genealogy for more than a century. To connect you with an area of particular interest, the site has a page called the Ellis Island Society Links Network.

Hiring a Professional Genealogist

This section contains information about professional genealogists and why you may want one. Through an alliance with the Association of Professional Genealogists, this page will connect you with individuals skilled in different geographic, ethnic, and other areas of research specialty.

Helpful Websites for Genealogy Research

This section introduces you to just a few of the places online that you are likely to find of general interest relating to your family history research.

Besides those helpful links, the opening page also has a link to the history of Ellis Island (Ellis Island), information about the organization that runs the site (About Us), the gift shop, and a place to donate to help keep the online search free for everyone.

The Immigrant Experience link has two sets of articles on the population of the United States. "Family Histories," the first set, gives real-life examples of people whose ancestors passed through Ellis Island. "The Peopling of America" is a companion series of articles showing the timeline of people coming to the United States from all over the world, beginning with those who crossed the Bering Straits 20,000 years ago. You can also look at a history of Ellis Island and a timeline that begins in 1630.

Using the Site

The site has two parts: free services and services available only to foundation members. Even without the free registration, however, you can find names and dates, and that's what's important.

Before you can gain access to the free searches, you must register. This involves choosing a logon name and password and giving your name and address; when you return, cookies on your computer will allow the site to show you saved searches.

Searches

As a registered user (remember, registration is free), you can use the Passenger Search. Simply put in a first and last name at the opening screen, and then click Search Archives. If you want to perform a more targeted search, click Passenger Search at the top of the page, and then click New Search. On that search page, you can input a first and last name, and then choose Male or Female (or don't use gender at all).

As the site says, if at first you don't succeed, don't give up! Remember that many passengers' names were misspelled, so try clicking the "close matches" or "alternate spellings" boxes at the top of the page to ask the system to search for spellings that have similar sound values (e.g., Dickson and Dixon would sound the same).

Free vs. Paid Membership

If you register as a regular user, which is free, you can keep copies of the passenger records, manifests, and ship images in "Your Ellis Island File." This can be opened on the computers at Ellis Island or on the website. You can purchase copies of these documents at the online gift shop or at the interpretive shop on Ellis Island.

If you join as a foundation member for $45 per year, you can:

- Annotate passenger records in the Ellis Island Archives

- Create and maintain your Family History Scrapbook

- Order one free copy of your initial scrapbook (printout or CD-ROM)

- Receive a 10 percent discount at the online gift shop or at the center

- Possibly get a tax deduction (check with your accountant)

- Help support the work of The Statue of Liberty-Ellis Island Foundation to preserve and protect the sites and their records

If the results list is too long, refine the search using the bar on the left side of the screen, filtering for year of arrival, ethnicity, and so on. Choosing one of the names gives you a screen where you can choose to see the original ship's manifest.

The information on passenger records comes from passenger lists, called ship manifests. Passengers were asked a series of questions, and their answers were entered into the manifests. Ellis Island inspectors then used the manifests to examine immigrants. Click the links on the left to view the passenger's ship and the manifest with the passenger's name. On some passenger records, click to read information added to the community archive by members of the foundation. (If you're a foundation member, you'll be able to add annotations of your own.) To save the passenger record, click Add To Your Ellis Island File. As a registered member, you can access this file at a later logon.

You can look at the transcription of the ship's manifest to see who is recorded near the person. You must look at two images for the complete records, which ran across facing pages of the original books.

Click the Ship link to view details about the vessel. Registered members can save their searches and results in an online file for later reference and use. All of these images, as well as an official Ellis Island Passenger Record, can be ordered in hard copy.

The Ellis Island search form lets you enter just the leading characters of the last name. It also allows you to search on ethnicity, ports, and ships. However, the search on the Ellis Island site requires you to first have an exact spelling match, whereas the Morse form (see the following section) does not. For example, if you are searching for Noelle de Nantes D'Avignonet, you will probably come up blank. But if you let it search for "den," it may come up.

Once you have the name, or a ship, or a date, you can probably find the manifest. Then you can look at either a transcription or the actual page, as in Figure 13-2.

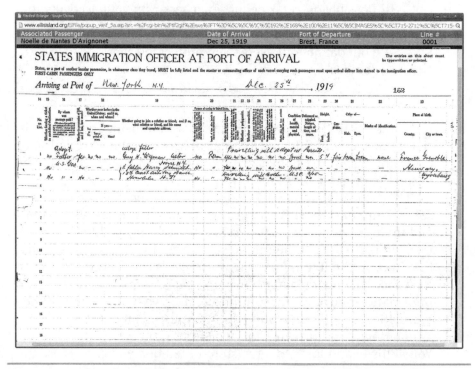

FIGURE 13-2. *You can look at an image of the original ship's record at the Ellis Island site.*

You can order either a print of the original page or a pretty certificate with a transcription in the gift shop. You can also store what you find in Your Ellis Island File so you can resume a search that you started earlier.

Community Archives

On the Ellis Island site, only members of the foundation can create annotations to the records, but all registered users of the website can view them. Annotations supplement information in the record, telling more about the passenger's background and life in the United States. This information has not been verified as accurate and complete—it's simply what the annotating member believes to be the facts. Click View Annotations on the passenger record (if no View Annotations button exists, the record hasn't been annotated yet). If you're registered with the site, you'll see a list of annotations. If you haven't yet registered, a screen will appear so that you can.

Ellis Island Family History

If you have paid for a membership to The Statue of Liberty-Ellis Island Foundation, you can contribute Family History Scrapbooks on the website or at the American Family Immigration History Center itself on Ellis Island.

Visiting in Person

The link for information is "Visiting Ellis Island" under "Ellis Island" in the bar at the top of any page on the site. As of this writing, the island was still rebuilding after Hurricane Sandy. That means some areas are restricted, but the American Family Immigration History Center is open for research into family immigration records. Also open is the Great Hall exhibit, "Journeys: The Peopling of America 1550–1890" and The American Immigrant Wall of Honor. Visitors can also enjoy the audio tour, join a ranger program, and watch the award-winning documentary *Island of Hope, Island of Tears.*

Morse's Forms

This search on the Ellis Island site is better now than it was the first summer the site went online, but it still has many steps you need to take, and sometimes the index is incomplete. Dr. Stephen Morse, with collaborators Michael Tobias, Erik Steinmetz, and Dr. Yves Goulnik, created One-Step Search Tools for the Ellis Island site (www.jewishgen.org/databases/eidb/). This project has several different search forms that overlap to a degree. Though this may get you a bit confused about which one to use, I suggest using several of them in this order:

- Ellis Island gold form (1892–1924) is an enhanced form for searching for Ellis Island passengers. If you put in your e-mail address at the top of the gold form, you will receive an e-mail with the results in addition to the display in your browser. This is the best one to use.

- Ellis Island white form (1892–1924) is the simpler form when searching for Ellis Island passengers.

- Ellis Island ship lists (1892–1924) allows you to search for the names of specific ships in the Ellis Island microfilms.

- Ellis Island additional details (1892–1924) searches the additional passenger information.

Note

Dr. Morse's pages are so much better at finding things than the Ellis Island site that I think you should go there to search. Register as a user at www.ellisisland.org and then search with One Step.

The forms on this site can search by town of origin, use "sounds-like" codes, and can search microfilms that are in the index but that are not accessible through the Ellis Island site's algorithms. An article on using these forms is at www.stevemorse.org/onestep/onestep3.htm with tips and explanations. It is definitely worth your time to read this article before you start, but I'll provide a quick overview here.

Other Forms

Morse has several other forms for searching the Ellis Island database, Ancestry.com (you have to input your ID and password for your paid subscription for those), and several other ports of immigration, including Baltimore, Galveston, Philadelphia, and more. He also has help on census forms, calendars, and translations. His site, www .stevemorse.org/index.html, is a bookmark you must have!

Wrapping Up

- Ellis Island Online is a wonderful resource on the Web.

- You can search for immigrants from 1892 through 1924—the peak years of Ellis Island's processing—by name, date, and ship.

- You can upload pictures, sounds, and text to an online scrapbook if you're a member of The Statue of Liberty-Ellis Island Foundation (it costs $45 to register) or if you visit the museum itself in New York.

- Stephen Morse and several others have created alternative search forms for the Ellis Island data, as well as other ships' lists and sites.

Chapter 14

Online Library
Card Catalogs
and Services

One of the wonderful things about the online world is the plethora of libraries now using online card catalogs (OCCs). This greatly speeds up your search while you're at any library.

It is so easy to look in the card catalog before actually visiting the library. You know immediately whether that library owns the title. With a few more keystrokes, you can find out whether the title is on the shelf, on reserve, on loan to someone, available by interlibrary loan, or found in a nearby branch library. Then, if you want to, you can get dressed and go to the library to pick up your resource!

You can connect to most libraries, both their online card catalogs and their services, through the World Wide Web using a browser interface. In many cases, the catalog will look exactly as it does in the library itself.

But almost as exciting: You can often download certain holdings as a PDF or other digital format; you can sometimes view an image of an actual artifact and save that digital file; and best of all, sometimes, you can use the library's online services, such as NewsBank, from your home if you have a library card with that institution.

Connecting to OCCs by Web Browser

Modern libraries use computerized card catalogs all around the world. Two sites to bookmark that will get you to most of them:

- An important site to bookmark is WorldCat (http://www.worldcat .org/). With this site, you can create an account and save your searches and results. This way, you have a research log of sorts for your book searches. Its opening page is shown in Figure 14-1.

- Another important one is LibWeb (www.lib-web.org/), a directory of worldwide libraries, library catalogs, and library servers. In Figure 14-2 you can see that the site has academic, national, and public libraries in its list.

FIGURE 14-1.   *The WorldCat site helps you search many libraries and formats at one time.*

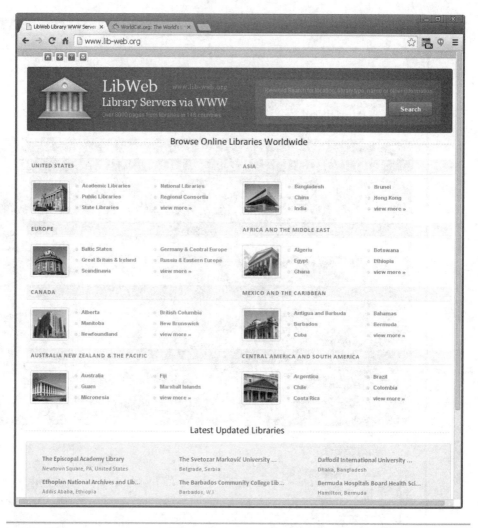

FIGURE 14-2. *The LibWeb site helps you search specific catalogs from around the world.*

In addition, many archives have their holdings cataloged online. You can browse these and more:

- **A2A** (http://www.nationalarchives.gov.uk/a2a) is a searchable collection of archive catalogs in England and Wales from the eighth century to the present. Type a word or phrase into the box; you can limit the search to specific archives or to English or Welsh counties, as well as specific dates.

- **Catalogue Collectif de France** (http://www.bnf.fr/pages/ zNavigat/frame/version_anglaise.htm?ancre = english.htmr) will let you use one interface to query the three largest online library catalogs in France, including the printed and digitized holdings of the national Library of France, the University SUDOC (System of Documentation) of French universities, and local libraries across France. It includes books printed from 1811 to the present in more than 60 public or specialized libraries.

- **LibDex** (http://www.libdex.com) is a worldwide directory of library home pages, web-based online public access catalogs (OPACs), friends of the library pages, and library e-commerce affiliate links, with a page for you to browse by country.

- **Lib-Web-Cats** (http://www.librarytechnology.org/libwebcats) is a directory of libraries worldwide. While the majority of the current listings are in North America, the numbers of libraries represented in other parts of the globe are growing.

- **The European Library** (http://www.theeuropeanlibrary.org) searches the content of member European national libraries. This includes books, newspapers, manuscripts, and more.

Google Books

Using Google Books for family history is fun and interesting. Google Books has full text search capabilities on millions of books. It is like an international library you can use and peruse from home.

The texts of all the books can be searched. Some of these books are public domain, and you can even download them as a PDF, in Google Play, or in some cases, to a Kindle or Nook. Others are still under copyright, but the pages that have your search term may be available to look at. Then you can click Find In Library to see if it is available to borrow, or Click Get This Book to find places where you can buy it.

Let's look at an example. Recently, I was researching Col. Guy H. Wyman. He is not a relation—he is the man who named and first surveyed Navarre, Florida, where I live. Opening www.books.google .com, there is a simple text box. Remembering the lessons from Chapter 7, the input could be as simple as GUY H.WYMAN. But to get better results, I would want to use quotation marks to search for the phrase. Because he was an officer in World War I, several government publications list him, including annual reports of his cavalry unit and a petition to the Treasurer of the United States for reimbursement for a horse. He is mentioned in the Official Bulletin of the National Society of the Sons of the American Revolution, in the Journal of the Senate when he is promoted, and best of all, in a local history that has an entire chapter on him (see Figure 14-3). If I click Find In A Library to the left, the browser goes to WorldCat, which lists six local libraries that have this book.

Google Books can be searched just as any card catalog can be: by subject, location, author, keyword, and so on.

Also, check out GooBooGeni (www.gooboogeni.com), a site that searches specific Google Books, such as city directories, surname genealogies, and so on. The opening page is a blog by the author, and this is a volunteer site, so updates are occasional. Still, it is a good idea.

The Library of Congress Card Catalog

The Library of Congress Online Catalog has about 14,000,000 records of books, serials, computer files, manuscripts, cartographic materials, music, sound recordings, and visual materials in one database with cross-references and scope notes. As an integrated database, the online catalog includes 3,200,000 records from an earlier database. These catalog records, primarily for books and serials cataloged between 1898 and 1980, are being edited to comply with current cataloging standards and to reflect contemporary language and usage.

Many items from the library's special collections are accessible to users, but are not represented in this catalog. In addition, some individual items within collections (microforms, manuscripts, photographs, etc.) are not listed separately in the catalog, but are represented by collection-level catalog records. You can use the simple search on the far left, or use Boolean terms and limiters in the middle and the right.

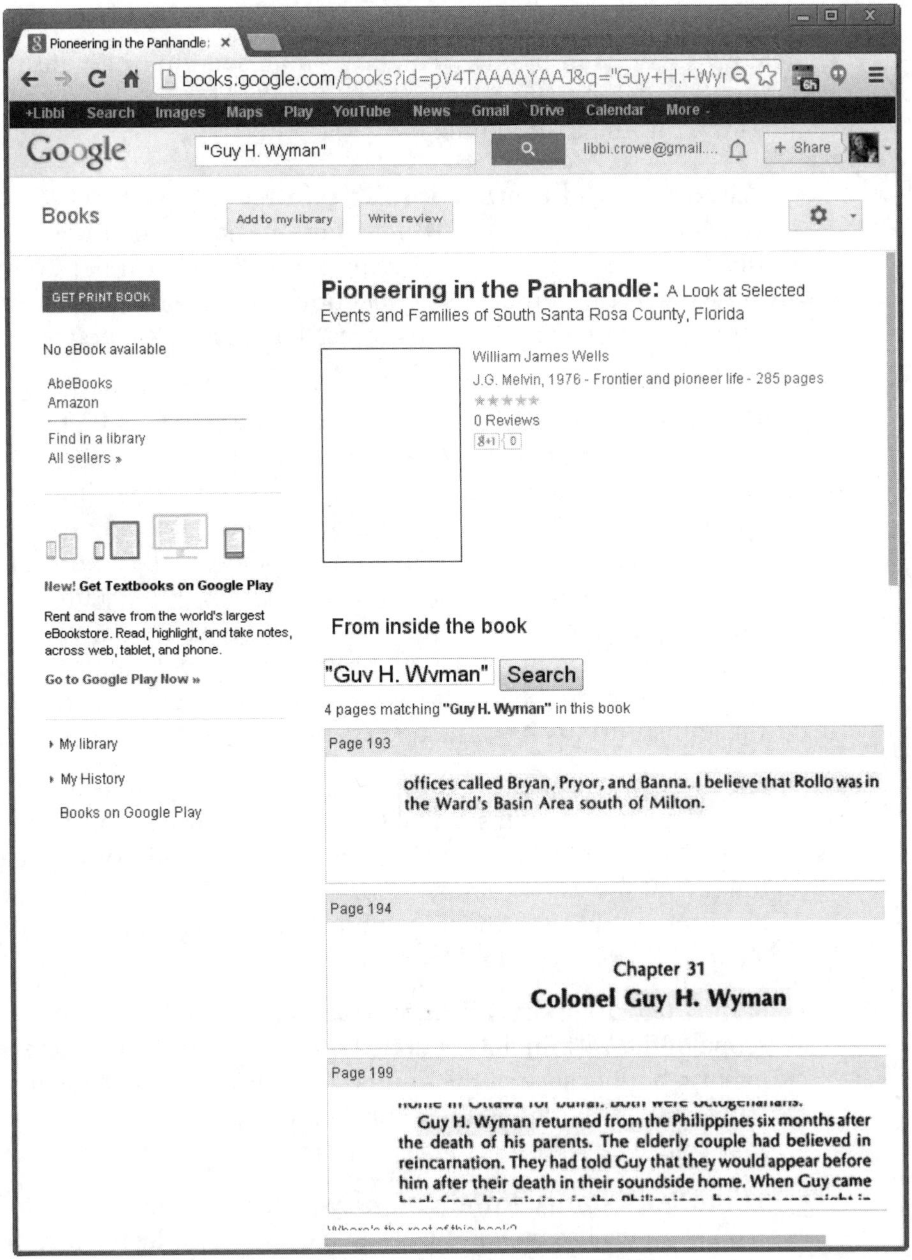

FIGURE 14-3.   *This book has a chapter on the subject of my search. Note on the left that Google Books has links for stores to buy this book, as well as Find In A Library.*

Don't Miss These Library Sites

Genealogy sections in libraries can be a small section or an entire floor, or even the library's reason for existence. Here are some card catalogs to examine from home:

- **Anne Arundel County Public Library** (Maryland) has the Gold Star Collection, which contains about 700 titles dealing with Maryland, including some Anne Arundel County genealogy. In their special collections are several Maryland family histories and local histories. The library catalog is located online at http://www.aacpl.net.

- **California University and State Libraries MELVYL** (California) at http://www.melvyl.worldcat.org/ is a searchable catalog of library materials from the ten UC campuses, the California State Library, the California Academy of Sciences, the California Historical Society, the Center for Research Libraries, the Giannini Foundation of Agricultural Economics Library, the Graduate Theological Union, the Hastings College of the Law Library, and the Lawrence Berkeley National Laboratory Library. And every single one of those institutions has a history/genealogy section.

- **Connecticut State Library** (Connecticut) has not only genealogy and local history of Connecticut, but also of the rest of New England. Their special collections include Connecticut town vital records to about 1900. The state library's catalog can be accessed through the state library home page at http://www.ctstatelibrary.org.

- **Samford University Library** (Alabama) does not have quite the scope of the Birmingham Public Library with regard to Alabama history, but because of the annual Institute of Genealogy and Historical Research held here has quite a collection of all things Alabama. The website is http://library.samford.edu/.

- **The Allen County Public Library** (Indiana) at http://www.acpl.lib.in.us/ has one of the best genealogical collections in the country. The link to the genealogy page gives you an overview of this wonderful treasure house. More than 50,000 volumes of compiled genealogies, microfilms of primary sources, and specialized collections, such as African American and Native American, make this library one you must see. But, like the

Family History Library in Salt Lake City, you must first plan your visit, or you will be overwhelmed. Search the catalog online for the names you need to see if they have something for you!

- **The Swem Library at the College of William and Mary Library** (Virginia) is one of the oldest universities in one of the oldest states, and the collection is astounding. The special collections include Virginia tax lists for the 1780s; census microfilms for Virginia (1814–1920), North Carolina (1790–1850), and other states (1790–1820); and compilations of Virginia county, marriage, land, probate, church, military, emigration, and immigration records. The library's catalog is located at https://swem.wm.edu/research/search-catalog.

- **The Daughters of the American Revolution Library** at http://www.dar.org/library has more than 160,000 books on American genealogy, and it's open to the public. Click Online Research in the menu to search the catalog.

- **The Library of Virginia** (Virginia) at http://www.lva.virginia .gov is home to a set of powerful online card catalogs. This site has scanned images of Civil War records, family bible records, letters, and other material, all indexed and searchable by name. I ran a test with "genealogy and Powell" as the search terms. If I want to refine my search further, I could also use Boolean terms, such as AND, NOT, and so on. Overall, the Library of Virginia's card catalog is easy to understand and read—and, I might add, a pleasure to work with.

- **The New York Public Library** (New York) at http://www .nypl.org/ contains a genealogy section called The Milstein Division. This department collects materials documenting American history on the national, state, and local levels, as well as genealogy, heraldry, personal and family names, and flags. The card catalog is searchable at the top of every page in the site.

- **The Newberry Library** (Illinois) in Chicago at http://www .newberry.org/genealogy/collections.html has more than 17,000 genealogies. Search the catalog to see if you need to make a visit!

- **The Sons of the American Revolution Library Catalog** at http://library.sar.org/ can tell you if this collection has genealogies of interest to you. The SAR Library maintains a noncirculating collection of genealogy and American Revolutionary War history and military records.

- **The University of Illinois at Urbana-Champaign Library Catalog** (Illinois) at http://www.uiuc.libguides.com/genealogy offers an outline of the UIUC online catalog, describing its major collections, and a helpful guide to American genealogy research. Note that the university also has extensive collections of material originating outside the United States that may be helpful for genealogical research once you get "back to the boat."

- **The Filson Historical Society Library** has material on the history of the entire Ohio Valley, especially the significant stories of Kentucky and the Ohio Valley history and culture (http://filsonhistorical.org). If you have any genealogy in that area, a personal visit to the Filson is something you will never forget. The library has 50,000 titles, a 1.5-million-item manuscript collection, a collection of 50,000 photographs and prints, and a museum with 15,000 items. The library has such items as original manuscripts, portraits, landscapes, photographs and prints, genealogical materials, printed family histories, local business records, and other primary historical materials about Kentucky, the Ohio Valley, and the Upper South. Search the catalog of the Filson at http://filson.ipac.dynixasp.com.

Where to Find More Online

There are more online library resources than you can shake a stick at. Be sure to Google the geographic area you need, plus "library" and "catalog." You are certain to get some hits! Also, search for the name of a state and "public library" because many states have a network of their libraries.

Card Catalogs

Librarians love to make lists and catalogs for each other! Try some of these:

- **Gateway to Library Catalogs** (http://www.loc.gov/z3950) is a page by the Library of Congress. In addition to links to the LOC catalog, you will find an alphabetical list of catalogs around the world. Also, check out the Research and Reference Services page for librarians at http://www.loc.gov/rr.

- **The Library of Michigan** website has a database with the locations of more than 3,700 Michigan cemeteries and lists sources at the library where a researcher can find the names of those buried in each. The database can be found at http://libraryofmichigan.state.mi.us/MichiganCemeteries/.

- **USGenWeb** (http://www.usgenweb.com) lets you search under the state and then the county you're researching to see if the library catalog is linked.

- **WWW Library Directory** (http://www.travelinlibrarian.info/libdir/) is a list more than 8,800 library websites sorted by geography, not topic. It is useful and international in scope.

Using Your Local Library Online

You can do more than just peruse the card catalog of your local and distant libraries. Find out if your local library offers online services for home use as well. Usually, the login to use these will be some combination of your local library card number and your identifier with their system (name, phone number, etc.).

Periodical Source Index on Microfiche

The PERiodical Source Index (PERSI) is a subject index to articles in genealogical periodicals and journals. Remember using the *Reader's Guide to Periodical Literature* (RGPL) in high school for writing research papers? PERSI is the same idea, but targeted to genealogy sources. It is searchable at http://persi.heritagequestonline.com/hqoweb/library/do/persi. With PERSI, you can look at indexes to articles in more than 2,000 periodicals, about 50,000 articles in all.

Note

PERSI is a subject index to articles, not an every-name or every-word index. You can search it by location and record type, surname as subject, or how-to topic.

Sample Search

In Figure 14-4, I have searched PERSI on Heritage Quest. I click Places; then I input Kentucky and keyword Jolly. The article titles, journals, and dates are listed with the result. Remember, this is not

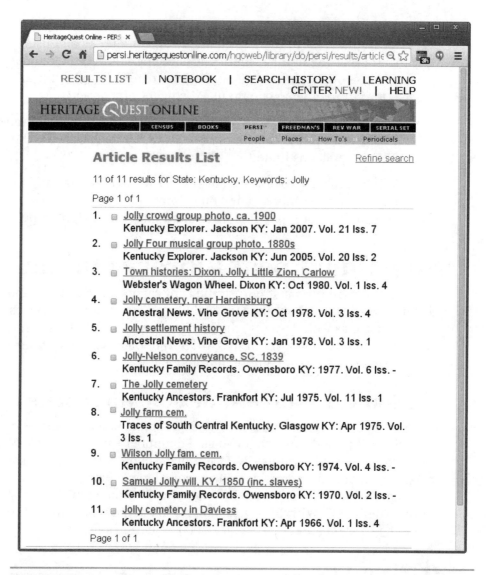

FIGURE 14-4. *Search PERSI for location and keyword, and results are presented most recent first.*

going to be a link to any actual article, but to the details on specific publications that have the articles.

So, I click the link for the title, getting details on the date, volume, and number. To read the actual article, I can click the title again and see whether the journal in question is held at a library near me. I can also search for the title of the journal in my local library catalog. If it is there, I can copy the call number from my local library's catalog and find out about reading and copying the article (the journal in question may not circulate, so I may have to read it there).

An alternative is the Family History Library. Most of the periodicals in PERSI also are available at the Family History Library. Look in the Author/Title section of the Family History Library Catalog. If the periodical has been microfilmed, you can order a copy to use at a local Family History Center. However, most genealogical periodicals are under copyright and are not microfilmed.

I can also write to the publisher to get a copy of an article. Names of publishers are listed with the periodical in most library catalogs, including the Family History Library Catalog. Often, the publishers are genealogical or historical societies, and their addresses are listed in the *Directory of Historical Organizations in the United States and Canada,* published by the American Association for State and Local History.

America's Genealogy Bank (NewsBank)

This resource contains more than four centuries of rare documents and records, including historical newspapers, books, pamphlets, and genealogies, as well as selected material from the American State Papers and U.S. Serial Set, the complete Social Security Death Index, and more than 29 million obituaries.

Success Story: Local History Online

Marian Pierre-Louis is a house historian and a realtor. Those two jobs combined mean that she gets to see a lot of old houses. Nothing makes her happier. Marian also regularly lectures on African-American and New England genealogy.

"My local library posted vital records from 1850–1900," Marian said. "While it doesn't show images, it's a very easy-to-scan chart (transcription). I use it all the time. Actually, they have a whole portal of local history for our town! (Search Facebook for "medwaylib.org" to see the pages.)

I've had also great luck with Heritage Quest and Sanborn Maps through the library. My library is now offering Ancestry, too, but I have my own subscription."

America's Obituaries & Death Notices (NewsBank)

An easy-to-use interface allows searching by name, date range, or text, such as institutional name, social affiliation(s), geographic location(s), philanthropic activities, etc.

Ancestry Library Edition (Available Only Inside the Library)

Ancestry Library Edition (ALE) gives individuals something truly priceless: the chapters of their own authentic, unique family stories. The world's largest online collection of family history records and resources, ALE is a popular research tool. It offers a wide variety of unique content to help users trace their family lineage.

Heritage Quest

This has digital, searchable images of U.S. federal census records with the digitized version of the popular UMI Genealogy & Local History book collection, U.S. federal census records from 1790–1930, more than 22,000 family and local history books, Revolutionary War Pension and Bounty Land Warrant application files with records for more than 80,000 individuals, and Freedman's Bank Records containing key African-American data.

ProQuest Obituaries

This service offers more than 10.5 million obituaries and death notices in full-image format from uninterrupted historical archives of top U.S. newspapers. With content dating as far back as 1851, this unique database provides researchers with valuable clues about their ancestors in the United States, including proper full name, maiden name, spousal information, relatives' names, occupation, religion, cause of death, and more.

Sanborn Fire Insurance Company Maps of Florida

These maps were created for insurance purposes from 1860 through 1923. They show the size, shape, and construction of buildings; dwellings (including hotels and churches); and other structures such as bridges, docks, and barns. The maps include street names, property boundaries and lot lines, and house and block numbers.

Wrapping Up

- Going to the library card catalog in your pajamas is fun!

- You can search the card catalogs of many libraries across the world from the Internet.

- Some libraries have begun scanning images and actual text of their genealogical holdings.

- Some libraries participate in interlibrary loans of books and microfilms.

- You can search for such libraries at several sites across the Internet.

- State libraries and provincial libraries are excellent online resources.

- Librarians like to maintain lists of online libraries for each other. You can use them, too!

- Beyond the card catalog, many local libraries allow you to use databases and indexes such as PERSI and Heritage Quest from your home as well as from the library. Check with your local librarian for details!

Chapter 15

International
Genealogy
Resources

Sooner or later, you'll get "back to the boat"—that is, you'll find your original immigrant in a certain family line. The first immigrant in your family might have arrived just a generation ago or centuries ago. Either way, that doesn't have to mean your genealogy is "done." When you find that first immigrant, finding the boat can be just as important. Although finding where he or she boarded won't tell you a birthplace, it is good information to have.

So where do you look? Many sites have ships' passenger lists and manifests. For general lists of such sites, you can check out Cyndi's List at www.cyndislist.com/ships. If you are fairly certain your ancestor entered the United States through New York during the right time period, search the Ellis Island site profiled in the last chapter.

For other centuries and other countries, you can investigate the Immigrant Ships Transcribers' Guild at www.immigrantships.net. Another such site is The Ships List (www.theshipslist.com), which not only has passenger lists, but also newspaper reports, shipwreck information, and information on shipping lines.

For U.S. immigration, you can search the National Archives and Records Administration (NARA) microfilm catalog for immigration records for arrivals to the United States from foreign ports between approximately 1820 and 1982. See www.archives.gov/research/immigration/#where for details on how to order microfilms that match. Also, look at naturalization records at the NARA page (www.archives.gov/research/naturalization), state archives, and county and state courts. The U.S. Citizenship and Immigration services have a good genealogy page at www.uscis.gov/historyandgenealogy.

Note

You can give back to the online genealogy community by getting involved in a project such as the Immigrant Ships Transcribers' Guild project.

USCIS Genealogy Program Frequently Asked Questions (FAQs)

The United States Citizenship and Immigration Genealogy Program (USCIS) is a way to pay the government to do research on immigrant ancestors. After the program launched in August 2008, there was a tremendous response, and the turn-around goal became to respond to all requests within 90 days.

The program accesses records from five different types of agency records:

- Naturalization Certificate files (C-files) from September 27, 1906, to April 1, 1956

- Alien registration forms from August 1, 1940, to March 31, 1944

- Visa files from July 1, 1924, to March 31, 1944

- Registry files from March 2, 1929, to March 31, 1944

- Alien files (A-files) numbered below 8 million (A8000000) and documents therein dated prior to May 1, 1951

An index search costs $20 and uses data you provide to come up with record citations. You also get instructions for how to ask for those records from the USCIS or National Archives, which costs between $20 and $35. If you do not have the right file number, find it with an index search.

If you have questions about index search results or record copies that you have already received, e-mail genealogy.uscis@dhs.gov and include your case identification number in your message.

Following the Past

Of course, the next step is to start researching in "the old country," outside the United States, Canada, or whatever country where you live. Can you do this online? Well, that depends on the country.

Some countries have online records for you to search, especially those countries where English is spoken. But some countries only have sites with the most general information, and you'll be lucky to find the address of the civil records offices. You'll probably wind up doing a combination of online and postal mail research and possibly some in-person research, too.

One thing that can help is the book *International Vital Records Handbook: Births, Marriages, and Deaths* by Thomas Jay Kemp (Genealogical Publishing Company, 2013). At this writing, the fifth edition is the latest. From Afghanistan to Zimbabwe, from Alabama to the U.S. Virgin Islands, Kemp has gathered not only the right offices and phone numbers and address, but if a website or fax exists, he has included that, too. Most important, Kemp has done the research for what records are released for genealogy research for each entry and included the proper form ready to be photocopied and mailed in. If your local library does not have this important resource, you can order it from Genealogical Publishing Company at www.genealogical.com.

Beyond the Boat

Once you have found the boat and the port of departure, you can really begin to search the life of your immigrant ancestor. In many of the online sites covered in previous chapters, you can find links to sites for genealogy beyond the United States. For online links, I recommend starting at Cyndi's List at www.cyndislist.com and RootsWeb at www.rootsweb.org. Other good places to look are discussed in the following sections.

National Archives

A country's national archives might have a webpage describing genealogy how-to's for that country. For example, I recently searched for "Poland National Archives" in Google. Quickly, I found the English version of the archives' website: www.archiwa.gov.pl/en/state-archives.html. This site has pages that explain how to start a genealogy search, what records you can ask for, and where to look for records.

> **Note**
>
> *Immigrate* means to come into and settle in a country or region to which one is not native; *emigrate* means to leave one country or region to settle in another.

Note ——————————————————————————

Be sure to check www.familysearch.org/ask for research guides and videos for the country you need.

Genealogical Societies

Search in any major search site (Yahoo!, Google, Bing, and so on) for the country of origin for your immigrant and "genealogy." Often, at the top of the list will be a genealogical society devoted to that particular nationality. These organizations can help you learn how to conduct research in those countries. Each place has its own method of recording vital statistics, history, and other information.

WorldGenWeb

The WorldGenWeb Project was created in 1996 by Dale Schneider to help folks researching in countries around the world. The goal is to have every country in the world represented by a website and hosted by researchers who either live in that country or are familiar with that country's resources. The site is www.worldgenweb.org, shown in Figure 15-1.

When the WorldGenWeb Project began, volunteers were recruited to host country websites. By coordinating with the USGenWeb Project, soon the major countries in the world had websites. Throughout the next year, WorldGenWeb continued to grow. In 1997, the WorldGenWeb Project moved to RootsWeb. The support of the RootsWeb staff helped WorldGenWeb expand to its present size. Divided into 11 regions (Africa, Asia, British Isles, Central Europe, Caribbean, Eastern Europe, Mediterranean, Middle East, North America, Pacific, and South America), WorldGenWeb provides links to local sites with local resource addresses of county/country public records offices, cemetery locations, maps, library addresses, archive addresses, association addresses (including Family History Centers or other genealogical or historical societies), and some history and culture of the region. Other resources may include query pages or message boards, mailing lists, historical data (including census records), cemetery records, biographies, bibliographies, and family/surname registration websites.

Between RootsWeb and WorldGenWeb, you should be able to find something about the country you need to search.

FIGURE 15-1. *WorldGenWeb is an eclectic collection of worldwide genealogy sites.*

Translate a Site

Don't be frustrated if you find a country's archive but can't find an English button. You can translate a page at most of the major search sites.

One way is "Translate A Page" using Bing Translator at www .microsofttranslator.com. Paste the original text in the text box. The site's software detects the original language, and then you choose what language to translate it to.

Google Translate at www.translate.google.com, Google's free online language translation service, instantly translates text and webpages. Simply input the uniform resource locator (URL) of the site you wish to translate, and Google Translate handles it. It also is built into the Chrome browser. When you open a page in another language in Chrome, a bar at the top will offer to translate it for you.

Several other browsers have add-ons that translate pages on the fly for you. Check your browser's help file.

Country-Specific Sites

In addition to the places mentioned so far, there are many good starting places for an international search. Some are general and provide all sorts of international research, and some are for specific locations. The following sections describe some to get you started.

Asian Genealogical Sites

- The Singapore Genealogy Forum (http://www.genforum .genealogy.com/singapore) allows those of all races to look for their relatives and ancestors who might have lived in Singapore.

- The AsianGenWeb (http://www.worldgenweb.org/index.php/ asiagenweb) is part of WorldGenWeb and has some sites, but needs hosts for many more.

- Origin of Chinese Surnames (http://www.yutopian.com/ names) is a fascinating page with the most common Chinese surnames and their history.

European Genealogical Sites

There are many sites where you can research your European roots. I recommend you start with the following:

- Europe Genealogy Links is a list of sites sorted by country and resource at http://www.genealogylinks.net/europe/index.html. You will find links to cemeteries, censuses, GenWeb pages, and personal sites.

- Benelux (Belgium, Netherlands, Luxembourg): Digital Resources Netherlands and Belgium (http://www.geneaknowhow.net/digi/

resources.html) is one place you can find resources from the Netherlands and Belgium, including more than 350 Internet links to online resources (with more than 150 passenger lists), nearly 900 online resources on Dutch and Belgian bulletin board systems, and hundreds of digital resources.

- Family Explorer Benelux (http://freepages.genealogy.rootsweb .ancestry.com/ ~jberteloot) is a list of links to databases, mailing lists, and other Benelux resources.

- The Federation of East European Family History Societies (FEEFHS) (http://www.feefhs.org) was organized in 1992 to foster family research in Eastern and Central Europe without any ethnic, religious, or social distinctions. You'll find a forum for individuals and organizations focused on either a single country or a group of people to exchange information and be updated on developments in the field. While it primarily serves the interests of North Americans in tracing their lineages back to a European homeland, it welcomes members from all countries. The site has historical maps, information on conferences and workshops, information on organizing tours to Europe for hands-on research, and a quarterly e-mail newsletter.

- The Ukrainian Roots Genealogy Webring can be found at http://www.rootsweb.ancestry.com/ ~ukrgs/ukrroots.html. The webring is community of webpages on Ukrainian genealogy research. The pages are personal home pages of people who want to share information that they have accumulated on their family history and Ukrainian heritage. You'll also find pointers to sources of information that would be of help to others doing research into their Ukrainian family history.

- Eastern Slovakia, Slovak, and Carpatho-Rusyn Genealogy Research (http://www.iarelative.com/slovakia.htm) has articles, links, message boards, and transcribed records.

France

Interest in French genealogy online is growing rapidly. This short list will get you started:

- Besides the usual sites, such as Cyndi's List and WorldGenWeb, check out FrancoGene at http://www.francogene.com. At FrancoGene, you'll find Quebec's pioneers and resources in

Europe; genealogy sites in former French colonies around the world, such as Quebec and Haiti; and links to genealogy societies and institutions.

- Much like Ancestry.com in the United States, Genealogy.tm.fr (http://www.genealogy.tm.fr) is a for-fee site that allows you to search documents and records in French. This was started in 1994, when Laurent Fondant began his own genealogy and found a need to transcribe, index, and scan documents. You pay a subscription for a period to access the documents you find in searching indexes.

- You can search for the geographic distribution of your surname in France (based on censuses from 1891 to 1990) at http://www.geopatronyme.com.

- Nomina (http://www.culture.fr/genealogie) is a meta-search of 13 million names in genealogy databases (GEDCOMs), marriages records, and military records. You can search them all at once, or narrow it down to one of four categories.

- Genealogie.com is much like Genealogy.com in the United States (http://www.genealogie.com). People upload their data for searching and exchanging information.

Germany

The Germans keep wonderful records, but wars and other disasters sometimes left holes in the lexicon. Still, using these sites may be helpful:

- Genealogy.net (http://www.genealogienetz.de/genealogy .html) is a treasure trove of information. From the home page, you can find the monthly newsletter in German, information on genealogical research in local regions, links to 35 different German genealogical societies, 60 mailing lists, a FAQ on German genealogy, a GEDCOM database, a gazetteer, a list of heritage books, and much more. Most of it is in German, so remember the translation sites mentioned earlier! You can search many of these databases with just one query in the meta-search engine.

- GermanRoots (http://www.germanroots.com) offers tips, links, and research hints. It has lists such as "The Best German Resources," "The Best General Resources" "History, Language, and Culture," and a basic guide for research in German genealogy by Joe Beine.

- The New England Historic Genealogical Society has a good history of the Hessian soldiers who fought and sometimes stayed in the Americas at http://www.americanancestors.org/hessian-descendants/.

- The telephone book for Germany can be found at http://www.dastelefonbuch.de.

- Kartenmeister is a free online gazetteer of German place names at http://www.kartenmeister.com/.

Italy

Italians love genealogy! Again, this is a short list to get you started:

- The Italian Genealogy Homepage (http://www.italgen.com) is the leading resource for those who research Italian genealogy. This page includes links to how-to articles, discussion groups, and history.

- Visit D'addezio, or The Italian Heritage and Genealogy page, at http://www.daddezio.com. It has links to atlases, cemeteries, genealogy articles, genealogy newsletters, genealogy software reviews, genealogy supplies, helpful organizations, history and culture resources, information on coats of arms, local (Italian) societies, maps, military records, passenger lists, research services, surname studies, vital records, and more.

- The Italy World Club has a page with links to archives in Italy by region at http://www.italyworldclub.com/genealogy.

Spain

The Spanish Empire in the New World, as well as in Europe, left many records that family historians can use. Here are some examples:

- The place to start is the Society of Hispanic Historical and Ancestral Research at http://www.shhar.net. This organization is nonprofit and all-volunteer, and is dedicated to family history. Besides good pointers for beginners and a message board, this is the only site I've seen with information on African-Hispanic families. The books and journals are worthwhile too. Don't miss the monthly online magazine at http://www.shhar.net/DVD.pdf.

- Spain Genealogy Links (http://www.genealogylinks.net/ europe/spain/) has tips, data, and links about Spain and more.

- A site called EuroDocs from Brigham Young University has a page on Spanish history at http://eudocs.lib.byu.edu/ index.php/History_of_Spain:_Primary_Documents. This has transcribed Spanish documents ranging from the Visigothic Code to wills of individuals.

- A list of mailing addresses for archives and libraries in Spain is on the Genealogy Forum at http://www.genealogyforum .rootsweb.com/gfaol/resource/Hispanic/SpainNA.htm.

Portugal

Portuguese ancestry is almost as widespread as Spanish. However, online resources are not as prevalent.

- Doug da Rocha Holmes' page at http://www.dholmes.com/ rocha1.html, called Portuguese Genealogy Home Page, is dedicated to Portuguese genealogy. The site proclaims, "This website was created with the Portuguese genealogist in mind. It is for anyone and everyone whose passion has become the search for their Portuguese ancestry no matter where they came from in the former Portuguese territories. Many projects are underway which will be of great interest to anyone concerned with this field of study. Check back from time to time to see the new developments."

- LusaWeb is a site dedicated to Portuguese culture, ancestry, and more at http://www.lusaweb.com. This is an organization with dues, like many genealogy societies. It is a place to celebrate common heritage, learn about Portuguese history and traditions, and share the memory of our Portuguese ancestors.

- The Portuguese-American Historical & Research Foundation has a page for genealogy questions and answers at http:// www.portuguesefoundation.org/.

- The National Library of Portugal is online at http://www
  .bnportugal.pt, in Portuguese, of course. Remember to use the
  translation tools mentioned previously!

Note ——————————————————————————————

Most European national libraries are searchable from The
European Library webpage at www.theeuropeanlibrary.org/.

Scandinavia

Census records of Norway are being transcribed and posted by
volunteers at these pages, which also have good information on
research in Norway:

- The Digital Archives is a public service from the National
  Archives of Norway. Here, you can search transcribed source
  material for free at http://www.arkivverket.no/Digitalarkivet.
  Click the English button at the bottom to read it in English, or
  use Chrome to browse there.

- Norwegian Research Sources (http://www.rootsweb.ancestry
  .com/~wgnorway/NorLinks3.htm) is an excellent starting
  place. It has links to articles on the Ancestors from Norway site
  and "Basics of Norwegian Research," among other things.

- Ancestors from Norway (http://homepages.rootsweb.ancestry
  .com/~norway) was created in 1996 to document and inform
  Norwegian ancestry. It now has excellent articles on research,
  links to more than 100 sites with information and records, and
  even recipes!

- The Norwegian Emigration and Genealogy Center offers
  information in Norwegian for descendants at http://www
  .emigrationcenter.com.

Note ——————————————————————————————

Are you finding lots of good information? Have you backed up
this week? This month? This year?

- Martin's Norwegian Genealogy Dictionary (http://www
  .martinroe.com/eidhalist.htm) can help you decipher words
  for relationships, occupations, and so on.

- ProGenealogists has a page for most European countries,
  including one for Denmark at http://www.progenealogists
  .com/denmark.

United Kingdom

Genealogy is as popular in the United Kingdom as it is in the United
States. Here are some good starting places for online information:

- The United Kingdom (UK) and Ireland Genealogy site
  (http://www.genuki.org.uk) is the best starting point. This
  site has transcribed data, such as parish records, plus links
  to individuals' pages where genealogy research (secondary
  material) is posted. Look at the index page (http://www.genuki
  .co.uk/contents) for specific counties, surnames, and so forth.

- The Free BMD (Free Birth, Marriage, and Death Records) Project
  (http://www.freebmd.org.uk) provides free Internet access to
  the Civil Registration Index information for England and Wales
  from 1837. The transcriptions are ongoing, and the updates are
  posted once or twice a month. You can volunteer to help!

- The National Archives of Ireland has a genealogy how-to page
  at http://www.nationalarchives.ie/genealogy1/introduction-to-
  genealogy. From the site, you can search the indexes of 1901 or
  1911 census returns; 1840s, 1850s, and 1860s Primary Valuation
  (also known as Griffith's Valuation); and 1820s or 1830s Tithe
  Applotment Books. There are also some marriage records, although
  a certain number of records were destroyed in "The Troubles."

- The UK National Digital Archive of Datasets (http://www.ndad
  .nationalarchives.gov.uk) has archived digital data from UK
  government departments and agencies. The site provides open
  access to the catalogs of all of its holdings, as well as free access
  to certain datasets, when you register online.

- The National Archives of Scotland (http://www.nas.gov.uk)
  has records from the fifteenth century. The family history
  page at http://www.nas.gov.uk/familyHistory has good how-to
  information. You can download PDF files of fact sheets on
  adoption, deeds, wills, and other topics.

Australia and New Zealand

Australia is rich with genealogy websites. Start with Cyndi's List at www.cyndislist.com/austnz.htm. Other sites include:

- The Society of Australian Genealogists (http://www.sag.org .au) offers materials, meetings, and special interest groups. The library catalog is online as well. This group has been helping people with Australian genealogy since 1932.

- The Dead Persons Society is a genealogy group with several branches. Each site has guides to searching Australian provinces; databases of cemeteries, census, and other records; and general articles on Australian genealogy. A full list of member webpages is at http://www.members.iinet.net .au/~perthdps/dps-socs.htm.

- Convicts to Australia, a guide to researching ancestry during the time when Australia was used as a large prison, can be found at http://www.convictcentral.com. The site has some how-to guides, many census and ships' passenger lists, and more. However, the site cannot handle individual questions or requests for research help.

- The National Archives of Australia (http://www.naa.gov.au) has an entire section on family history and what records to look for.

Africa

- South African Genealogy (http://www.sagenealogy.co.za) is dedicated to helping folks find South African ancestors. "Here you will find lists of passengers arriving or departing the port of Cape Town mostly during the 1800s, books and CDs of colonial records and local history, links to specialist South African and International genealogical websites and more ... all aimed at making your South African Family History research a little easier," the site says.

- Conrod Mercer's page (http://home.global.co.za/~mercon) is a personal collection of tips on doing South African (white) genealogy.

- The African Atlantic Genealogical Society (http://freepages
  .genealogy.rootsweb.ancestry.com/~gfli/africanatllantic
  .html) has newsletters, queries, and census data to help you
  get started.

- You may want to check out Cyndi's List (search for the African
  nation of interest) and WorldGenWeb first.

North America

The following sites are good places to start to search for information
on ancestors from Canada and Mexico.

Canada

Canadian history is as long and varied as U.S. history. Here are some
good starting places:

- Canadian Genealogy and History Links (CGHL) (http://www
  .islandnet.com/~cghl) lists online sites for vital records,
  genealogies, and general history, sorted by province. The CGHL
  search engine will look for your search term in the descriptions
  or titles of pages listed on the site.

- Immigrants to Canada (http://jubilation.uwaterloo.ca/~marj/
  genealogy/) offers information extracted from various
  government records, as well as from shipping records. You
  can read and search such documents as ships' lists, immigration
  reports, and first-person accounts. It also has links to other
  genealogy sites. It is from the University of Waterloo.

- The Canadian Genealogy Centre (http://www.collectionscanada
  .gc.ca/genealogy/) is a page from the National Archives and
  Library of Canada. You can read a PDF file of the free booklet,
  "Tracing Your Ancestors in Canada," which describes the major
  genealogical sources available at the National Archives and
  other Canadian repositories. You may also want to see the main
  page, http://www.collectionscanada.gc.ca/, which combines the
  Archives and Library of Canada sites.

Mexico

Mexican records are fairly detailed when it comes to church matters (births, baptisms, marriages, burials, and so on). However, some states in Mexico have less information on civil matters.

- Archivo General de la Nation (http://www.agn.gob.mx) is the National Archives of Mexico site. It's as rich and deep as the NARA site in the United States. Note that the site is in Spanish.

- Archivo Historico de Arzobispo (http://www.arquidiocesismexico .org.mx/) has the archives of the Archbishop of Mexico, a treasure trove of church records. This site is also in Spanish and has a corresponding Facebook page at http:// www.facebook.com/ pages/Archivo-Historico-del-Arzobispado-de-Mexico/204431596423.

- The Texas General Land Office has a page at http://www.glo .texas.gov/ for their archives. This state office has records dating back to Spanish times. The page tells you how to write for these records, including the proper addresses and what is available. It also has a searchable catalog of historic maps of the region.

- The Genealogy of Mexico (http://garyfelix.tripod.com/index63 .htm) is one genealogist's compilation of starting places. He covers the conquistadores, coats of arms, a DNA surname project, and more.

- The Hispanic Genealogical Society of New York (http://www .hispanicgenealogy.com) includes Mexico, Puerto Rico, and other North American Hispanic genealogy. You can learn about their regular meetings and publications, as well as find links to resources.

A Success Story: German Ancestry Discovered

Denzil J. Klippel had quite a bit of success in his international genealogy search, but it didn't happen overnight. Denzil started with what he knew, researched back to the boat, and finally found his family's village of origin. How he did this is fascinating.

Denzil only knew his parents, his grandmother on his mother's side, and her brother and sister. "In the beginning, I didn't take advantage of the resources on the [Internet] like DearMYRTLE and so forth, and ask questions. But I soon learned everyone in the online genealogy community is willing to help answer questions. We don't need to reinvent the wheel—just ask if anyone has done this or that," Denzil says. So he did eventually ask DearMYRTLE, who pointed him to research at a local Family History Center (FHC). Denzil visited a local FHC in New York City.

There he found his grandmother's family, but not his grandmother, on one of the microfilms. Requesting the name and address of the submitter, he contacted him with a query, including his e-mail address. Soon, another researcher contacted him by e-mail, and everything began to fall together. Denzil sent for his father's death certificate (New York) and found the father's place and date of birth (California). Then he found his grandfather's place of birth (upstate New York), as well as his father's mother's maiden name (Settle) and place of birth (California). He was able to order some of these records online through various vital records sites maintained by these states.

"After going back to my great-grandfather and finding he came from Germany, I hit a brick wall. Not knowing what to do, I went to one of the search engines—Yahoo!—and put in the name Klippel. It gave me 6,000 places where the name appeared on the [Internet], most of them regarding an illness discovered by a Klippel. I captured all of the Klippel e-mail addresses and sent them a message saying I was researching the Klippel family name and, if they were interested in working with me, perhaps we could find some common ancestors or at least discover where the Klippels originated."

Denzil says he does not recommend this approach, however. "This shotgun approach never works," he said. What did work, though, was searching for the surname on Google and looking for the genealogy sites. After e-mailing people with Klippel genealogy sites, as opposed to every Klippel he could find online, Denzil heard from people who had been searching the line. Several were cousins he didn't know he had, and since that time, he now calls all Klippels he comes in contact with "cousin." "One of these cousins had the name of the town in Germany where my Klippel line came from (Ober-Hilbersheim). I found this village had a website and sent a letter to the mayor. He responded via e-mail and said he knew of my line and told me there were still Klippels living in the village," Denzil said. "In the meantime, other Klippels in Europe contacted me, and before I knew it, I was planning a trip to visit some of them and Ober-Hilbersheim. When they heard I was going to visit, they all said I had to stay with them. I bought my airline tickets online via Priceline.com and my train pass online."

(Continued)

Now Denzil was really into the in-person, offline mode! Through electronic and regular mail, he made appointments at all the archives he planned to visit in Germany. When he arrived, they were ready for him and, in most cases, they'd already done all the lookups. As Denzil gathered the research material, he mailed it home to himself. This was important insurance against losing or misplacing any of the papers during his sojourn. "My trip started in Ober-Hilbersheim, and I stayed with the mayor. He took me to all the archives and helped me get all the Klippel family history back to 1550! My distant cousins in the village welcomed me with open arms. I then went to the Netherlands and stayed with the Klippels there, and they took me to the Island of Tholen, where the first Klippel came from in the 1400s. Then on to Hamburg to visit Helmut Klippel and the archive there," Denzil said.

"And last, but not least, on to Sweden to stay with Alf Klippel, who had given me a wealth of information about the origins of the Klippel name via e-mail and did most of the translating of the old German documents I had been receiving over the [Internet]." It took some footwork and perseverance, but after seven years, Denzil feels he accomplished a lot in his international search, and the online resources made it possible.

Wrapping Up

- Once you find your immigrant ancestor, you can use archives and ships' passenger lists to identify the home town.

- Many national archives have webpages describing research techniques for that country.

- At FamilySearch, you can download and print research guides for immigrant origins and for specific countries, as well as word lists of genealogical terms in non-English languages.

- You can find specific sites on genealogy for many nationalities.

- Translating pages are found at most web search sites.

Chapter 16

Ethnic Genealogy Resources

The international sources cited before can also help you with ethnic research within the United States and Canada for a well-documented ancestry. For some groups, however, the search is a little more complex.

Special Challenges

As I described in the Introduction, sometimes you need to search unexpected resources based on other genealogies, history, and, yes, the infamous "family legend." None of these things alone will solve the challenges of ethnic research, but taken together, they might lead to that one document, vital record, or online resource that solves the puzzle. It worked for Bill Ammons, the success story in the Introduction, and it might work for you, too.

For example, African-American genealogy often presents special challenges. When researching the genealogy of a former slave, it's necessary to know as much about the slave owner's family as you do about the slave. Wills, deeds, and tax rolls can hold clues to ancestry, as do legal agreements to rent slaves. Tracking down all these items can be difficult. You need to know the history of the region and the repositories of the records, and you need to consider family legends to be clues, not answers.

As another example, Native American genealogies are also difficult, because in many cases, very little was written down about individuals in the tribes in the eighteenth and nineteenth centuries. A genealogist must contact the tribe involved and look at many different kinds of records.

Mixed ethnic heritages, such as Melungeon, are problematic to research because these mixed groups suffered from stigma for many years. If you are researching a Melungeon family line, the true genealogy may have been suppressed or even forgotten by your ancestors. These special cases have led to many online resources as genealogists have tried to solve the problems and shared their results.

The sites mentioned in this chapter provide good information on how to begin to search for specific genealogy information, as well as the history and culture of different groups. The challenges you will face can be discussed in the forums and mailing lists; you will often find tips on which records to seek and how to get them. Don't forget, however, that new pages are being added to the Web all the time.

Search for "genealogy" plus the name of whatever ethnic group you're seeking on your favorite search engine about once a month to see if new information has become available.

And stay on the mailing lists and newsgroups for the ethnic groups; when you hit a brick wall, perhaps someone on the list can help. And when you break one down, you can share that!

African-American Genealogy

African-American genealogy presents some special challenges, but online genealogists are working hard to conquer them. Search for "African-American genealogy" in any search engine, and you'll find many good resources. Also try these sites as starting places. To begin, the African-American Research Area (www.archives.gov/research/african-americans/) on the National Archives and Records Administration (NARA) site provides a list of articles and other resources not to be missed.

Note

You will find many African-American resources in the "Caribbean Genealogy" section later in the chapter, and you'll find plenty of Caribbean information among the African-American genealogy pages listed in this section.

AfriGeneas

AfriGeneas (see Figure 16-1), www.afrigeneas.com, is the major portal for African-American research. Transcribed records, discussion groups, monthly articles, and more will help you get started. The site has a searchable database of surnames (in addition to slave data) from descendants of slaveholding families, as well as from other sources, both public and private. Tips and topics to help people in their search for family history are distributed through mailing lists, chats, newsletters, and the Internet. Volunteers do all of this; they extract, compile, and publish all related public records with any genealogical value. The site also maintains an impressive set of links to other Internet resources to help African Americans in their research.

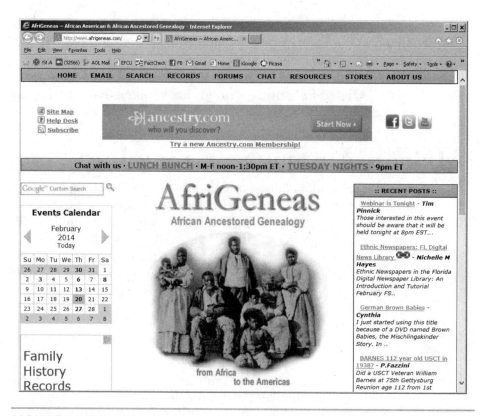

FIGURE 16-1.   *AfriGeneas has databases, forums, chats, and more.*

The sections of this site are an important body of work. They include:

- **E-mail**   AfriGeneas has a page for you to create an e-mail account at so that your address is <yourname>@afrigeneas.com, through Google Mail. The advantage: You can use this address only for genealogy and not for other correspondence. That way, you don't have so much worry about spam coming in with the stuff you really want to read.

- **Search**   The search page lets you search the mailing list, surnames, death records, and the entire site for your surnames or places of interest.

- **Records**   This drop-down menu can help you search the Census Records, Death Records Database, Library Archives, Marriage Records Database, Photos, Slave Data Collection, Surnames Database, State Websites, and World Websites of the AfriGeneas collection.

  Be sure to read the page, "African American Genealogy: An Online Interactive Guide for Beginners" by Dee Parmer Woodtor, author of *Finding a Place Called Home: An African-American Guide to Genealogy and Historical Identity* (Random House Reference, 1999). This step-by-step guide to genealogy in general, and African-ancestored genealogy in particular, is full of good advice.

- **Resources**   Under this heading on the navigation bar, you can find a site map, with every page on the site and a What's New link. It also can take you to the Beginner's Guide, a slideshow-like presentation that steps you through online genealogy. It's a no-nonsense approach, showing what can and can't be done online. It also includes some success stories. The Resources tab also has links to state resources, a clickable map with links to each state in the United States with history, links to state resources, and queries. The World Resources link does the same for other countries, such as the Bahamas. Volunteers are actively being sought for other countries. From the Resources tab, you also get to some important databases:

  - **Forums**   This drop-down menu lists the major topic divisions from African-Native connections to surnames and family research, and the mailing lists. You can also choose to look at the most recent posts in all topics to quickly catch up on what's going on in the different forums.

  - **Chat**   The AfriGeneas Chat Center is open 24 hours and seven days a week for any AfriGeneas member who cares to use it, except during times set aside for regularly scheduled or special chats, and the menu will take you to a chart of when those are. Use is specifically restricted to discussion of African-American or African-ancestored genealogical or historical topics. If anyone abuses the privilege, off-hours access to the chat spaces will be curtailed by AfriGeneas .com. To reserve a room, host a chat, or make comments about or suggestions for future chats, you can contact the chat manager at forum@afrigeneas.com.

- **Resources** This menu has links to books, guides, directories of sites, links to genealogical and historical societies, humor, history, and the help desk, to name just a few. You could spend a week just exploring the items under this drop-down menu!

- **Stores** Links you to both the onsite bookstore and Amazon.com.

Among the most valuable resources on the site are:

- **Slave Data** This area will help you find the last owned slave in your family. Records kept by the slave owner are frequently the only clue to African-American ancestors, particularly during the period 1619–1869. The site is also designed to help descendants of slaveholders and other researchers. Users share information they find containing any references to slaves, including wills, deeds, and other documents. This site also houses a search engine and a form for submitting any data you might have. To use the database, click the first letter of the surname you're interested in. This takes you to a list of text files with surnames beginning with that letter. Now click a particular filename. The text file may be transcribed from a deed book, a will, or some other document. The name and e-mail address of the submitter will be included, so you can write to that person for more information, if necessary.

- **Census Records** These are transcribed census records. As a file is submitted, it's listed at the top of the What's New list on this page. Not all states have volunteers transcribing right now, so you can only click those states that show up as a live link.

- **News Briefs & What's New** These headings on the home page keep you updated on the latest news and additions.

Note

AfriGeneas also has a Facebook page, www.facebook.com/afrigeneas, where queries, news, and reviews are posted regularly. Be sure to become a fan!

Africana Heritage

A project at the University of South Florida (USF), this site is at www.africanaheritage.com. The USF Africana Heritage Project is an all-volunteer research project and website sponsored by the Africana Studies department at the University of South Florida. The volunteers concentrate on recovering records that document the names and lives of slaves, freed persons, and their descendants and then share those records on the site. You are invited to share documents with the site, and material is there from readers, scholars, archives, universities, and historical societies. For more information, contact Toni Carrier, Founding Director, USF Africana Heritage Project, 4202 E. Fowler Avenue, FAO 270, Tampa, FL 33620. Or you can e-mail info@africanaheritage.com.

More Good Resources

Other good African-American sites are in this list:

- The **Afro-American Historical and Genealogical Society** (AAHGS) is a group for the preservation of the history, genealogy, and culture of those with African heritage. The society's main emphasis is in recording research (as in transcribing sources and so on) and sharing completed genealogies. You'll find AAHGS at http://www.aahgs.org. They have an annual conference, local chapters, a journal, and newsletter.

- **Slaves and the Courts** (http://lcweb2.loc.gov/ammem/ sthtml) is an online collection of pamphlets and books at the Library of Congress about the experiences of African and African-American slaves in the United States and American colonies. It includes trial arguments, examinations of cases and decisions, and other materials concerning slavery and the slave trade. You can locate information by using the collection's subject index, author index, or title index, or you can conduct your own search by keyword. You can look at the items as transcriptions or as images of the original pages. Knowing this sort of history can often give you a clue as to where to look for other records.

Cases from America and Great Britain are included with arguments by many well-known abolitionists, presidents, politicians, slave owners, fugitive and free-territory slaves, lawyers and judges, and justices of the U.S. Supreme Court. Significant names include John Q. Adams, Roger B. Taney, John C. Calhoun, Salmon P. Chase, Dred Scott, William H. Seward, Theodore Parker, Jonathan Walker, Daniel Drayton, Castner Hanway, Francis Scott Key, William L. Garrison, Wendell Phillips, Denmark Vesey, and John Brown.

- **African-American Griots** (http://www.rootsweb.ancestry .com/ ~ aagriots) discusses the storytellers, or griots. Their roles are hereditary, their surnames identify them as griots, and they sing and tell the histories of their tribes. This site provides a list of links to databases for individuals and records pertaining to groups of people, background on the history of the griots, and, of course, e-mail lists.

- **The Freedman's Bureau Online** (http://www.freedmensbureau .com) allows you to search many records. The Freedman's Bureau took care of education, food, shelter, clothing, and medicine for refugees and freedmen. When Confederate land or property was confiscated, the Freedman's Bureau took custody. Records include personnel records and reports from various states on programs and conditions.

- The **African-American Genealogical Society of Northern California** is a local group, but its website has monthly articles, online genealogy charts, discussion groups, and more. It is worth a visit. Find it at http://www.aagsnc.org.

- **AAGENE-L** is a moderated mailing list for African-American genealogy and history researchers. Subscribe to the list by sending a message to aagene-l@upeople.com with SUBSCRIBE in the subject line. Details can be found at htttp://ftp.cac.psu .edu/ ~ saw/aagene-faq.html.

Arab Genealogy

- **Linkpedium** (the best-kept secret of online genealogy) has a page of Arab genealogy links at http://www.linkpendium .com/. You can also use the search box.

- **GenForum** has a discussion group on United Arab Emirates genealogy at http://www.genforum.genealogy.com/uae.

- Check **Cyndi's List Middle East** page (http://www.cyndislist .com/middle-east) for a list of sites dedicated to history, culture, and genealogy research on the Middle East.

Australian Aborigines

- The **Aboriginal Studies WWW Virtual Library** (http://www .ciolek.com/WWWVL-Aboriginal.html) has links to resources and articles concerning Australian aborigines.

- The **New Zealand WorldGenWebPage** (http://www.rootsweb .ancestry.com/ ~ nzlwgw/resources.html) has links to many resources about New Zealand genealogy.

- The **National Library of Australia** has a page on genealogy, located at http://www.nla.gov.au/oz/genelist.html, that includes links to many specific ethnic and family sites.

- The **Australian Institute of Aboriginal and Torres Strait Islander Studies** (AIATSIS) has a page just for family historians at http://www.aiatsis.gov.au.

Caribbean Genealogy

- **Caribbean Genealogy Resources**, located at http://www .candoo.com/genresources, lists links to archives, museums, universities, and libraries with historical and genealogical information for countries in the Caribbean. Another page from this site is http://www.candoo.com/surnames, which is a list of Caribbean surnames. The text files list surnames, places, and dates, as well as e-mail contact information for researchers looking for them.

- **Caribbean WorldGenWeb** (http://www.rootsweb.com/ ~ caribgw). Search RootsWeb for mailing lists for related queries and discussions.

British Virgin Islands Genealogy

- **British Virgin Islands Caribbean GenWeb** (http://www .rootsweb.ancestry.com/~bviwgw) has general resources, online records, query boards, and a mailing list.

- **Caribbean Genealogy-Resources-Microfilm Indexes** (http:// www.candoo.com/genresources/microfilms.htm) is a list of surnames in the Caribbean listed by surname and researcher.

- **Genforum.genealogy.com** (http://www.genforum.genealogy .com) features a forum finder, and you can search by surnames. It also offers information on general genealogy topics, such as immigration, emigration, migration, religions, and wars.

- **BVI Civil Registry** (http://crisvi.gov.vg/netdata/db2www .pgm/c2_public.ndm/start2) provides information on the BVI records going back to 1859. This would be an offline research opportunity. If you make an appointment, you can do research there. The General Civil Registry Office holds records of births, marriages, deaths, and wills from 1859 to present. The Anglican and Methodist churches hold records of baptisms, marriages, and deaths as follows: Anglican Church: baptisms (1825–1861), marriages (1833–1946), and burials (1819–1867); Methodist Church: baptisms (1815–1895 and 1889), marriages (1877–1934), and burials (1845–1896).

- The **Inland Revenue Office** records ownership of houses, land, and other property.

- **Tax lists** containing pertinent information are published annually.

- The **Land Registry** holds property identifiers, including indexes and maps from 1972, public library information (newspapers from 1959 and various name indexes), BVI history books, and, from the Survey Department, ordinance 1953 maps and boundary maps from 1975. You can write to them at The Archives Unit, Deputy Governor's Office, Burhym Building, 49 deCasro Street, Road Town, Tortola. (284) 468-2365 (phone) and (284) 468-2582 (fax).

Creole/Cajun Genealogy

The Acadians/Cajuns were the French settlers ejected from Nova Scotia by the British in the mid-eighteenth century. Some went to Quebec, and some to Louisiana.

"Creole" means different things in different places. In Latin America, a Creole is someone of pure Spanish blood. In the Caribbean, it means a descendant of Europeans; in the Guineas, it means someone descended from slaves, whether African or native to the islands. In the southern United States, the term refers to aristocratic landowners and slaveholders before the Civil War, part of the overall French/Cajun culture of the Gulf Coast. For almost all Creole research, parish records are your best bet—those and mailing list discussions!

- **Acadian-Cajun Genealogy and History** (http://www .acadian-cajun.com) publishes records, how-to articles, history, mailing lists, maps, genealogies, and more.

- **The Encyclopedia of Cajun Culture** (http://www.cajunculture .com) will give you good background information.

- **Acadian Genealogy Homepage** (http://www.acadian.org) has census records, books, maps, and more.

Note

Have you backed up your data this week? This month? This year?

- **The Cajun and Zydeco Radio Guide** also has a list of family histories that have been posted to the Web at http://www .cajunradio.org/genealogy.html.

- **Canadian GenWeb** is at http://acadian-genweb.acadian-home .org/Links.html. Here you will find links to surname forums, several personal websites, some census records and DNA studies.

- The **Louisiana Creole Heritage Center** is located on the campus of Northwestern State University in Natchitoches, Louisiana, and on the Web at http://creole.nsula.edu. The Facebook page is http://facebook.com/creoleheritagecenter.

- The **Confederation of Associations of Families Acadian** (http://www.cafa.org) promotes the culture and genealogy of Acadian families in America.

- Search the **RootsWeb mailing lists**; there are several for Acadian/Cajun research and data in Louisiana and Canada.

Cuban Genealogy

- The **Cuban GenWeb** (http://www.cubagenweb.org) has good pointers, tips, and exchanges on Cuban genealogy.

- The **Cuban Digital Library** page (in Spanish—remember, the Chrome browser will translate for you) is at http://www.bibliotecadigitalcubana.blogspot.com/. This page has some digitized scholarly manuscripts much like Google Books. See Figure 16-2.

- Search **Google Books** for "Cuba" and "genealogy" or "history" for some good hits.

- The **Cuban Genealogy Club of Miami** has a good website at http://www.cubangenclub.org/. Begun in 2001, the club works for the preservation of shared memories and experiences. The club also fosters an interest in the preservation of records and testimonies that document Cuban family history.

- **Florida International University**, **University of Florida**, and other Florida colleges have good special collections with Cuban and Caribbean heritage items. For example, at FIU, check out the article "FIU Library Holds Unexpected Treasures" http://news.fiu.edu/2013/05/fiu-library-holds-unexpected-treasures/62827.

Doukhobors Genealogy

The history of this small sect of Russian pacifist dissenters is outlined in an article at http://rootsweb.ancestry.com/~cansk/Saskatchewan/ethnic/doukhobor-saskatchewan.html. The RootsWeb message boards at Ancestry.com have several topics on this group as well.

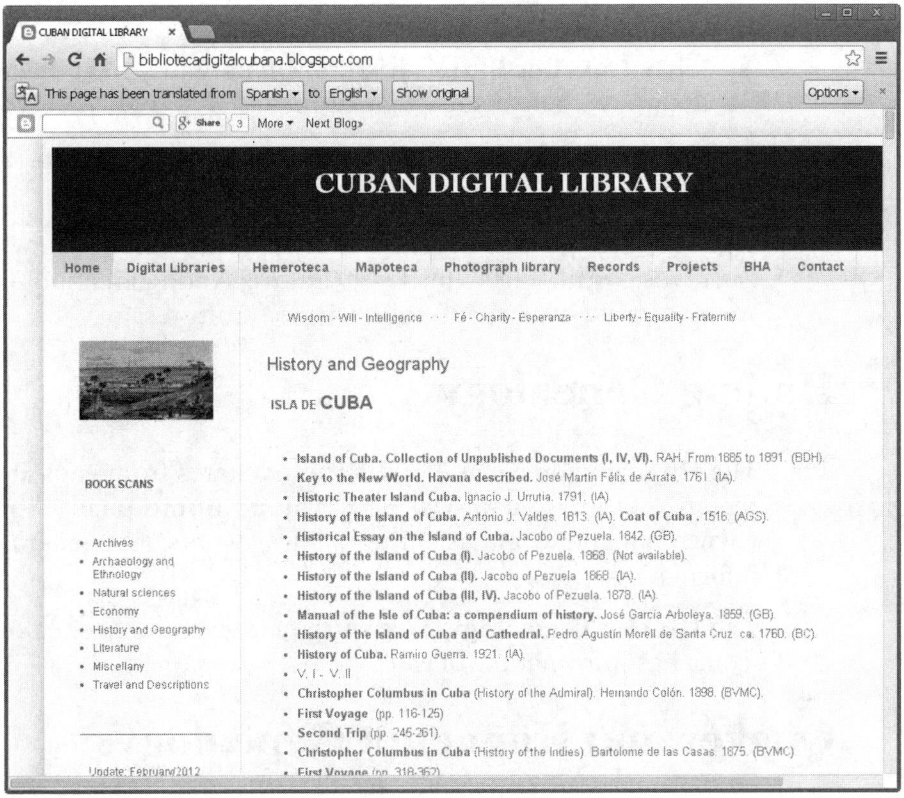

FIGURE 16-2. *The Cuban Digital Library has digital books you can search.*

Gypsy, Romani, Romany, and Travellers Genealogy

- **The Gypsy Lore Society** maintains a list of links on Gypsy history, genealogy, and images at http://www.gypsyloresociety .org/.

- **Romani culture and history** are covered at http://www .romanygenes.com.

- Learn about the **Irish Travellers** at these sites:

    - **Irish Traveller** (http://irishtraveller.org.uk/find-out-about-irish-travellers/history-and-culture/)

    - **Romani & Traveller Family History Society** (http://rtfhs.org.uk)

- From the **Surrey County Council** site page at http://new.surreycc.gov.uk, click Heritage, Culture, And Recreation; then Archive And History; and then Diverse Cultures.

Hmong Genealogy

- The Hmong people came to the United States from Laos at the end of the Vietnam War. The **Hmong home page** (http://www.hmongnet.org) has culture, news, events, and general information.

- The **Hmong Genealogy** page (http://www.hmonggenealogy.com) has information as well.

Quaker and Huguenot Genealogy

- **My Quaker Roots** (http://robt.shepherd.tripod.com/quaker1.html) is a site covering New England families of Maris, Palmerton, Jenkins, Smith, Nichols, Newlin, Rogers, Kinsey, Sherman, Palmer, Pugh, Fawkes, Mendenhall, and other Quakers.

- **The Quaker Collection** (http://freepages.genealogy.rootsweb.ancestry.com/~jrichmon/qkrcoll/qkrcoll.htm) offers a collection of Family Group Sheets on the founders of certain larger Quaker families.

- **The Quaker Corner** (http://www.rootsweb.ancestry.com/~quakers/) has many resources for Quaker genealogical research.

- **The Huguenot Society of America** has a website and an e-mail newsletter at http://www.huguenotsocietyofamerica.org/.

- **The Genealogy Forum: Huguenot Genealogy Resources: Huguenot Timeline** (http://www.genealogyforum.com/gfaol/resource/Huguenot/hug0006.htm) is a good overview of the movement.

- *Huguenot Ancestry* by Noel Currer-Briggs and Royston Gambier (Phillimore & Co., Ltd., 1985) is available on Google Books.

- A very good roundup of information is at http://www.familytreemaker.com/glc/links/c/c-people,ethnic-religious-groups.html.

- **The National Huguenot Association** (http://www.huguenot.netnation.com). Here they have background information, links to records and databases, and more.

Jewish Genealogy

- The first site to visit for Jewish genealogy is **JewishGen.org** (http://www.jewishgen.org). Mailing lists, transcribed records, GEDCOMs, and more are at the site. You can also find links to special-interest groups, such as geographic emphasis or genetics.

- Your next stop should be **The Israel GenWeb Project** website (http://www.israelgenealogy.com), which serves as a resource for those researching their family history in Israel.

- **Sephardic Genealogy** (http://www.sephardicgen.com) has links to articles and historical documents, as does **Sephardim .com** (http://www.sephardim.com), which has an article on Jamaican-Jewish history.

- Canadian-Jewish genealogists should begin at the **Jewish Genealogical Society of Montreal** (http://www.jgs-montreal.org), which contains a history of the first Jewish settlers there.

Native American Genealogy

- **Indians/Native Americans** on NARA is a reference page with links to various government records resources. It can be found at http://www.archives.gov/research/alic/reference/native-americans.html.

- A good source on culture/heritage is a search engine called **Native Languages of America**, located at http://www.native-languages.org/.

- **The Congress of Aboriginal Peoples** is a site that presents categorized links to Canadian aboriginal, Native American, and international indigenous sites on the Web. The genealogy page is at http://www.abo-peoples.org.

- **The African-Native American History & Genealogy** webpage, located at http://www.african-nativeamerican .com/, is mostly concerned with the history of Oklahoma and surrounding areas.

- **Access Genealogy's Native American Genealogy** page, located at http://www.accessgenealogy.com/native, has transcribed records and a state-by-state list of online sites.

- **The All Things Cherokee** genealogy page is at http://www .allthingscherokee.com/genealogy.html.

- **The Potowami** has a site at http://www.potawatomi.org, with a history of the tribe.

- Many other tribes also have sites. Simply use any search engine for the tribe name, plus the word "genealogy," and you'll likely get a hit.

Metis Genealogy

Metis is a name for those of Native American heritage, but mixed tribes. A good place to start researching this is at http://metisnationdatabase.ualberta.ca/MNC/ which is the link for The Metis Nation Database.

Melungeon Genealogy

The origins of the people, and even the name, are controversial, but the Appalachian ethnic group called Melungeon seems to be of European, African, Mediterranean, and Native American descent. One legend is that Sir Francis Drake marooned Portuguese, Turkish, and Moorish prisoners on the North Carolina shore in the 1560s, who then married the Native Americans.

Melungeons are documented as far back as the eighteenth century in the Appalachian wilderness. They are found in the Cumberland Plateau area of Virginia, Kentucky, North Carolina, West Virginia, Tennessee, and, some argue, North Alabama. Melungeon genealogy took on new and exciting relevance with the publication of *The Melungeons: The Resurrection of a Proud People* by Dr. N. Brent Kennedy (Mercer University Press, 1997). One interesting theory in the book is that Abraham Lincoln bears the Melugeon characteristics of his mother, Nancy Hanks.

- **Melungeons and Other Mestee Groups** (http://www .melungeonmestee.webs.com) by Mike Nassau is an online book on the subject that you can download.

- One of the best places to start besides those listed here is the **Melungeon Heritage Association**, at http://www.melungeon .org.

- An informational page called "**Avoiding Pitfalls in Melungeon Research**" is at http://www.melungeonstudies.blogspot .com/2009/08/avoiding-pitfalls-in-melungeon-research.html. This is the text of a talk presented by Pat Spurlock Elder at "Second Union, a Melungeon Gathering" held in Wise, Virginia, in July 1998.

- **The Melungeon Resource** page includes a FAQ file, located at http://homepages.rootsweb.ancestry.com/~mtnties/ melungeon.html.

- **The Appalachian Mountain Families** page includes information on Melungeons and is found at http://freepages .genealogy.rootsweb.ancestry.com/~appalachian.

- Some rare diseases are characteristic of Melungeons. The **Melungeon Health Education and Support Network**, at http://www.melungeonhealth.org, describes some of these diseases and has links to resources about them.

Wrapping Up

- Many ethnic groups have started mailing lists, newsgroups, and history sites.

- Once a month, use your favorite search engine to find new sites by searching for the ethnic term and "genealogy."

- Stay on mailing lists to discuss your ethnic "brick walls" and share your breakthroughs.

Chapter 17

The National Genealogical Society

The National Genealogical Society (NGS) is one of the most important genealogical societies in the United States. This service organization, which is over 100 years old, leads and educates the national genealogical community and assists members in tracing family histories.

On its website (www.ngsgenealogy.org), you'll find announcements of NGS seminars, workshops, and programs; information on its home-study course; youth resources; and other NGS activities. This is an excellent site for learning genealogy standards and methods.

NGS was organized in Washington, D.C., in 1903. The preliminary first meeting was held on April 24, and then it formally organized that year on November 11. Now, the NGS has over 17,000 members, including individuals, families, genealogical societies, family associations, libraries, and other related institutions.

About the NGS

The NGS is one of the best broad-based organizations for family history. Its workshops, meetings, and publications are invaluable. You can see its home page in Figure 17-1.

On the home page, you'll find links to the newest and most relevant items on the site, including upcoming meetings, trips, courses, and competitions. On every page of the site, you'll find a navigation bar at the top that leads to the following sections.

Note

It seems intuitive to use www.ngs.org as the Uniform Resource Locator (URL) for this organization, but the National Geographic Society got there first.

Educational Courses

Free to NGS members, the online, self-paced, self-graded Family History Skills course is good for beginners or for those who need a refresher course. Other online courses cover population census records, special agricultural or mortality census schedules, deeds,

FIGURE 17-1. *The National Genealogical Society website has searchable data as well as information about the organization.*

and more, and range in price from free for members to $50 per course for nonmembers.

The famous NGS American Genealogy: Home Study Course is now on CD-ROM. Members and nonmembers can opt for the course to be either self-graded or graded by a professional genealogist. You can buy the three-CD course one at a time for $85 apiece or in bundles for as much as $565 (graded course, nonmember price).

Some Reasons to Join

Some of the benefits of membership are:

- A free online course for members of the NGS on basic genealogy skills and techniques.

- Periodicals include the *National Genealogical Society Quarterly,* the *NGS Magazine,* and the "UpFront with NGS" online blog.

- The Members Only section of the NGS website has publication archives, the *National Genealogical Society Quarterly* searchable index, the *NGS Magazine* online, and special exclusive videos of interviews with leading genealogists.

- Members can also access databases such as The National Intelligencer, an abstracted database of marriage and death notices from 1800–1850; NGS Bible Records (indexed by names with PDF scans); and NGS Member Ancestry Charts (MACs).

- Members can also download research aids and forms to help you create an abstract for a census, learn how to file your finds, and more.

- Discounts from Boston University, Fold3, and FlipPal and, of course, on NGS courses, trips, and seminars.

Publications and Videos

Written and edited by leading experts in the genealogical field, NGS periodicals and books show you the best techniques to help you research and record your family history. The publications and videos cover the latest technology tools, case studies of how to solve a difficult research problem, and reference books on particular geographic areas. You can view for free the video *Paths to Your Past* in this section of the site.

Conferences and Events

Many people first learn about the NGS as an organization at the conferences and events held around the country every year.

The NGS Family History Conference is the biggest event of the year for the society. Everyone from neophytes to those who want to become Certified Professional Genealogists will find something interesting at this conference. The location changes yearly, and fee ranges from $100 for one day to $275 for nonmembers for the whole conference.

You can also sign up for a research trip where a professional genealogist leads a tour to help you research in the Family History Library in Salt Lake City, Utah. Two are held each year.

Family reunions and other genealogy groups also publicize their events on the NGS events calendar, so this is a place to bookmark for future reference.

Awards and Competitions

NGS awards are given each year at the annual conference. They are:

- **Award of Honor**   To recognize an individual or organization for dedicated and sustained service in support of an NGS Family History Conference.

- **Award of Merit**   To recognize exceptional contributions to the field of genealogy by an individual or nonprofit genealogical or historical organization over a period of five years or more.

- **Certificate of Appreciation**   To recognize an individual or organization for service during an NGS conference. A nominee need not be a member of NGS. This award may be presented to an individual or institution more than once.

- **Distinguished Service Award**   To recognize outstanding contributions to the work of NGS. A nominee must have been a member of NGS for at least one year.

- **Fellow of the National Genealogical Society (FNGS)**   To recognize outstanding work in the field of genealogy or the related fields of history, biography, or heraldry, in addition to outstanding service to the National Genealogical Society.

Several competitions, such as the Family History Writing Contest and scholarships for students and adults, are also outlined in this section.

Calendar

You might want to bookmark the calendar at www.ngsgenealogy.org/cs/event_calendar, where not only NGS events but also events from other genealogical organizations are listed.

My Account, My Orders, My Downloadable Products

Whenever you order from the website, whether a member or not, the transactions are stored here. This is one reason to fill out the registration when you first visit the site so that you can trace your activity later.

Store

The NGS has several excellent publications for sale. Members receive a discount, but nonmembers can also buy the research guides (available as PDFs and in hard copy) and the excellent book, *Mastering Genealogical Proof* (National Genealogical Society, Inc., 2013)—now available for the Kindle—among others. If you want to order, you need to create a profile with your e-mail and contact information. This does not sign you up as a member of the National Genealogical Society or give you access to the members-only section of the website; it just helps you keep track of your purchases and redownload your PDFs later.

Wrapping Up

- The NGS is a broad-based American institution for education and resources in genealogy.

- You can take online and at-home genealogy courses from NGS, take research trips, and attend NGS conferences to learn about genealogy.

- Certain databases can be searched online at the site by members; you can also pay a fee to have NGS staff do research for you.

Chapter 18

Ancestry.com and RootsWeb

The Ancestry.com family of sites and products is a collection of billions of historical records—digitized, indexed, and put online—available by subscription and through libraries around the world. The company developed their own systems for digitizing handwritten historical documents, and established relationships with national, state, and local government archives; historical societies; religious institutions; and private collectors of historical content around the world to build this collection. The records and documents, combined with their web-based online search technologies and software, let subscribers research family history, build family trees, and use the ancestry.com sites for social networking.

Is a paid membership worthwhile? One friend of mine compared it to the premium movie channels. If you only watched one movie a month, a premium movie channel would not be a good buy. If you have a 60-inch screen and your own popcorn machine, however, because movies are your favorite thing to do, then a premium movie channel would save you money over going to the theater or buying individual pay-per-view movies. Ancestry.com is the same: If you have been seriously bitten by the genealogy bug, you will use it so much you will wonder how people ever found records without it. If you just wonder who your great-grandparents are, then don't get your own subscription. Use it at the local library or your local Family History Center on those rare occasions when you feel like doing some research.

Note

Ancestry.com can be found on several social platforms, including Facebook (www.facebook.com/Ancestry.com)
Livestream (www.livestream.com/ancestry)
Pinterest (www.pinterest.com/ancestrycom/)
Twitter (www.twitter.com/ancestry)
YouTube (www.youtube.com/AncestryCom)

With 24,000 searchable databases and titles, Ancestry.com is a major online source for family history information. Since its launch in 1997, Ancestry.com has been the leading resource for family history and has worked hard at gathering diverse data with many easy-to-use tools and resources. The Ancestry.com part has the only complete online U.S. federal census collection (1790–1930), as well as the world's largest online collection of U.S. ship passenger list records, featuring more than 100 million names (1820–1960). Based in Salt Lake City, Utah, it is a wide-ranging collection of genealogy resources. You can do some things for free, but fees apply for certain searches, some levels of disk space, and some other services.

Ancestry.com

Registering for Ancestry.com is free. That will allow you to build a family tree, connect with community members, and access all of the free content. A list of free records and a search box is at www .ancestry.com/freerecords. Just a few of the types of indexes of records you can search there include:

- Find a Grave, 1770–1790

- Census of the Cumberland Settlements, 1864

- Census for Re-Organizing the Georgia Militia, 1880

- United States Federal Census, 1881

- Channel Islands Census, 1881

- England Census, 1881

- Isle of Man Census, 1881

- Wales Census, 1891

- New South Wales, Australia Census, 1901

- New South Wales, Australia Census

The list includes hundreds more (see Figure 18-1).

To find out about all of Ancestry's newest features, records, and more, follow the official Ancestry.com blog at http://blogs.ancestry .com/ancestry. Regular genealogy columns by writers such as George G. Morgan, Dick Eastman, Kip Sperry, Juliana Smith, Elizabeth Kelley Kerstens, and Drew Smith are available free of charge, too. You can participate in the Ancestry.com Livestream hosted weekly with Crista Cowan at www.livestream.com/ancestry. Crista walks viewers through new topics and features, followed by a Twitter session where you can tweet more detailed questions and Crista will answer.

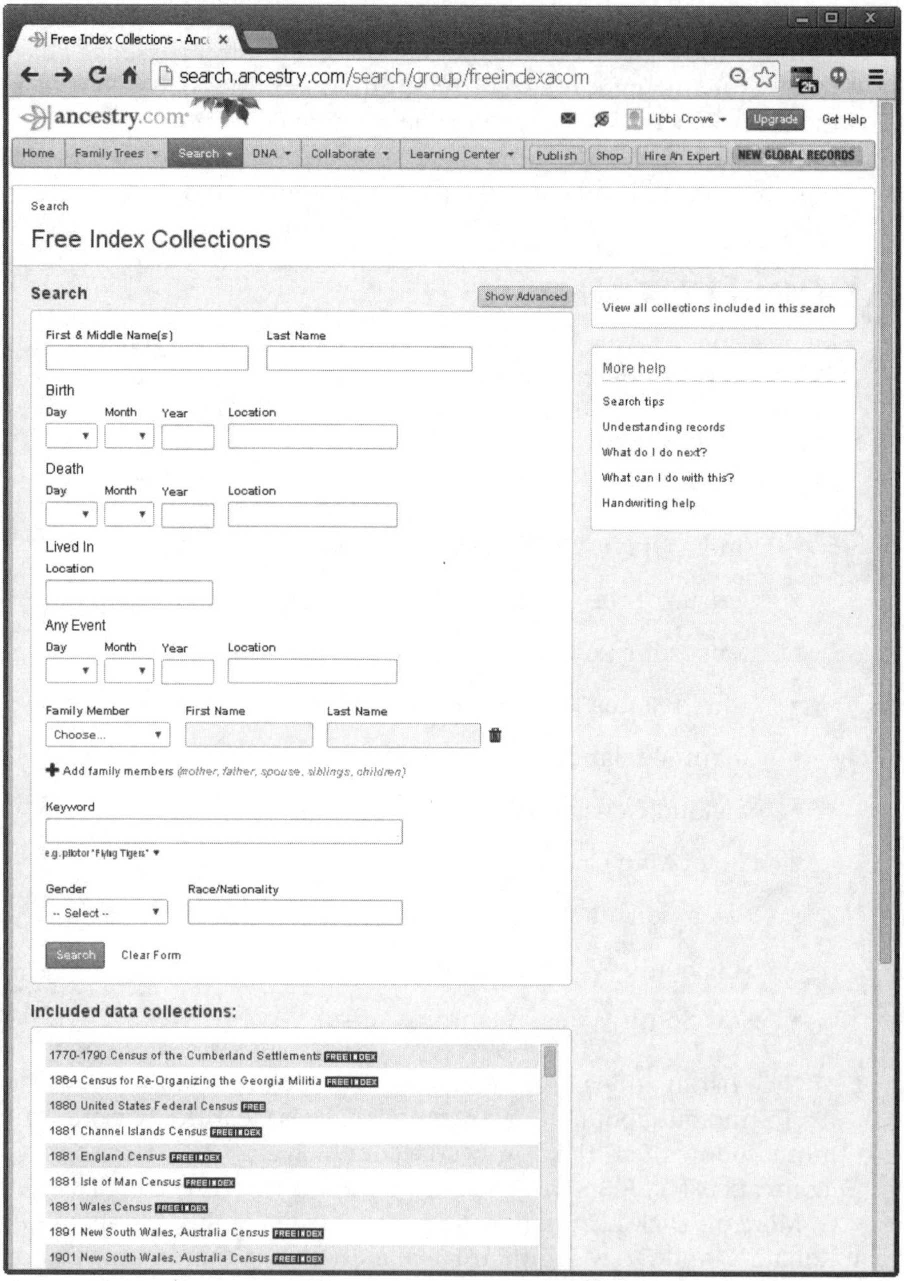

FIGURE 18-1. *Ancestry.com has many records and indexes you can search for free, as well as subscription-based databases.*

Family Tree Maker

As noted in Chapter 2, Family Tree Maker (FTM) syncs with your online Ancestry.com tree. FamilyView, a family group sheet with pictures, makes navigating easier, especially when you want to see extended family members, such as cousins. FTM lets you copy and paste facts and sources from one individual to another, and you can let family and friends view the online version of your tree without software or a subscription.

Within FTM, you can sort children automatically by birth order and view people by location, grouping them by country, state, county, and city. The charts and reports options and views let you display an individual's ancestors, spouses, and children together. You can use the Index of Individuals Report to see anniversary, birthday, contact lists, and more. You can also export a single branch of your tree. It's available for Windows and Mac, and the price ranges from $40 to $80, depending on how many features you want. Ancestry.com also has three apps for smart phones and tablets:

- **Ancestry.com** This is a great way to take Ancestry.com with you. The program will sync instantly with your online tree.

- **Find A Grave** This can help with your gravesite discovery and headstone indexing.

- **ShoeBox** Scan photos and documents and upload them to your Ancestry.com tree.

Using Ancestry.com

When first starting out with genealogy, it's tempting to start researching your grandparents or further back. Start with what you know and build a tree. It can be difficult to keep all of the information straight, so the free tree feature on Ancestry.com will help you keep track of dates, stories, and relationships. Start with yourself and then move backward in time. Enter names, dates, places, and, if you have them, photographs and scanned comments. Right away, "shaking" leaves will show up on the names in your tree to help walk you through your family history (see Figure 18-2). This means that Ancestry.com has already done

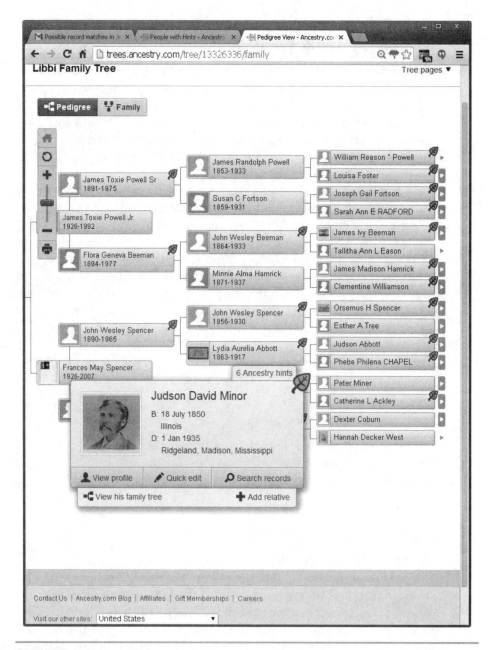

FIGURE 18-2. *"Shaking" leaves mean some records may have matched your ancestor.*

some searches for you, but you can do more detailed ones yourself later on, too. Talk to the oldest members of your family, and start building a family tree branch by branch.

> ## Note
>
> The average Ancestry.com member needn't worry about copyright issues. You are able to use the images and documents to record your own family history, including creating family history books, printouts, posters, etc. If you want to use documents found on Ancestry.com for commercial use or mass publications, send an e-mail to permissions@ancestry.com.

Building Your Tree

Work on one generation at a time, and work backwards slowly. Look at each suggested record and thoroughly read and vet each one. If you decide one of them is right, you simply click Add, and the record (and image if available) can be attached to a specific person.

But, as great as those shaking leaves are, they won't show you everything, so search for records from profiles of people in your family tree. Searching for data on an individual using the profile will allow you to use all of the data you already have on that person as search criteria to find more. Also, if another member has data that seems to match one of your individuals, you can connect with that person to collaborate.

Another interesting view: From an ancestor's profile, click the green Story View button. This will pull all of the information you have on that individual into a storyboard format in a sort of executive summary. This will make sharing the family story with others simpler. A sample is in Figure 18-3.

Search

The main use for Ancestry.com is to find data. Sure, it has many helpful tools for analyzing, comparing, and printing out what you find, but you will mainly use Ancestry.com for searching. New in 2014 is an integrated search with sliding filter feature. You can slide the control from broad to exact for spelling, dates, and places instead of typing in ranges or doing a separate search for different spellings. This is a great time-saving tool.

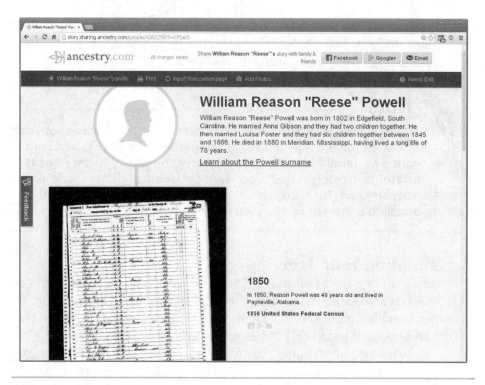

FIGURE 18-3. *Reason Powell's story view.*

The new search will also know which of the hits in the search are already attached to someone in your trees. For example, if you already have a 1940 census attached to your grandfather, search results aren't going to bring that up again since he should only be in the 1940 census once.

With more than 13 billion historical records on Ancestry.com, it's easy to think that they have every record. The company works with archives, courthouses, and private entities to acquire records that will have the most significance for family historians. Sometimes, records are not on Ancestry.com due to time constraints, privacy laws in certain states, or unformed partnerships with archives. To make sure the site has the collection you need, use the Ancestry.com card catalog. Hover over the Search button at the top of the page. Click Card Catalog in the drop-down menu. Then you can select location, year, record type, and more. This will help you narrow your searches to specific databases or learn if the type of record you need has been digitized yet.

Those who have the world deluxe subscription can get records on all international sites. For example, you can search England for emigration records. Again, using the card catalog to see if the records exist can be a big help. However, remember that if a record is in Italian, for example, the record will not be translated into English—only the index fields such as date and location will.

Collaborate

The Collaborate menu in Ancestry.com includes messages boards and original articles on genealogy, all of which are accessible for free. Features include the following:

- **Card Catalog** is the last menu option here, but may be the most useful. Besides the records noted earlier, you can search other members' trees for dates and names to find potential matches. If the tree is set to Public, then you can look at it and compare for common ancestors. If it is set to Private, you can send a message to the owner explaining why you think you should connect.

- **Recent Member Connect Activity** shows you a list of the people in your Connect list. When these members save records, upload photos, or add persons to their trees, the activity shows up on your recent list.

- **Online Support Community** is a message board about software, research techniques, and all the services offered by Ancestry.com. If you have a question or problem with Ancestry.com products, the answer is probably here.

- **Message Boards** includes surnames, geography, and many other topics.

- **World Archives Project** is Ancestry.com's volunteer indexing program. It works much like FamilySearch's volunteer indexing program.

- **Member Directory** allows you to search for others in Ancestry .com's membership who may be searching the same families as you are or who may live nearby. You fill out your Public Profile so that others can find you with this feature and with the Card Catalog.

Learning Center

Do not forget to check out the Learning Center tab on the menu bar. As mentioned, the What's New option shows you the latest blogs and articles. First Steps has links to several good beginners' guides, as does Family History 101. You can watch online archived webinars under one option. Another one will take you to the Ancestry.com wiki, where members and employees post answers to questions, definitions, and other useful information. Finally, of course, there's Help.

DNA

Also, take a look at Ancestry.com DNA. Your DNA can tell you some surprising things about your heritage. You swab your cheek and mail the swab in. The resulting report from Ancestry.com DNA tells you

Success Story: Smashing a Brick Wall

I smashed a brick wall recently using Ancestry.com. I have a basic subscription. There has been a story in my husband's family for as long as anyone can remember that the name Flynt isn't really the family surname, that it is really Damon. No one knew any more than that. Ancestry.com put an index to Maine court records online. I did a search for the great-great-grandfather Daniel Flint/Flynt. I was rewarded with "Daniel Flint (Alias)." I copied down the book and page numbers and contacted the State of Maine Archives for copies of the court records. The records showed a conviction for bigamy and included marriage records for the first marriage as Delafayette Damon to Esther Damon in Reading, Massachusetts, in 1805 and his second unlawful marriage as Daniel Flint to Lydia Anne Williams in Farmington, Maine, in 1812. He appealed the conviction on the grounds that the first marriage took place in Massachusetts and Maine didn't have jurisdiction. He was granted a new trial, but the attorney general didn't pursue the matter, and Daniel Flint went home to Abbot, Maine, to raise his second family, from which my husband was descended. With this information, I was able to find his ancestors through his mother back to Thomas Flint, one of the early settlers of Reading, Massachusetts, and his first wife's family, as well as their three children. This has all been from secondary sources and not yet proved, but at least now I know where to look for proof.

—Alta Flynt

about your ancient ancestry. Your DNA could also connect you with genetic cousins you never knew you had. Using this service, you can trace mothers with mDNA and your father's with YDNA. The maternal line of DNA can go back 50,000 years, but these results are not as useful for beginners. The paternal report can trace 33 markers on the DNA or 45 markers. How many times the markers repeat will tell you who has the same number of repetitive sequences at the same location, meaning those who are more closely related to you.

RootsWeb

How would you like a place where you can search dozens of databases of genealogical materials, look through hundreds of genealogical webpages, and subscribe to thousands of mailing lists? How about a place where you can publish your own page, upload your own data, and create your own mailing list? And all for free!

Note
www.rootsweb.com and www.rootsweb.org take you to the same site: www.rootsweb.ancestry.com.

Welcome to RootsWeb (www.rootsweb.org). Once upon a time, RootsWeb was a site for a group of people working at the research center RAND who dabbled in genealogy on the side and had a club for family history. They had a little mailing list, hosted by the University of Minnesota, and a little database on the RAND server for their club. That was 20 years ago. Today, RootsWeb is the largest all-volunteer genealogy site on the Web.

RootsWeb started and continues as a volunteer effort. But the costs of servers, disk space, and connections got so high that what was once a little club of genealogy enthusiasts that worked together merged with Ancestry.com. It's not a completely black-and-white situation; there are still plenty of transcribing projects that are free to access, such as ship's passenger lists, census transcriptions, and so on. And Ancestry.com hosts some of the free stuff—for example, all the message boards. For the RootsWeb user, little has really changed except the format.

Note

Remember, any time you post genealogical data anywhere, you still need to be sure that data on living people isn't included in your submissions because anyone can copy publicly posted data.

The mission of RootsWeb is summed up in the following statement, published on its home page: "The RootsWeb project has two missions: To make large volumes of data available to the online genealogical community at minimal cost. To provide support services to online genealogical activities, such as Usenet newsgroup moderation, mailing list maintenance, surname list generation, and so forth."

A quick guided tour of RootsWeb only scratches the surface of all the helpful and informative services available on this site. The following story gives you an idea of the unique possibilities RootsWeb offers.

Success Story: RootsWeb Leads to a Reunion

About three years ago, I started searching for my Powell ancestors on my father's side, but about the only thing I knew how to do was search the surname and message boards. One night, after having done nothing in about two months, I decided to get online and read the [RootsWeb] surname message boards. On a whim, I went into the Hubbard message boards on my mother's side.

The first message I read was about someone searching for descendants of my grandmother's parents. When my grandmother was about three or four, her mother passed away and she went to live with an aunt and uncle. Eventually, my grandmother lost contact with her brothers. She did see her oldest brother once when she was about 15, but after that she never saw or heard from him again. That night, I found him—a person my grandmother had not seen in over 70 years. We flew to Washington state and met all kinds of new cousins, aunts, and uncles. Over the next two years, my grandmother spoke with her brother many times. Unfortunately, he passed away soon after, but she did see him twice and was able to speak with him on numerous occasions.

We figured out that the message I responded to had been posted for about a minute before I discovered it. The surname message boards are a wonderful tool in searching for the ancestors and relatives you never knew you had, or those you had but didn't know who they were.

—Jennifer Powell Lyons

Digging in RootsWeb

RootsWeb has more genealogical information than you can shake a stick at. Some of this is secondary source information, such as the genealogy databases (GEDCOMs) members have submitted. Some of this information is close to primary source information, though still derivative—for example, transcripts of wills, deeds, census forms, and vital records, some with citations of where exactly the physical record can be found. Some of it is primary information (for example, Ancestry.com's census images) and you have to pay a subscription fee to Ancestry.com to access it.

At the top of all RootsWeb pages, you'll see a navigation bar with these categories: Home, Searches, Family Trees, Mailing Lists, Message Boards, Web Sites, Passwords, and Help (see Figure 18-4). Home, Passwords, and Help are self-explanatory.

When you look at the RootsWeb home page in your browser, you'll find two search templates to input a surname, first name, or any keywords. The search will look in all the RootsWeb pages or Ancestry .com databases and show you the results. It's a great way to get started on your genealogy!

Finding information on RootsWeb can be that simple. However, you can use many different tools on the site to get more targeted results.

Getting Started at RootsWeb

On the Home page index is a section called "Getting Started." The sections there—Getting Started at RootsWeb, Ancestry Tour, RootsWeb's Guide To Tracing Family Trees, RootsWeb Review Archives, Subscribe, and What's New—will give the beginner a good grounding in RootsWeb. Getting Started At RootsWeb is a short page on how to share, communicate, research, and volunteer with the site. Ancestry Tour is a multimedia overview of what the commercial side offers. RootsWeb's Guide To Tracing Family Trees is really a collection of

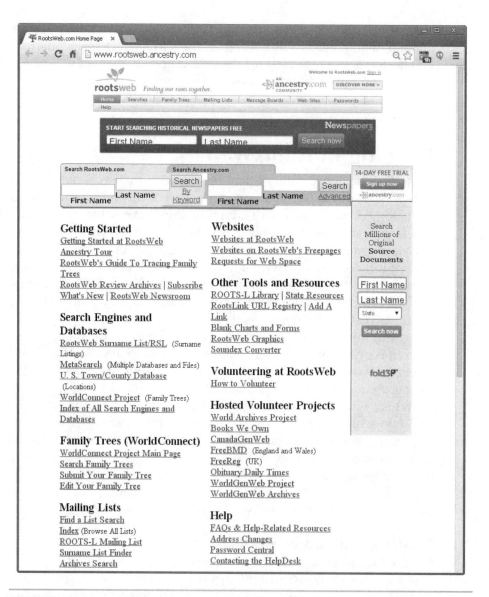

FIGURE 18-4. *All RootsWeb pages have a navigation bar at the top.*

guides sorted by general genealogy, sources, and countries. What's New lists the newest additions to the pages and databases on the volunteer side, and subscribing to RootsWeb Review will bring the same information to your e-mail inbox.

Available Files and Databases

ROOTS-L has tons of files and databases, which you can get access to by e-mailing the appropriate commands to the list server that runs ROOTS-L. You can search the ROOTS-L library for everything from a fabulous collection devoted to obtaining vital records, to useful tips for beginners, to book lists from the Library of Congress, and more. Some of the available files include:

- **Surname Helper** (http://surhelp.rootsweb.com)   Looks at the RootsWeb message boards and personal websites.

- **U.S. Town/County Database** (http://resources.rootsweb.com/ cgi-bin/townco.cgi)   Looks for locations. It's a sort of online gazetteer.

- **The WorldConnect Project** (http://worldconnect.rootsweb .com)   Searches GEDCOMs of family trees submitted by RootsWeb members.

- **The USGenWeb Archives Search** (http://usgenweb .org)   Looks for pages posted across the United States in the GenWeb Project.

- **WorldGenWeb** (http://worldgenweb.org)   Searches for genealogy resources in nations outside the United States.

- **RootsWeb Surname List**   The RootsWeb Surname List (RSL), located at http://rsl.rootsweb.com, is a registry of who is searching for whom and in what times and places. The listings include contact information for each entry. When you find someone looking for the same name, in the same area, and in about the same time period, you might be able to help each other. That's the intent of the list. You don't have to pay to submit your own data or to search for data. To search the list, you can use the form on the search page or go to the page directly. On the RSL page, type the surname you want to search for. You can narrow your search by including a location where you think the person you are looking for lives or lived, using the abbreviations you'll find in the link below the location box. Use the options to choose whether you want to search by surname (names spelled exactly as you've typed them) or by Soundex or Metaphone (names that sound like the one you've typed but spelled differently). In future attempts, you can limit the search to new submissions within the last week, month, or two months. The list is updated once a month. The Migration field shows you the path the family took. SC > GA, for example, shows migration from South Carolina to Georgia.

- **WorldConnect Project**   The WorldConnect Project is one of several GEDCOMs discussed in Chapter 11. When searching it from the RootsWeb home page, you can only input first and last names. The results page has another input form at the bottom, enabling you to fine-tune the search by adding places and dates. If you go to the WorldConnect page at http:// worldconnect.rootsweb.com, you can find links to tips and hints for using the site. Remember, all the data here is uploaded by volunteers, so errors might exist!

- **Social Security Death Index**   The Social Security Death Index (SSDI), located at http://ssdi.rootsweb.com, searches the federal records of deaths. Anyone who died before Social Security began in the 1930s won't be in this database. When searching from the RootsWeb home page, all you can input is the first and last name, but the results page will let you link to the Advanced Search page, where you can narrow the search by location and date. This is an excellent tool for researching twentieth-century ancestors.

- **GenSeeker**   GenSeeker looks for your search terms on the thousands of personal genealogy webpages at RootsWeb, plus any other registered documents, such as records transcriptions. You can also perform Boolean searches.

Other Search Engines

RootsWeb has several other ways for you to search both the site and the Web at large. Search Thingy looks at all the databases and text files, and MetaSearch looks for names across RootsWeb. The Surnames search index, United States Counties/States index, and the Countries index all search different subsets of RootsWeb information. These searches can be helpful in your research, but they assume you're a rank beginner with no more than a name or a place to launch your inquiries. Perhaps you know for sure that you're looking for a land record in Alabama or a cemetery in Iowa. RootsWeb has several searchable resources for items such as these. All these are worth looking at, and all can be accessed from http://searches .rootsweb.ancestry.com/.

Message Boards and Mailing Lists

Among the best resources on RootsWeb are the mailing lists and message boards, now hosted on Ancestry.com. A message board is a place where messages are read, sent, and answered on the Web, using a browser. A mailing list is where messages are e-mailed to and from the members. A mail client is used to read them.

Click the bottom of any message board's page to read the frequently asked questions (FAQs), request a new board, read the rules, or get help. The mailing lists, located at http://lists.rootsweb .com, cover many topics, such as the RootsWeb newsletters, described later in this chapter. Lists exist for specific surnames; every state in the United States; other countries (from Aruba to Zimbabwe); and topics such as adoption, medical genealogy, prisons, and heraldry. From the Mailing Lists page, you can click a link to each one, and you'll get instructions on how to use the list, including subscribing, unsubscribing, sticking to the topic, and so on.

Besides ROOTS-L, which is the grandparent of genealogy mailing lists on the Internet, RootsWeb hosts literally thousands of mailing lists. The index, located at www.rootsweb.com/~maillist, has thousands of lists you can join, along with instructions explaining how to subscribe.

A good rule of thumb: Be choosy in joining lists! Take on only a few at a time. Read the lists for a while, sign off if they don't prove useful, and then try some others. Some lists are extremely active—sometimes overwhelmingly so. One RootsWeb user who signed up for every possible mailing list for the United Kingdom had 9,000 e-mails in his inbox within 24 hours! Be careful what you wish for...

And remember, some lists are archived, so you needn't subscribe to see if that list is talking about subjects of interest to you. Just search the archive for your keywords, and save the important messages. You might even want to start a mailing list of your own someday, which contributors can do. You can learn more about what's required of a list owner by going to the Help page and clicking the Request A Mailing List link or by going to http://resources.rootsweb.com/adopt.

Newsletters

A newsletter, like a mailing list, comes straight to your e-mail inbox. Unlike the lists discussed previously, however, they are not for discussion; the communication is one-to-many. Like a print magazine, a newsletter will have news, notes, stories, and the occasional (text) advertisement. RootsWeb has several e-mail newsletters, all of which are worth reading. Here are some descriptions of them.

RootsWeb-Sponsored Pages

Books We Own (http://rootsweb.ancestry.com/~bwo) is a list of resources owned and accessed by volunteers who are willing to look up genealogical information and then e-mail or snail mail it to others who request it. It works like a worldwide research library, where your shelf of genealogy books is one branch and you're one librarian of thousands. This is a volunteer service, and participants might ask for reimbursement of copies and postage if information is provided via snail mail. The project began in 1996 as a way for members of the ROOTS-L mailing list to share their resources with one another, and now some 1,500 people are involved.

FreeBMD (http://freebmd.org.uk) stands for Free Births, Marriages, and Deaths. The FreeBMD Project's objective is to provide free Internet access to the Civil Registration index information for England and Wales. The Civil Registration system for recording births, marriages, and deaths in England and Wales has been in place since 1837. This is one of the most significant single resources for genealogical research back to Victorian times.

Immigrant Ships Transcribers Guild (http://immigrantships .net) is a group of volunteers dedicated to making the search for our ancestors' immigration easier. The aim is to make as many ships' passenger lists as possible available online—and not just for U.S. ports. There are databases for Australia, Canada, Irish passengers to Argentina, and more. This group would also be happy to have your help!

State Resource Pages (http://rootsweb.ancestry.com/roots-l/ usa.html) is one of the main areas of RootsWeb. It offers a wealth of information to those researching in the United States.

Freepages are genealogy pages by volunteers. These pages must fit the RootsWeb mission; cannot contain copyrighted, commercial, or multimedia material; and cannot redirect to another site. If you

meet these and all the other rules stated on http://accounts
.rootsweb.ancestry.com, you can have free web space at RootsWeb.
The freepages include sites of major RootsWeb projects, such as
USGenWeb and WorldGenWeb, as well as genealogical or historical
organizations.

You can find kids' pages, lessons and help pages, memorials, and
timelines among these pages. If you already have a genealogy-related
website and want it linked from RootsWeb, you can register it as well.

The Help Desk

The Help Desk (http://helpdesk.rootsweb.com/) maintains a page to
help you find a FAQ file about RootsWeb and its services. If you have
a question or problem, check here first. If you can't find an answer
here, you can follow the links from this site to the message board,
where you can post a question for the Help Desk team to answer.

This quick tour is just enough to whet your appetite, but isn't even
half of what's there. Spend some time getting to know RootsWeb.

Wrapping Up

- Ancestry.com and RootsWeb have digitized, transcribed, and
  abstracted records for you to search, as well as message boards
  and other interactive services.

- Many Ancestry.com articles and helpful files are free, but the
  bulk of the data is only available to paying members.

- RootsWeb is the oldest gathering of volunteer pages, data, and
  programs in the world of online genealogy.

Chapter 19

Genealogical Publishing Houses and Their Sites

You will definitely want to read some books on genealogy as you pursue your family history (like this one!). And someday, you may even want to publish your own book on your family history or on the expertise you have gained in the process.

Publishing a Genealogy Book

There are several ways to go about publishing a book. For a long time, your usual route to publishing a genealogy was to pay a book publisher anywhere from $5,000 to $10,000 to typeset, print, and bind your books. Sometimes, you could find a short-run publisher, that is, a publisher who specialized in printing 1,000 or fewer copies of an old, out-of-print, and out-of-copyright book that someone wanted revived for libraries and archives. Again, this involved paying thousands of dollars up front.

Note

If you only want enough copies of your genealogy for your immediate family, consider using a genealogy program—for example, RootsMagic, The Master Genealogist, Heredis, and so on—that can output your data as a narrative. It will not be very professional in appearance, but it will certainly be cheaper. This will entail much more effort on your part to create a nice "master copy" (indeed, physically cutting and pasting may not be out of the question), but the result can be run off at your local office supply store. Binding can be as simple as having the store drill holes and then buying enough three-ring binders to hold your copies.

If your topic is more about how to do genealogy than the family history of one surname, sometimes, a book publishing house will accept a genealogy methods book, pay an advance, foot the cost of the production, and pay royalties on the proceeds to an author just as is the practice for novels and textbooks.

Even more rarely, an interesting family history book will be printed commercially, as in *The Spencers: A Personal History of an English Family* (St. Martin's Press, 2000) by Lady Diana's brother Charles Spencer. (Note: Do not bet the farm on this happening to you, unless you can prove a connection to a royal family!)

All these publishing options are still available and thriving.

The drawback about the traditional self-publishing route, besides the obvious costs, is that you wind up with a basement full of books to sell (including collecting taxes, managing credit card sales, and so on), market, ship, and store. Lucky for us, in the twenty-first century, we also have print-on-demand (POD) publishers. These hold an electronic version of your book, usually in PDF format, on their servers and handle the sales, printing, and marketing for you, paying royalties, but, as the name implies, usually print out copies only when someone has actually plunked down some money for them. If 100 copies are sold this week, then 100 copies will be printed. If none sell, none are printed. Sometimes, the POD publisher can also sell and ship to traditional bookstores, as well as to individual buyers. Obviously, this makes the price for each book higher, but on the other hand, it makes life simpler.

POD publishers also handle things like payment by credit card or PayPal, taxes, and so forth. Furthermore, updates can be handled much more quickly should more information on your ancestors be found after you complete your manuscript.

"Print-on-demand looks like a great service for genealogists," says Eastman's Online Genealogy Newsletter (EOGN) editor Dick Eastman. "The old-fashioned, short-run printing services normally charge $5,000 or more (sometimes much more) to print the first run of a few hundred books. The author is saddled with the task of selling these books in order to recover expenses. A 'print-on-demand' publisher can be a much more cost-effective alternative."

Most of the time, a fee of some sort is involved for the author, from $100 to more than $300, for publication design, cover art, binding, and the like. As you would imagine, the more of this you do yourself in the way of layout, creating a master copy, an index, and so on, the less the POD publisher will charge.

And then there are e-books, which involve no materials at all except electrons and the machinery to zip them around between seller and buyer. When a book is published electronically, it can be for a specialized reader such as the Kindle or just as a large PDF file the buyer can read on the computer or print out as he chooses. Usually, e-books are much lower in cover price than a physical book, as no paper, shipping, or binding is involved for the producers of the book, only for the buyer. Therefore, often, the author gets a larger percentage of the cover price for each sale.

E-books are not as durable as physical books, which is something to consider if your genealogy work is meant for the ages. A computer crash or a Kindle in the pool, and the purchaser of your genealogy book could be out of luck. Also, the buyer must have an e-book reader or a computer to access his purchase. However, searching an e-book for surnames is incredibly fast and easy, and your references can link to websites as well as cite paper sources, which is a great convenience for the reader.

Success Story: A Gift of Biography

Jane Fraser of Pueblo, Colorado, has experience in publishing online for genealogy purposes, and loved the experience, she said.

"My father, John M. Fraser, was born in Scotland; grew up in Brooklyn; and worked as an engineer on fascinating projects in the telephone industry, at Bell Labs, Hughes Communication Satellites, and as a consultant," Jane said. "From his influence, I, too, am an engineer. After my sister died in 2004 (she was only 57), he was, of course, devastated, and I suggested he write his autobiography as a way to get his mind off her death. He agreed that 'it would keep him out of trouble.'

"The goal was to tell his life story. We knew from the start that mainly relatives would be interested, but he has been involved in some big projects (the first transatlantic telephone cable in the 1950s), so he was also writing for people who would care about the engineering history."

Choosing an online publisher seemed to Jane to be the way to go. It was simple, fast, and within her budget, she decided.

"I looked at a number of online publishers (Lulu, CreateSpace, and others). I thought the prices and services were best with CreateSpace, [see Figure 19-1] although many of them looked good. I liked the facts that CreateSpace took care of getting an ISBN and that CreateSpace would put the book on Amazon (CreateSpace is owned by Amazon); neither of those options cost extra." Jane said.

So the process began.

"Dad was very computer literate and had his own computer. Because his eyesight was starting to fail, he bought Dragon NaturallySpeaking Speech Recognition software and a microphone headset so he could dictate rather than type. I think that approach was really good, because the book reads as he spoke. We talked often on the phone while he was writing,

FIGURE 19-1. *CreateSpace is an online publisher owned by Amazon.com.*

and I reminded him of events to include. My stepmother did a lot of editing for him. As he was writing, I was also working on photos. We have always taken many family photos; sometimes, I had to hunt through boxes of photos and slides to find exactly the one he was thinking of. I scanned the photos that he wanted to use in the book. I tried scanning slides, but found that very hard to do, so I projected each slide and took a photo of it with my digital camera.

"Dad e-mailed me the completed manuscript, *Muddling Through* (95,000 words), in September 2008," Jane said. "I was thrilled with it; I thought I knew all his stories, but there was so much new in the book.

I really wanted to do a good job in publishing it. It took me a little over four months from when I received the manuscript to publication. I work full-time, so I worked on the book after work and on weekends."

This is an important point for the self-publishing genealogist: You are your own staff on this project. Editing, layout, and error control are all your responsibility and in your power!

"Proofreading, proofreading, and proofreading," Jane said. "I read the book extremely carefully three times, word by word, and I still found a few errors in the published version. I started to do some fact checking, but then decided not to. My father's memory was astounding. When he said that Miss Asti (one of his schoolteachers) had lived next door to his future brother-in-law (my father and this friend married sisters), the 1930 census confirmed that he was correct. I would have written some sentences differently, but I decided the book was my father's and it was his voice that should be heard. I did fix spelling and grammar. I picked a style (font for text, headings, and subheadings; layout of the first page of each chapter; etc.) and put the entire book in that format. I followed CreateSpace's advice and advice from CreateSpace user discussion boards for what to put on the copyright page."

You will learn quickly, as Jane did, that book design has certain parameters. The size of the book in finished form affects the choices you make in typesetting and layout.

"CreateSpace limited the number of pages in an 8 by 10 color book to 178, so that requirement pretty much dictated the choice of font size and line spacing," Jane said. "I would have used a larger font and bigger line spacing otherwise since I recognized that many of the readers of the book may have failing eyesight, but more pages would have increased the cost of the book. I think the font size and spacing I chose still make it readable.

"Laying out the photos was tricky. I had to learn how to insert and format photos in Microsoft Word. I put some of the photos on pages with text, but also made several other pages just containing photos. For a while, we contemplated publishing and assembling the book ourselves (through a copy chain such as Kinko's); thus, we were thinking about having some pages in black and white only and some pages in color only to reduce copying costs. With CreateSpace, the entire book is classified as either black and white or color, so keeping the photos separate didn't matter, but we liked the separate pages of photos so kept some of them."

Another technical consideration is that sometimes your equipment and software may not be entirely compatible with the online publisher's. There are always workarounds, but be prepared for some trial and error.

"I had trouble downloading a cover template from CreateSpace and using it in Photoshop," Jane said, "so I created my own cover in Photoshop. Dad wanted to keep the front cover simple, with title, his name, and subtitle; he selected the font for the title. I put a photo of my father on the back cover, with a brief description of the book. I had to figure out the dimensions to make sure the material on the back and front covers would be centered. CreateSpace tells you how to figure out the spine width and other dimensions, so the cover came out fine.

"[Using] Photoshop and Word, I created PDF files for the cover and the interior and uploaded them to CreateSpace; those steps were easy. CreateSpace automatically reviewed both files for technical problems. For example, it told me a few photos were not of high enough resolution to print well, so I made them a little smaller. I got stuck for a while in converting the Word file to a PDF in the correct format. Page 1 should be on the right, but it kept coming out on the left. The margins are different on left and right pages (to allow for binding), so this point was very important. This was my moment (actually a month) of greatest frustration. I kept inserting a blank page, resubmitting the PDF file, and getting the same error. I finally figured it out after finding detailed instructions on a CreateSpace discussion board (you have to tell Word in some obscure place that it should put the first page on the right). The users of CreateSpace are very helpful. I had to learn a lot of printing terms (for example, "full bleed"), but again, the CreateSpace website and discussion boards helped. I had to read and reread some instructions several times," Jane said.

"Another difficulty arose because I wanted to include a short article from the *New York Times.* My father had been mayor of our town in New Jersey and an amusing dispute (over licensing cats) actually got quite a bit of coverage in major papers. I requested permission from the *New York Times* to use it (the NYT website has an online form to do so), but their charge (over $300) was, we thought, crazy, so I took it out. I think they saw that the book would be on Amazon and thought there would be some money to be made."

But note that Jane was careful to follow that step of finding the copyright holder and asking for permission. This is very important if you are including photos, text, or other material in your publication.

CreateSpace required that Jane order (and pay for at a reduced price) a proof copy, approve the proof, and then publish. The total was about $20 for this.

"I ended up having to do three proof copies due to my errors (and due to having to remove the *New York Times* piece), and I got a little frustrated then," Jane said. "When I finally figured out the right/left page stuff, I felt I could finish the book—but I did have doubts for a while. And Dad was getting very eager to have the book. I signed up for the ProPlan for free during a promotion on CreateSpace (they had waived the $39 fee). That plan increases the royalties I get."

Jane ordered 12 copies for her father at $13.17 each, plus $8.20 in shipping and $12.25 in tax, for a total of $178.49. Tax was charged because these copies were sent to her father in California, where Google is headquartered. Jane ordered another 30 copies for herself at $13.17 each, plus $15.43 in shipping and $0 tax for a total of $410.53. Google charged no tax on this order because these copies were shipped to Jane in Colorado, so it was an interstate sale.

Note

Congress is considering whether to pass a bill in the future to charge sales tax on interstate sales.

"I was very pleased with the quality of the product from CreateSpace. The interior paper is good quality, the soft cover is also good, the printing is clear, and the binding is sturdy. The book looks good and it feels nice to hold," Jane said.

Setting the price of the book at $30 gave Jane a return of $4.83 for each copy sold on Amazon and $10.83 for each copy sold through the CreateSpace storefront she set up.

"Two copies have been sold through the e-store and four on Amazon, so this has not been a money maker, but I didn't do it for that purpose," Jane said. "On sales through the e-store, the sales report tells me who bought it, but I don't get that information for Amazon sales. The book is currently #3,395,134 in Books on Amazon, which I find very amusing."

When the book first came out, Amazon listed it at a discounted price for promotion purposes ($24) but didn't cut the amount of the royalty. Now it is listed at the $30 price and can be found at www.amazon.com/Muddling-Through-Autobiography-John-Fraser/dp/1438258496/ref=sr_1_1?ie=UTF8&s=books&qid=1264888477&sr=8-1.

Amazon.com does some promotion on its sites, and Jane did a little publicizing of her own as well. "I sent copies to relatives and to friends of my father, in this country and in Scotland," Jane said. "I also sent five copies to museums and company archives related to my father's work. I got back nice thank-you notes from everyone. I posted the URL in a few online newsgroups about the telephone industry and history."

Overall, Jane said, the process was not hard, but neither was it exactly easy. Learning to make Word and Photoshop do what she wanted took time and research, almost more than the book itself. Getting it to look right required a lot of attention to detail, but she wanted to do that for her father because this was a project of love.

"The best part was working with my father on the book. He had some health problems in the last year of his life, and I was traveling to his place often to visit and to help. Working on the book together was great. It was finally published in January 2009. Dad got to see a copy before he died early in March, at age 92. He was thrilled with it. I am so happy to have it as a legacy from him. The book has been a great comfort for me. I reread it often," Jane said.

Would she do it again?

"In a heartbeat," Jane said. "It was a remarkable gift that my father and I gave each other."

Buying Genealogy Books

Here is a list of some notable publishers of genealogy titles. These are not the whole of the universe of publishers who have books on family history, but a representative sample. These publishers specialize in genealogy topics; other publishers like McGraw-Hill Education and BookLocker have a broader scope, but will publish a genealogy book if it fits their market.

Avotaynu

Avotaynu
155 N. Washington Ave.
Bergenfield, NJ 07621
Phone: 201-387-7200

Avotaynu, Inc. (www.avotaynu.com) is the leading publisher of products of interest to persons who are researching Jewish genealogy, Jewish family trees, or Jewish roots. The books include beginner guides and books about Jewish surnames. Avotaynu has an Internet newsletter for Jewish genealogy entitled "Nu? What's New?"

Genealogical Publishing Company

Genealogical Publishing Company
3600 Clipper Mill Road, Suite 260
Baltimore, MD 21211
Phone: 410-837-8271

Genealogical Publishing Company (GPC) and Clearfield Company (see Figure 19-2) publish genealogy books and CDs—in fact, more than

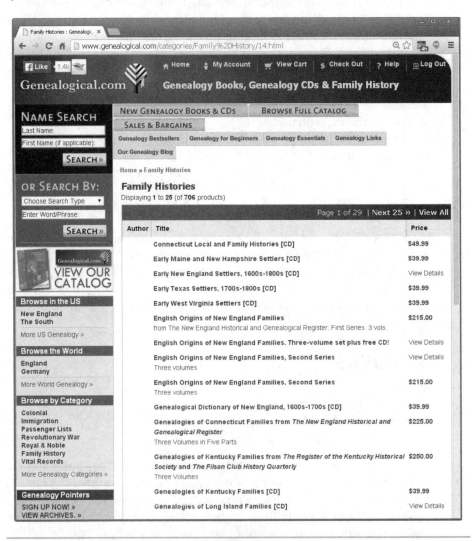

FIGURE 19-2. *Genealogical Publishing Company publishes titles written by amateurs and professionals in genealogy.*

2,000 different genealogy books and CDs featuring colonial genealogy, Irish genealogy, immigration, royal ancestry, family history, and genealogy methods and sources. Their books are found in every library in the country with a genealogy and family history collection, and are written by both amateur and professional genealogy authors. You can contact them at info@genealogical.com.

The books and CDs cover the entire range of American genealogy, but one of the principal areas of strength is found in their collections of individual family histories. Typical of such collections, and among the best known in American genealogy, is Donald Lines Jacobus' *Families of Ancient New Haven*, a three-volume work that covers every family in pre-Revolutionary New Haven, Connecticut. Similarly, Robert Barnes's *British Roots of Maryland Families* establishes the origins of hundreds of pre-eighteenth-century Maryland families, much like the comprehensive collection of magazine articles printed in the three volumes of *Genealogies of Pennsylvania Families*.

GPC's 1973 publication of Val Greenwood's *Researcher's Guide to American Genealogy* set the standard for commercial book publishing in genealogy. I still have my mother's well-marked edition. Each year, GPC publishes as many as 40 new original works in genealogy written or compiled by experts in the field; it also reprints dozens of genealogical classics. Typically, GPC's emphasis is on early American genealogy, especially the colonial and federal periods.

You can also find here Frederick Dorman's acclaimed *Adventurers of Purse and Person, Virginia, 1607-1624/5* (3 vols.). The Dorman work documents six generations of the founding families of Virginia and is considered the most important work ever to appear on Virginia genealogy.

For titles on the techniques of genealogy, check out the Genealogy Essentials page and the Genealogy for Beginners page, notably their guidebooks on German, English, Irish, Scottish, Italian, Polish, and Hispanic genealogy, as well as manuals and textbooks featuring both traditional instruction in genealogy methodology and contemporary instruction in the use of the Internet for genealogical research.

Print on Demand Comes to Genealogical.com

Genealogical Publishing Company and its affiliate, Clearfield Company, started offering print on demand in 2008. They use print on demand to publish reprints of many old favorites for which there is a clear and evident demand, as well as personal genealogies. Sample titles in this category include:

- *In Search of Your Canadian Roots, Third Edition*

- *German-American Names, Third Edition*

- *Black Genesis: A Resource Book for African-American Genealogy, 2nd Edition*

- *The Hidden Half of the Family: A Sourcebook for Women's Genealogy*

- *The Complete Beginner's Guide to Genealogy, the Internet, and Your Genealogy Computer Program*

- *My Ancestors Came with the Conqueror: Those Who Did, and Some of Those Who Probably Did Not*

Family Roots Publishing

Family Roots Publishing
P.O. Box 830
Bountiful, UT 84011
Phone: 801-992-3705

Both an online bookstore and a publishing house, the Family Roots Publishing Company (www.familyrootspublishing.com) provides a select catalog of genealogy research books and supplies at prices below retail. With new products nearly every day and a "daily special" on the home page, this site is worth a bookmark. They do not do print on demand at this time, and they specialize in how-to books, the owner, Leland Meitzler, told me.

"We publish genealogy guidebooks (how-to) only," he said. "Anyone interested in submitting a manuscript should contact me at Lmeitzler @gmail.com with an overview of the proposed book. If I like what I see and wish to publish the book, I'll most likely request a sample chapter prior to a contract being signed. We are presently seeking good manuscripts with wide appeal within the family history community."

Among the outstanding publications from Family Roots Publishing is Bill Dollarhide's latest book, *Genealogical Resources of the Civil War Era*. They also published Bill Dollarhide's two-volume *Census Substitutes and State Census Records* books in 2008.

This publisher is also well known for its *Map Guide to German Parish Registers*. In addition to the Map Guides, they sell many genealogy-related guides printed by other publishers.

Family Roots Publishing is also the exclusive distributor of limited numbers of new copies of back issues of *Heritage Quest Magazine,* as well as the *Genealogy Bulletin*. Thirty-three back issues of the "Bulletin" are now found on this website, while *Heritage Quest Magazine* back issues are now beginning to be posted. The co-owner of Family Roots Publishing is Patty S. Meitzler, former editor of *Heritage Quest Magazine* and wife of Leland K. Meitzler, former managing editor of *Heritage Quest Magazine* and the *Genealogical Helper Magazine.*

Martin Genealogy Publishing

Martin Genealogy Publishing
4501 SW 62 Court
Miami, FL 33155-5936
Phone: 305-662-6115

William and Patricia Martin specialize in Alabama and Florida resources for genealogical and historical research. They also sell used books relating to genealogy. Patricia's families are from Alabama, while William's are from Florida. Both family lines extend back through Georgia, the Carolinas, and up the eastern coast of the United States.

MGP (www.wtmartin.com/home/martin-genealogy-publishing) started publishing works for genealogical and historical research in 1990. The website now lists a collection of old books and will be adding collectibles as they become available. Products include:

- 1885 Florida State Census Index in one volume for the entire state or as individual counties.

- The Gadsden Times (Etowah County, Alabama) Abstracts. Currently, four volumes are available: Vol. I 1867–1871, Vol. II 1872–1875, Vol. III 1876–1880, and Vol. IV 1881–1885.

- The Cubahatchee Baptist Church Book 1838–1850 (church minutes book) of Macon County, Alabama.

- The Ebenezer Church (of Talladega/Clay County, Alabama) 8 Aug 1878–13 Aug 1899.

The company's first publications were simple indexes created as research tools. The 1885 Florida State Census Index was the first major publication. Other federal census indexes followed for a number of Florida counties in 1910. Then opportunities arose to expand into Alabama resources, and that has been the focus for several years. The Gadsden Times Abstracts is now available in four volumes, starting in 1867. The fifth volume, starting in 1886, is in production, the site says. Many libraries around the country have copies of the 1885 complete volumes, and several individuals have bought single-county volumes as needed.

Heritage Books

Heritage Books, Inc.
100 Railroad Avenue, Suite 104
Westminster, MD 21157-4826
Phone: 800-876-6103

For nearly 40 years, Heritage Books, Inc. (www.heritagebooks .com) has been a major publisher of titles in genealogy, history, military history, historical fiction, and memoirs. The company will publish 40 to 50 titles a month; some are completely new compilations, and others are historical reprints, though often with added name indexes or other improvements. Heritage Books now has over 3,900 titles under four publishing imprints. These cover historical accounts, vital statistics of immigrants, and even fact-rich historical novels. The imprints are:

- **Heritage Books**   Historical works and genealogical titles

- **Willow Bend Books**   Historical and genealogical titles now being imprinted under Heritage Books

- **Eagle Editions**   Memoirs

- **Fireside Fiction**   Historical fiction

To submit your book, read the submissions requirements at www .heritagebooks.com/publishing.html.

BookLocker

BookLocker.com (www.booklocker.com) is a general publisher, but they have accepted genealogy titles. They specialize in print-on-demand and e-books. Costs run from about $300 for doing everything yourself to about $500 for using their cover design service for a black and white book.

Genealogy titles you can buy from them include:

- *The Genealogist's Guide to Digital Photography*

- *Find Your Roots Now!*

- *Roots Recovered! The How To Guide for Tracing African-American and West Indian Roots Back to Africa and Going There*

- *Cleburne Memorial Cemetery of Johnson County, Texas*

The print books are listed on Amazon, Barnes and Noble, and other major online bookstores. Buyers can also special order books from the local bookstores. BookLocker can provide an ISBN at no additional charge.

Lulu.com

One of the largest self-publish, print-on-demand, and e-book houses, Lulu.com (www.lulu.com) has become very popular with aspiring authors. They use a completely automated online system. As a high-tech version of the traditional vanity press, Lulu.com offers printing services and on-demand CDs, DVDs, e-publications, and more. Lulu .com's prices are low, but you can expect to do all the work, such as designing book covers, creating page layouts, and marketing. Lulu .com does some marketing work, but does not publish catalogs or online websites for genealogists. Like BookLocker, it does offer its books through many bookstores, online booksellers, and so forth. Among the authors using Lulu.com is Dick Eastman of Eastman's Online Genealogy Newsletter.

Some recent titles in genealogy include:

- *The Church of Ireland in Co Limerick Edited Research Correspondence January 2012 to December 2013* by J. A. Murphy

- *My Father's Branch: The Lineage, Lore, and Life of Larkin Eugene Williams* by Doyle W. Williams

- *A Fox Family History* by Kevin A. Fox

- *A Gift to My Descendants* by Barbara Samper

- *My Mother's Swedish Family* by James D. Hedberg

- *Carleton Gonya Cramer: An Uncommon Common Man* by Donald M. Cramer

iUniverse.com

iUniverse (www.iuniverse.com) bills itself as "supported self-publishing." About 231 titles in their catalog match the keyword "genealogy."

The iUniverse.com service includes a custom cover and book design; an ISBN number; registration in the Ingram Books and Bowker's Books in Print databases; and listings on Amazon.com, Borders.com, and BN.com (Barnes and Noble's online site). The site says that the books are "available" through 5,000 bookstores (that is, available through special order to bookstores). iUniverse.com can be more expensive than other print-on-demand services, with prices starting at $599 in advance and going up to $2,099 in advance. More pricing information is available at www.iuniverse.com/Packages/PackageCompare.aspx.

Smaller Publishers

Creative Continuum, Inc.
2910 E. La Palma Ave. Suite C.
Anaheim, CA 92806
Phone: 866-799-2738

Creative Continuum (www.creativecontinuum.com) concentrates on family history books and other smaller publishing projects. A "vanity press" (the author pays the costs and uses the company's expertise and equipment), they provide a number of publishing services, including professional book design, layout and typesetting, and printing on archival paper. The company's website says they can assist an author with organizing a genealogy and family history, developing data into a publication-ready format, and publishing an heirloom book of genealogy and family history.

Family Heritage Publishers

Family Heritage Publishers
573 West 4800 South
Salt Lake City, UT 84123
Phone: 801-685-6151

A traditional vanity press, Family Heritage Publishers (www .familyheritagepublishers.com) is the binder for the Family History Library in Salt Lake City. They offer archival-quality printing for any size publishing job, from 1 copy to 1,000. This publisher will print and bind books of all kinds—including family histories, town histories, biographies, and family reunion booklets. They can also help you prepare your manuscript for publishing. They do only physical books, not e-books or POD.

Modern Memoirs, Inc.

Modern Memoirs, Inc.
34 Main Street #9
Amherst, MA 01002-2367
Phone: 413-253-2353

This is a vanity press with an emphasis on memoirs. Services include editing, printing, and binding. They specialize in memoirs and family histories and can handle offset printing and digital print on demand. You can contact them by e-mail at kitty @modernmemoirs.com.

Shortrunbooks.com

Shortrunbooks
215 E. 3rd Street
Des Moines, IA 50309
Phone: 800-247-5087

This division of Dilley Manufacturing Company (www.dilleymfg.com) provides binding-only services for your self-printed family history. Print at home or your local copy shop, and then send the manuscripts to them for hard-cover binding.

Finding More

To find more options for self-publishing your genealogy work, try:

- Cyndi's List page (www.cyndislist.com/books.htm#Publishers).

- Search Google, Bing, or Yahoo! for `"print on demand" +publisher`.

- Talk to your local university or college to see if they have a press that prints local history and similar topics.

To find more books about genealogy, use your favorite search engines for the surnames, places, and/or date you need.

Wrapping Up

- Several publishing companies specialize in genealogy.

- Publishing your family's genealogy will likely involve a vanity press (self-publishing) outfit.

- Print-on-demand and e-books are economical ways to go about it.

- If you want to share your genealogy expertise, you may find a traditional publisher. Or, you could still go the self-publishing route.

Chapter 20

A Potpourri
of Genealogy

As you've no doubt noticed while reading this book, genealogy websites come in all categories. You will find portals that aim to be your web home. You will find sites with images of original documents or transcribed records (perhaps both!), and sites with completed, annotated genealogies. You will find sites where folks have slapped up any data they found, regardless of accuracy or relevancy. You will find primary records, secondary records, family legends, and scams. It's truly an embarrassment of riches out there.

You must remember to judge each source you find critically and carefully. Compare it to what you have proven with your own research. Look for the original records cited in an online genealogy to see if they have been interpreted correctly (remember the lesson about census records!). Most of all, look for application to *your* genealogy. How helpful is it?

This list of websites reflects what I've found to be valuable. Some of these sites are portals and will link you to sites I haven't found or that didn't exist at press time. Other links may be "dead" (as they say in web parlance) by the time you read this. Don't be discouraged by this. That's part of the fun of online genealogy: There's always something new!

Note

Most online genealogists have at least these five links bookmarked:
Cyndi's List (http://www.cyndislist.com), DearMYRTLE (http://www.dearmyrtle.com), FamilySearch.com (http://www.familysearch.com), NARA (http://www.archives.gov), and RootsWeb (http://www.rootsweb.com).

Alexa.com Top 25 Genealogy Sites Early 2014

Alexa Internet, started April 1996, crawls the Web and reports the most popular of sites back to the database. The website not only has current trends in web surfing, but also historical measures of the popularity of sites in thousands of categories. If you are brand new to online genealogy, these are good places to start, which is why some of them got a dedicated chapter in this book. Among the top genealogy sites measured by Alexa for early 2014 are:

- **http://www.ancestry.com**   As covered in a previous chapter, this is the subscription-based resource of worldwide census, marriage, newspaper, and various other records. The site has some free searchable databases, columns and articles, GEDCOMs, and forums.

- **http://www.legacy.com**   Legacy.com collaborates with more than 800 newspapers in North America, Europe, and Australia to provide ways for readers to express condolences and share remembrances of loved ones.

- **http://www.familysearch.org**   The Church of Jesus Christ of Latter-day Saints provides an online search of the millions of names in its International Genealogical Index, and of genealogical websites. It also has information on its Family History Library and local branches.

- **http://www.rootsweb.ancestry.com**   Genealogical resource with searchable databases, family trees, mailing lists, and message boards.

- **http://www.archives.com**   This site is a resource guide, allowing the sharing of family photos and documents.

- **http://www.geneanet.org**   Features a network of online genealogy databases.

- **http://www.genealogy.com**   Offers FamilyTreeMaker software, subscription-based access to searchable databases, plus forums, news, and research tips.

- **http://www.wikitree.com**   A free, collaborative worldwide family tree project by a community of genealogists and their family members.

- **http://boards.ancestry.com**   Centralized collection of genealogical message boards hosted by Ancestry.com. Forums include specialized topics such as surnames, locales, and organizations. A versatile search engine allows for locating specific resources, including bible records, deeds, and marriage bonds, among others.

- **http://blog.eogn.com**   Newsletter with family history news, tips, and reviews from genealogist Dick Eastman.

- **http://www.ancientfaces.com**   Ancient Faces builds a visual representation of history through the collaboration of the online community. Share vintage photos to discover the faces and places related to your history at this website.

- **http://www.familytreedna.com**   DNA is the ultimate link in the family and social network. DNA can show relationships between individuals, whether close or distant. It also establishes fingerprints for the purpose of determining ancestral pedigrees. Any person can have a simple DNA test with a simple and painless cheek swab. The company has headquarters in Houston, Texas.

- **http://www.findmypast.co.uk**   Family history research online. Enables you to create a family tree using birth, marriage, and death indexes; census returns; and many more historical UK family history records.

- **http://www.genforum.genealogy.com**   Over 14,000 online forums devoted to genealogy, including surnames, U.S. states, countries, and general topics.

- **http://www.genealogyintime.com**   An online genealogy magazine with free search engines, articles, tools, and listings of the latest genealogy records on the Internet.

- **http://www.newspaperarchive.com**   Registered members may access a database of searchable and downloadable archived newspapers from the 1700s to today. Many libraries have access for patrons.

- **http://www.genealogy.about.com**   Written by famed genealogist Kimberly Powell, this blog and link site features links for researching family history, including genealogical societies, ethnic sites, and access to genealogical software.

- **http://www.kabalarians.com**   Approximately 300,000 names and what purports to be analysis of the names' meaning and significance. I don't know why this one is listed in the "genealogy" category, as it is about New Age philosophy as applied to names. It's a parlor game, not useful data to do family history.

- **http://www.cyndislist.com**   A large, categorized, and cross-referenced directory of sites useful for genealogical research, with hundreds of thousands of links.

- **http://www.jewishgen.org**   Provides a wide range of resources, including databases, Family Finder, articles, societies, projects, and discussion groups.

- **http://www.royal.gov.uk**   This official site covers the monarch's role and the history of the monarchy, gives biographies of the Royal Family, and tourist information for Royal Palaces and the Royal Collection.

- **http://www.worldvitalrecords.com**   This website offers users international record databases, references to top genealogical resources, a blog, podcasts, videocasts, webinars, expert advice, training, and user-generated content.

- **http://www.surnames.behindthename.com**   Searchable database featuring the etymology and history of last names.

- **http://www.ellisisland.org**   Runs the American Family Immigration History Center on Ellis Island, which offers access to the passenger records of the ships that landed some 22 million immigrants, crew members, and other passengers at the Port of New York and Ellis Island from 1892 to 1924.

- **http://www.progenealogists.com**   Official research firm for Ancestry.com. Professional genealogists specializing in family history research worldwide. Based in Salt Lake City, Utah, at the Family History Library. Genealogists for the NBC TV show *Who Do You Think You Are?*, the member genealogists have accumulated over 500 years' worth of research experience.

Golden Needles in the World Wide Haystack

In the manner of websites everywhere, these sites will all lead you to other sites, where (I hope) you'll find the information you need. Note that this isn't even close to an exhaustive list. For that, see Cyndi's List and Genealogy Resources on the Internet. I have sorted these sites by topic.

Adoption

The following are places that concentrate on reuniting birth families:

- **Adopting.org** This site includes a birth-family search guide.

- **Adoption.com** This site has a discussion board for adoptees, including birth mother searches.

- **American Adoption Congress** (http://www .americanadoptioncongress.org) The American Adoption Congress (AAC) is an advocacy group for adoption reform. AAC members support those whose lives are touched by adoption or other loss of family continuity. The organization promotes honesty, openness, and respect for family connections in adoption, foster care, and assisted reproduction. It educates members and professional communities about the lifelong process of adoption and advocates legislation that will grant every individual access to information about his or her family and heritage.

- **Bastard Nation** (http://www.bastards.org) This organization fights to open all adoption records. It's a strident site, but has some good articles and book reviews. A sample from their "About Us" page: "We at Bastard Nation believe that there is NOTHING shameful about having been born out of wedlock or about being adopted. We selected our name because we will no longer be made to feel shamed by the odious state laws that permanently seal our original birth records. We do not fling the word 'bastard' at anyone. Rather, we wear it proudly as we work to achieve our goal of equal and unconditional access to original birth records for all adult adoptees."

- **Karen's Adoption Links** (http://www.karensadoptionlinks .com/worldwide.html) This site has a section for adoptees.

- **Facebook** (http://www.facebook.com) Facebook has some groups and pages for adoptees to network, many sorted by geography (states, countries, etc). Simply search Facebook for "adoptees" to find several.

- **RootsWeb Adoption Discussion Lists** (http://lists
  .rootsweb.ancestry.com/index/other/Adoptions/)   This site
  provides four different lists for those researching adoptions in
  their genealogy: Adoption-Gen, Aus-Vic-Adoptions, Il-Rhbal
  (Illinois-Research hindered by adoption laws), and Pre-1940_
  Adoption_Genealogy.

Beginners' "Classes," How-to Articles, Tips, Etc.

- **About.com Genealogy** (http://www.genealogy.about
  .com)   This site has tips, discussion groups, and weekly
  articles on genealogy.

- **Ancestors Series Teacher's Guide** (http://www.byub.org/
  Ancestors/teachersguide)   This site is a set of pages designed
  to help teachers and students in grades 7–12 use the ten-part
  Ancestors series to create their genealogies as a school project.

- **DearMYRTLE's Genealogy Lessons** (http://www.dearmyrtle
  .com/lessons.htm)   This is a self-guided course for beginners.

- **Eastman's Online Genealogy Newsletter** (http://blog
  .eogn.com/)   This is a weekly newsletter on genealogy topics.
  A typical issue will cover reviews of genealogy computer
  programs; news items of note to genealogists; a list of websites
  to visit; reviews of books, CD-ROMs, TV programs; and more.
  Eastman publishes a short free version and a "Plus Edition" for
  $20 a year.

- **GeneaWebinars.com**   If you ever wake up one morning and
  say to yourself, "Self, I want to learn more about genealogy
  today," then head over to http://www.geneawebinars.com.
  There you will find a Google Calendar schedule of online
  meetings, classes, hangouts, seminars, and webinars. Many
  are free, although some are fee based. Note: The times on the
  calendar are in U.S. Eastern Time Zone (New York). If you
  need a time zone converter, see http://www.timeanddate.com/
  worldclock/converter.html.

- **Genealogy Dictionary** (http://freepages.genealogy .rootsweb.ancestry.com/~randyj2222/gendict.html) This site gives you definitions for all those confusing terms such as "cordwainer" and "primogeniture."

- **Genealogical Glossary** (http://www.rootsweb.ancestry .com/~nsdigby/lists/glossary.htm) This page is similar to the Genealogy Dictionary.

- **Genealogy Lesson Plan** (http://www.teachnet.com/lesson/ misc/familytrees040199.html) Located at TeachNet.com, this site has a lesson plan on family history for different curriculum areas.

- **Genealogy Today** (http://www.genealogytoday.com) This site announces and rates genealogy sites, has news updates and links to databases, lets readers vote for their favorite sites, and so forth.

- **Kindred Trails** (http://www.kindredtrails.com) This site has links, a kinship calculator, articles, message boards, and more.

- **Lineages, Inc**. (http://www.lineages.com) This is the website for a group of professional genealogical researchers who, for a fee, will help you find your roots. Many of them hold professional certification. In addition, their site includes some free information, such as "First Steps for Beginners," a free genealogical queries page, and more.

- **Association of Personal Historians** (http://www .personalhistorians.org) This site helps you find a professional to write your personal history.

- **Treasure Maps** (http://www.amberskyline.com/treasuremaps) This how-to genealogy site is one of the best sites on the Web for novices. To keep track of the latest news on Treasure Maps, you might want to subscribe to its monthly newsletter.

Blogging and Genealogy Blogs

Genealogy bloggers can help you with techniques, news, and more, as noted in Chapter 9. Here are a few more blogs to consider:

- **Ancestry Insider**, at http://www.ancestryinsider.org, reports on the two big genealogy organizations: Ancestry.com and FamilySearch. The unnamed author, who is a genealogical technologist, has worked for both companies, but strives to be objective in his analysis. It is always worth a read.

- Arlene H. Eakle is a speaker, blogger, and president and founder of The Genealogical Institute, Inc. Arlene's blogs include **Arlene H. Eakle's Genealogy Blog** (http://www .arleneeakle.com/wordpress/), **Tennessee Genealogy** (http:// www.tnblog.arleneeakle.com/), **Virginia Genealogy** (http:// www.virginiagenealogyblog.com/), and **Kentucky Genealogy** (http://www.kyblog.arleneeakle.com). She is on Twitter at http://www.twitter.com/arleneeakle. Dr. Eakle is a professional genealogist with more than 30 years' experience in research, consulting, lecturing, and writing and is an expert in tracing families from New York, the Southern United States, the British Isles, Switzerland, and parts of Germany.

- Cheryl Rothwell has three blogs: **Logan County Genealogy** (http://www.logancountygenealogy.blogspot.com/) is about Logan County, Illinois, and the companion blog, **Graveyards of South Logan County** (http://www.southlogancounty.blogspot .com/) focuses on the cemeteries there. **Ancestor Hunting** (http://www.genealogysleuth.blogspot.com/) is more general and covers "the never-ending, incredibly addictive search for information about our ancestors, their family and friends, neighbors, and total strangers, commonly known as genealogy." It's witty, informative, and fun. Also, she's my friend and neighbor!

- **Documenting the Details** (http://www.lfmccauley.blogspot .com) is the blog by Linda McCauley about her own genealogy, the use of technology in research, the value and fun of genealogy events such as conferences and workshops, and delightful musings.

How Blogs Can Be Cousin Bait

Linda McCauley has had lots of contact from people because of blog posts, but the best was probably an e-mail she received on Christmas Day a few years ago. The writer found a blog post Linda had written about a fourth great-grandmother months earlier. Linda knew the great-grandmother's husband's name, their children, and where they lived in Kentucky and Illinois, but nothing about her parents, not even a surname. This writer not only knew her maiden name, he had a copy of her father's will that clearly identifies her. Her father died in Pennsylvania and lived in Maryland before that. Chances are Linda might never have found that on her own.

Diane MacLean Boumenot, whose blog is One Rhode Island Family (http://www.onerhodeislandfamily.com) was really lost about her great-great-grandmother from Pictou, Nova Scotia. She didn't even have enough material for an individual blog post, but instead included her in a blog post about ten of Diane's brick walls. Then a fifth cousin contacted her and told Diane about a family history book written in 1956 by her great-great-grandmother's nephew. "I got the book, and although I still have a few mysteries, I learned a lot," Diane said. "I also got to meet the fifth cousin, and he and his wife had traveled to Scotland and gave me pictures of the graves of our mutual ancestors. The book in question was rare, only in a handful of libraries. Since a common last name was involved, I may never have found her."

- Elyse Doerflinger of **Elyse's Genealogy blog** (http://www.elysesgenealogyblog.com) shares both her personal family history and her knowledge of research techniques. An elementary schoolteacher as well as an administrator of WikiTree, she has a fresh and breezy approach to genealogy.

- Gena Philibert Ortega writes for the blogs at **Gena's Genealogy** (http://www.philibertfamily.blogspot.com) and contributes to the **World Vital Records blog** (http://blog.worldvitalrecords.com). She wrote the books *Putting the Pieces Together* (Lulu, 2007) and *Cemeteries of the Eastern Sierra* (Arcadia Publishing, 2007). Follow her on Twitter: @genaortega and @WVRNewsletter.

- **Geneabloggers** (http://www.geneabloggers.com) is Thomas' MacEntee excellent blog about blogging... for genealogists, by genealogists, about genealogists, and so on! A good description is at http://www.geneabloggers.com/about/. This is a must-see site! Thomas MacEntee specializes in the use of technology and social media for better family history research and to cooperate with others in the genealogy world. He is on Facebook at http://www.facebook.com/tmacentee and on Twitter at http://www.twitter.com/tmacentee.

- Jean Wilcox Hibben blogs at **Circle Mending: Where Music and Genealogy Meet** (http://www.circlemending.org). Hibben lives in Riverside County, California, and is a Board-Certified Genealogist, with a doctorate in folklore and a master's in speech communication. She is also president of the Corona Genealogical Society and the Southern California Chapter of the Association of Professional Genealogists.

- Lee R. Drew writes the **FamHist Blog** (http://www.famhist .wordpress.com/about/) and **Lineage Keeper Blog** (http:// www.lineagekeeper.blogspot.com). You can reach Lee at the Twitter account http://www.twitter.com/lineagekeeper.

- Lisa Alzo writes **The Accidental Genealogist** (http://www .theaccidentalgenealogist.com) and is on Twitter at http:// www.twitter.com/lisaalzo and Facebook at http://www .facebook.com/lisaalzo. Lisa has written seven books, including *Baba's Kitchen: Slovak & Rusyn Family Recipes and Traditions* (Gateway Press, 2005) and *Finding Your Slovak Ancestors* (Heritage Productions, 2005). She teaches classes for GenClass .com and the National Institute for Genealogical Studies. Lisa has presented at numerous national and international conferences, genealogical, and historical societies.

- Lisa Louise Cooke (http://www.lisalouisecooke.com) owns **Genealogy Gem**. She writes blogs and magazine articles, hosts podcasts and videocasts, and works closely with *Family Tree Magazine*. She is the author of *Genealogy Gems: Ultimate Research Strategies* (privately published, 2007) and several other books. You can find Lisa on Twitter at http://www.twitter.com/ LisaCooke and on Facebook.

- Renee Huskey blogs at **http://www.photoloom.wordpress .com/** and on Twitter (http://www.twitter.com/PhotoLoom). Renee writes about preserving the images and stories in order to turn genealogy data into family history.

- Renee Zamora writes **Renee's Genealogy Blog** (http://www .rzamor1.blogspot.com) and is on Twitter at http://www.twitter .com/rzamor1. Renee has been secretary for the Utah Valley PAF Users Group and a Family History Consultant at the Alpine Family History Center. Her blog is often about the Church of Jesus Christ of Latter-day Saints (LDS) family history scene. She began researching at age 15, mainly in Warren and Washington Counties, New York.

Other blogs to check out:

- Amy Johnson Crow writes the blog **No Story Too Small** about the small stories that make up family history. She shares the stories and the techniques to find them for your genealogy. Find it at http://www.nostorytoosmall.com.

- **FootnoteMaven.com** is a wonderful blog about citations, sources, reference works, and genealogy. It is much more entertaining and fun than that sounds. You can also follow the author on http://www.facebook.com/footnoteMaven and http://www.twitter.com/footnoteMaven.

- Marian Pierre-Louise writes **Roots and Rambles** (http://www .rootsandrambles.blogspot.com) and **Fieldstone Common** podcast (http://www.fieldstonehistoricresearch.com). Her podcast gives away weekly book prizes for listeners!

- Thomas J. Kemp blogs for **http://www.genealogybank .com/gbnk/**.

- Maureen Taylor is the author of **The Photo Detective** (http:// www.photodetective.com).

- Randy Seaver writes the **Genea-musings Blog** (http://www .geneamusings.com).

- Colleen Fitzpatrick writes **The Forensic Genealogist** (http:// www.forensicgenealogy.info).

- Paula Hinkle writes the **Southern California Genealogy Jamboree** (http://www.genealogyjamboree.blogspot.com/).

- Stephen Danko PhD writes a genealogy blogger at **http:// www.stephendanko.com/blog**.

Birth, Death, Marriage, and Other Records

Here are just a few of the sites where volunteers are uploading data. Be sure you visit RootsWeb and Cyndi's List often for updates and new pages:

- **Australian Office of Regulatory Services** has a page where you can search vital records at http://www.ors.act.gov.au/ community/births_deaths_and_marriages/historic_death_index.

- **Danish Demographic Database** (http://www.ddd.dda.dk/ ddd_en.htm) has several ways to search for information in different sources. You can search for individuals when you have some information. Information is being added regularly by volunteers, so keep searching!

- There are three good sites for finding cemetery information. **Cemetery Junction: The Cemetery Trail** (http://www .daddezio.com/cemetery/trail/index.html) has transcriptions of tombstones found in cemeteries across the United States, Canada, and Australia, collected and uploaded by volunteers, links to other sites focusing on cemeteries, and some interesting articles on the subject. **Find a Grave** (http://www.findagrave .com/index.html) is all about cemetery research and recording gravesites, new and old. Here, people volunteer to find headstones for each other. Finally, check out **http://www .BillionGraves.com**, a site searchable on FamilySearch and Ancestry.com. BillionGraves also has its own smart phone/ tablet computer app.

- **Census Bureau Home Page** (http://www.census.gov/ genealogy/www) site has a list of frequently occurring names in the United States for 1990, a Spanish surname list for 1990, an age search service, and a frequently asked questions (FAQs) file on genealogy.

- **FreeBMD** (http://www.freebmd.rootsweb.com), which stands for Free Births, Marriages, and Deaths, is made up of volunteers transcribing the Civil Registration Index information for England and Wales from the years 1837 to 1898 onto the Internet. Progress is sporadic; volunteer if you can.

- **GENWED** (http://www.genwed.com/) is a free genealogical research database for marriage records and a directory to other marriage records online for the United States, Canada, and the United Kingdom. Some of the records can be obtained for free; others will require some sort of cost. Most of the records are volunteer submitted and are therefore considered secondary material.

- **The Bureau of Land Management Land Patent Records** (http://www.glorecords.blm.gov) is a searchable database. It's invaluable, especially for information in the Western states when they were territories and when local records were scarce.

Also, do not forget that many states, provinces, and territories have online sites for the official archives of vital records. Even if you cannot find the actual record online at some of them, usually, you can at least search an index of them and then write for a copy. On occasion, this is also true of larger libraries.

DNA

DNA research is becoming part of online genealogy. These are sites you can explore for this topic:

- **Chris Pomeroy's DNA Portal** (http://www .dnaandfamilyhistory.com)   What was a website of articles turned into a book, a free e-mail newsletter, and a set of articles on the cutting edge of DNA genealogy.

- **Family Tree DNA** (http://www.familytreedna.com)   This is a company you can pay to look for matches with people you suspect are relatives. In searching my mother's genealogy, we had long suspected that our Abraham Spencer was related to a certain Abner Spencer. Using this site, my uncle and another man submitted saliva samples. The other man (who wishes not to be named) was a proven descendant from that Abner.

The results showed that he and my uncle have an ancestor in common. Many professional genealogists scoff at such proof (for example, the white descendants of Thomas Jefferson), but we feel this has finally solved our 30-year brick wall on Abraham's parents.

- **Genealogy DNA Mail List** (http://lists.rootsweb.ancestry .com/index/other/DNA/GENEALOGY-DNA.html)   This is a discussion group about the topic of DNA hosted by RootsWeb.

- **Oxford Ancestors** (http://www.oxfordancestors.com)   This is a company that does the same thing as Family Tree DNA, but in the United Kingdom.

- **Sorenson Molecular Genealogy Foundation** (http:// www.smgf.org)   Brigham Young University (BYU) has a site explaining its DNA genealogy research. You can learn how this project is progressing and how you can participate in your area. You can also read about how BYU hopes to use the data to further the Mormons' quest to have a family history for all mankind.

Ethnic/National

Here's a list of some important ethnic pages:

- **Australian National Library** (http://www.nla.gov.au/ guides/#Genealogy_-_Australia)   This is a subject guide page with links to Australian genealogy resources, organizations, military service records, and so on, as well as an online card catalog.

- **Center for Basque Studies** (http://www.basque.unr .edu)   This site, at the University of Nevada, Reno, covers history, anthropology, and other aspects of Basque culture.

- **Center for Jewish History** (http://www.cjh.org)   This site has a special section on family history at http://www.cjh.org/ collections/genealogy/.

- **Christine's African-American Genealogy Website** (http://www.ccharity.com)   This is an excellent site about African-American history and genealogy.

- **Federation of East European Family History Societies** (http://www.feefhs.org)   This site has databases, maps, and directories to help with genealogy in this region. The group is also on Facebook.

- **History and Genealogy of South Texas and Northeast Mexico** (http://www.vsalgs.org/stnemgenealogy)   This is an interesting source if you're looking for relatives from the South Texas/Northeast Mexico area. The database has over 11,000 names, all linked as lineages.

- **Hungarian Genealogy** (http://www.rootsweb.ancestry .com/~wghungar)   This is a good place to start if your research leads you to Hungary.

- **India Office Family History Search** (http://indiafamily .bl.uk/UI/Home.aspx)   This site has data taken from a card index at the British Library. The card index was compiled by members of staff at the India Office Records from the mid-1970s onwards to meet the growing interest in genealogy. Although less than 10 percent of the biographical sources available in the India Office Records were incorporated into the index, the site notes that future additions are in the works.

- **Johannes Schwalm Historical Association** (http://www .jsha.org)   This is a registry for descendants of Hessian soldiers, the German auxiliary troops the British used in the Revolutionary War. Many of them remained here, became citizens, and are the ancestors of thousands of Americans. JSHA maintains an archive of materials and resources at the Franklin and Marshall College Library. You can search the inventory of the archives at http://www.library.fandm.edu/ archives/jsha.php.

- **New Zealand History Online** (http://www.nzhistory.net .nz/handsonhistory/genealogy-links)   This is a page of links to various sites with shipping lists, cemetery records, tribal history, archives, and so on in New Zealand.

- **Scotland's People** (http://www.scotlandspeople.gov.uk)   This is one of the largest online sources of genealogical information, with almost 80 million records. This is the official government source for genealogy data in Scotland.

- **Spanish Heritage Home Page** (http://www.shhar.net)   This is a great site with articles, links, and networking resources for those researching Hispanic family history in the Western Hemisphere.

Historical Background

Certain historical events may have an impact on your genealogy. The following sites can give you some information on the people in history:

- **The History Detectives TV series** (http://www.pbs.org/opb/historydetectives/)   This is a favorite of genealogy junkies across the United States. They take an object from a submission (click the link on the home page) and trace its history, provenance, and origins. Based on viewer submissions, the History Detectives investigated Goering's gun, Lewis and Clark's cane, an antislavery flag, Jean Lafitte's spyglass and a Revolutionary War prisoner letter.

- **American Civil War Home Page** (http://www.sunsite.utk.edu/civil-war)   This site has links to fantastic online documents from many sources, including those of two academics who've made the Civil War their career.

- **British Civil War, Commonwealth, and Protectorate** (http://www.british-civil-wars.co.uk)   This site offers timelines, biographies, and military history on the United Kingdom from 1638 to 1660.

- **Calendars Through the Ages** (http://www.webexhibits.org/calendars)   This site explores the fascinating history of how we have tried to organize our lives in accordance with the sun.

- **Castle Garden** (http://www.CastleGarden.org)   This is the educational project of The Battery Conservancy. Castle Garden was a major port of entry for immigrants before Ellis Island opened. The free database has information on more than 11 million immigrants, spanning most of the nineteenth century.

- **Glossary of Terms Used in Past Times** (http://www.johnowensmith.co.uk/histdate/terms.htm)   This site, written by John Owen Smith, is a page of definitions of "assart," "toft," and other terms you may come across in old records.

- **Dan Mabry's Historical Text Archive** (http://www
  .historicaltextarchive.com/)   This is a compilation of articles
  and documents on various topics. Of special interest are the
  collections on African-American history and genealogy.

- **Daughters of the American Revolution** (http://www.dar
  .org)   This is the organization for those who can prove an
  ancestor fought in the American Revolution. A free lookup in
  the DAR Patriot Index is just one of the site's many features.

- **Fold3.com**   This is a site for original documents and
  photographs concerning American military history. The free
  membership allows you to create your own Footnote pages;
  search and browse all images, and documents; upload images to
  your gallery; annotate member images; upload, annotate, and
  print your own images; and view and search member images.
  The paid membership allows you more interaction, notations,
  and control.

- **Hauser-Hooser-Hoosier Theory: The Truth about Hoosier**
  (http://www.geocities.com/Heartland/Flats/7822)   This site
  explains how genealogy solved the mystery regarding the term
  "Hoosier" in a whitepaper titled "Migration, Ministry, and a
  Moniker."

- **Immigration: The Living Mosaic of People, Culture &
  Hope** (http://www.library.thinkquest.org/20619)   This is a
  student project about immigration in the United States.

- **Mayflower Web Pages** (http://www.mayflowerhistory
  .com)   These pages contain the passenger lists of the
  Mayflower, the *Fortune,* and the *Anne,* plus many related
  documents.

- **Medal of Honor Citations** (http://www.history.army.mil/
  moh.html)   This site contains the names and text of the
  citations for the more than 3,400 people who've been awarded
  the Congressional Medal of Honor since 1861.

- **Migrations** (http://www.migrations.org)   This site has two
  separate parts. First is a database of migration information
  submitted by volunteers (secondary source information, of
  course!), searchable by name and place. Second is a list of links
  to resources on migration.

- **The Olden Times** (http://www.theoldentimes.com/ newsletterpage.html)   This site has historic newspapers online that can be searched for free.

- **Pitcairn Island Website** (http://www.lareau.org/genweb .html)   This is one place to go for information on over 7,500 descendants of the crew of the *H.M.S. Bounty*, of *Mutiny on the Bounty* fame. Another good site for history and to buy stamps and coins is found at the island's government site: http://www.government.pn/.

- **Sons of the American Revolution** (http://www.sar .org)   This site has information on this organization's genealogical library, articles from its quarterly magazine, the history of the American Revolution, and more.

- **United States Civil War Center** (http://www.lib.lsu.edu/ cwc)   This site from Louisiana State University publishes book reviews, research tips, and articles about studying the War Between the States.

Libraries

Search the web catalogs (Yahoo!, Lycos, Google, and so on) for "library" plus "state" or "national" or the region you need. Some state libraries also have special genealogical collections, which you might find with a search such as "Michigan State library genealogy." These are some of the best library sites for genealogy:

- **Abrams Collection, Archives of Michigan** (http:// www.the-abrams-foundation.org/grantees/archives-of- michigan/)   The Library of Michigan's genealogy collection is known as the Abrams Foundation Historical Collection. The Abrams Collection provides a variety of resources for researchers to explore their family history. Materials are mostly for states east of the Mississippi River. This includes the Great Lakes, New England, Mid-Atlantic, Southern states, and the Canadian provinces of Ontario and Quebec. The Abrams Collection Genealogy Highlights lists what researchers can find at this wonderful library. From assistance on specific genealogy topics to an online newsletter, this page lists resources at the Library of Michigan and at other libraries and research centers.

- **Allen Public Library Genealogy Division** (http://www
  .genealogycenter.org)   This is one of the leading genealogy
  departments in a public library in the United States. Be sure to
  use the library's online catalog to prepare before you make a
  trip to this outstanding facility. This will help orient you to the
  scope of the collection and help you plan your actual research
  time in the department. Also, be sure to check the library's
  main webpage (http://www.acpl.lib.in.us) for any important
  news and announcements regarding hours or closures.
  Librarians experienced in genealogical research are always
  on duty to answer your questions.

- **Clayton Library Center for Genealogical Research** (www2
  .houstonlibrary.org/clayton)   This library is in Houston, Texas,
  but with much more genealogy information than just Texas
  research resources. The site has searches for their collections,
  microprint collection, periodical collection, and online catalog.

- **Connecticut State Library History and Genealogy Unit**
  (http://www.cslib.org/handg.htm)   This page explains
  the special collections and services the state library has for
  genealogists.

- **Elmer's Genealogy Corner** (http://www.elmersgenealogycorner
  .com/)   This site, established by Elmer C. Spear, features
  Madison County, Florida, and several other categories of
  records. Elmer is a past Genealogist of the Year in Florida.

- **Gateway to Northwestern Ontario History** (http://images
  .ourontario.ca/gateway/search)   This site has more than 1,000
  photographs and drawings, as well as the full text of several
  books.

- **Indiana State Library Genealogy Division** (http://www
  .in.gov/library/genealogy.htm)   This site has searchable
  databases and an online card catalog.

- **Midwest Genealogy Center** (http://www.mcpl.lib.mo.us/
  genlh/mgc.htm)   This is a branch of the Mid-Continent Public
  Library, based in Independence, Missouri. The branch has
  its own page, building and card catalog and participates in
  interlibrary loans.

- **Mobile Local History and Genealogy** (http://www
  .mplonline.org/lhg.htm)   This site covers the area from
  Pascagoula to Pensacola. The Local History Collection
  includes works by local authors, Mobile histories, periodicals,
  an extensive clippings file, Mobile newspapers on microfilm
  from 1819 to the present, city directories back to 1837, and
  the federal census records for most of the southeastern states.
  A recent addition to the collection is the Mobile Historic
  Development Commission's survey of historic architecture in
  Mobile, with 10,000 images stored and indexed on CD-ROM.

- **Repositories of Primary Sources** (http://www.webpages
  .uidaho.edu/special-collections/other.repositories.html)   This
  site is a listing of over 5,000 websites describing holdings of
  manuscripts, archives, rare books, historical photographs, and
  other primary sources. Sorted by geographical region, this site
  is worth a look.

- **South Carolina State Library** (http://www.statelibrary
  .sc.gov)   This is the online card catalog for the South Carolina
  Library, which houses an extensive collection of genealogy
  holdings. Be sure to look at the pages under the menu choice
  "S. C. Information" for links to sites with obituary records,
  history of counties and towns, and libraries across the state.

- **Texas Archival Resources Online** (http://www.lib.utexas
  .edu/taro/index.html)   This site is just a really large index in a
  way. You use a drop-down box to search specific repositories for
  descriptions of archival materials, manuscripts, and museum
  collections held in repositories across the state.

- **Texas General Land Office** (http://www.glo.texas.gov)   Just
  like the federal GLO, this site has volumes of land records. In
  fact, one genealogy speaker, James Harkins, said they scan
  5,000 records a week. Poke around in the collections; search the
  Texas Land grant database, the online map database, the online
  surname index, and all archival collections located at the GLO,
  and learn how to use the GISweb Mapping Viewer. Also, look
  into buying one of their research guides.

- **Texas State Library and Archives** (http://www.tsl.state
  .tx.us)   This site for the library in Austin, Texas, has a

genealogy page with various links, such as an index for county records on microfilm. These films are available for free via interlibrary loan within Texas. The TSLA also has microfilm of the federal census schedules for all states through 1910, selected states from the 1920 and 1930 censuses, printed family and county histories, and a variety of Texas government records. As with all state archives and manuscripts, the riches here are mind-boggling.

- **Virginia Memory** (http://www.virginiamemory.com)   A starting point where you can search Virginia colonial records, as well as bible records, newspapers, court records, and state documents.

Sources of Free Online Books

When a book outlives its copyright in the country where it was registered, it becomes public domain. Many sites on the Internet are dedicated to gathering audio and textual versions of such books, and genealogy books are among these projects. Here is a list of sites you might consider searching for terms such as "genealogy" and "history":

- **Books Should Be Free** (http://www.bookshouldbefree.com) has thousands of titles, including public-domain audiobooks and e-books in formats for iPhone, Android, Kindle, and MP3 players. When I searched for genealogy, I got only about 30 results, but some of them were quite interesting titles, such as *The Tribes and Castes of the Central Provinces of India*.

- **Digital Public Library of America** (http://www.dp.la/) is a project to allow access to digital resources of American libraries and archives. This includes, among many others, the New York Public Library, University of Michigan, Harvard University, and the Library of Congress. *Bookshelf* is the catalog to search, as it has over 1.6 million items. Clicking a search result will redirect you to the page of the institution that holds that specific item.

- **Europeana** (http://www.europeana.eu/) and **The European Library** (http://www.theeuropeanlibrary.org) are online catalogs of digitized and physical items from European museums, libraries, and archives. Sometimes, you find books; sometimes, other media. Some are digitized, like Project Gutenberg, but some are not. The best way to search is to choose Text and Public Domain before putting in your search terms.

- **Internet Archives** (http://www.archive.org) is a nonprofit Internet library. It offers access to historical collections in digital format. The last time I searched for "genealogy" there, I got 85,000 hits, many of them single surname genealogies. Searching for "Powell genealogy" got nearly 100 hits. These results were almost all available for download. Based on U.S. copyright, it nevertheless has materials in many languages.

- **Open Library** (http://www.openlibrary.org) is actually a lending library of all titles, digital or not, held by many U.S. libraries. First, determine whether your library participates, usually by entering the number under the barcode on your library card. Then start searching to find titles, many of which you can load onto your e-reader for two weeks.

- **Project Gutenberg** (http://www.gutenberg.org) is the original online access to public-domain books. Started in 1971 by Michael Hart, it is a collection of books that are out of copyright in the United States. There are over 42,000 of them, and many are self-published genealogies.

- **Projekti Lönnrot** (http://www.lonnrot.net) is a collection of public-domain books in Finnish and Swedish. It's a cooperative, volunteer effort, so what is there represents what someone was willing to scan, index, and upload.

- **World Public Library** (http://www.worldlibrary.org) is what it says. Audio, video, and text are available online—some of it is in the public domain, but not all. The materials under copyright may only be on your device or computer for a limited time, or may only available to read in your browser. Still, it is a fantastic collection of materials, with a plethora of hits on "genealogy" in all media.

Maps, Geography, and More

"Where is that township?" is sometimes a hard question to answer. It can be even harder to find a community that no longer exists, or where county or state lines were moved. Searching for "historical maps" and the name of the county, state, province, or nation in question may turn up a hit in Google, Yahoo!, or other search sites. An excellent article on this topic can be found at http://www .joycetice.com/articles/place.htm. It's titled "You Gotta Know the Territory—The Links between Genealogy, Geography, and Logic." Some other good sites to help with maps include:

- **Deed Platter** (http://www.genealogytools.net/deeds)   If the deed with your ancestor has the metes and bounds, you can have this site draw a map. Learning to do this can sometimes help you see a connection you didn't see before.

- **The Hargrett Rare Book and Manuscript Library** (http:// www.libs.uga.edu/hargrett/index.shtml)   This library at the University of Georgia has a collection of over 800 historic maps spanning five centuries.

- **Global Gazetteer Version 2.2** (http://www.fallingrain.com/ world/index.html)   This is a directory of over a quarter million of the world's cities and towns, sorted by country and linked to a map for each town.

- **GEONET Names Server** (http://earth-info.nga.mil/gns/ html/)   This site lets you search for worldwide geographic feature names, and it responds with latitude and longitude coordinates. For names in the United States and Antarctica, visit the U.S. Geological Survey site (http://www.usgs.gov) or the Geographic Names Information System site (http:// geonames.usgs.gov). The GNS contains 4 million features with 5.5 million names.

- **U.S. Census Bureau Gazetteer** (http://www.census.gov/geo/ www/gazetteer/gazette.html)   This is where you can search by entering either the name and state abbreviation (optional) or the five-digit ZIP code.

- **A Vision of Britain** (http://www.visionofbritain.org.uk) This project started in 1994 with the goal of creating a major database of Britain's localities as they have changed over time. This website was created by the Great Britain Historical GIS Project (GIS stands for Geographical Information System), based in the Department of Geography of the University of Portsmouth.

- **Historical Maps of the United States** (http://www.lib .utexas.edu/maps/united_states.html)   This site, hosted by the University of Texas at Austin, has dozens of maps under the headings Early Inhabitants, Exploration and Settlement, Territorial Growth, Military History, Later Historical Maps, and Other Historical Map Sites.

- **Old Maps UK** (http://www.old-maps.co.uk/)   This site lets you search online for maps and order hard copies.

Regional

If you need a regional resource, first go to Google, Yahoo!, Lycos, or another web catalog and search for "archives." The following links are good examples of what you can expect to find:

- **Alabama Department of Archives and History Genealogy Page** (http://www.archives.alabama.gov/research.html)   This is a collection of tutorials for how to search the Alabama archives for family history, as well as links to various online records. Most state and province archives have something similar.

- **Canadian Heritage Information Network** (http://www .rcip-chin.gc.ca/index-eng.jsp)   This is a bilingual French/ English guide to museums, galleries, and other heritage-oriented resources in Canada.

- **European Archival Network** (http://www.euan.org/)   This page lists national archive sites by alphabet and region.

- **Filson Historical Society** (http://www.filsonhistorical .org)   This is a library, manuscript collection, and museum concentrating on Kentucky history and genealogy. It has a searchable online card catalog of library materials.

- **GENUKI** (http://www.genuki.org.uk)   This site is all about genealogy in the United Kingdom and Ireland.

- **Irish Genealogy** (http://www.irishgenealogy.ie/en/)   This is a portal with message boards, transcribed records, surname origins, and a newsletter.

- **National Archives of Singapore** (http://www.nas.gov.sg)   This site offers relatively recent records.

- **New England Historic Genealogical Society** (http://www .americanancestors.org/home.html)   This site is designed to be a center for family and local history research in New England. The society owns 200,000 genealogy books and documents. If you're a New England genealogist, you should check it out.

- **Surnames.com** (http://www.surnames.com)   This site discusses general genealogy, with some focus on the Arizona area. It includes a surname search and a map of genealogical organizations in the United States. The site also has a useful beginner's section.

- **Utah State Archives** (http://www.archives.utah.gov)   Here you can access the research center for the archives' public services. This site includes research, places where questions can be answered, and places where records can be ordered. Not everything here is free, but it's very convenient!

Starting Places

Here are some good places to begin your search for people, places, and pages:

- **WikiTree** (http://www.wikitree.com)   This is a free, cooperative genealogy site. You put in or upload your data, with sources, photos, scans of documents, family stories, and more. Other members searching the site for their ancestors may find your data and suggest a merger between your entry on a person and another entry that seems to be the same person. If you agree, then the sources, data, and connections are merged into one entry, eliminating duplication and sometimes eliminating mistakes or typos. Then, it can calculate the relationship between you and the owner of the other record. It has a wonderful, active message area, too. It is easy and intuitive to use. If you have not been thrilled with the usual suspects of online genealogy sites, give WikiTree a try.

- **Archives.com** (http://www.archives.com/)   This is a competitor to Ancestry.com with many of the same features and services.

- **Genealogy Links.Net** (http://www.genealogylinks.net)   This site includes over 9,000 links, most of them to online searchable databases, such as ships' passenger lists, church records, cemetery transcriptions, and censuses for England, Scotland, Wales, Ireland, Europe, United States, Canada, Australia, and New Zealand.

- **Genealogy Pages** (http://www.genealogypages.com)   This site provides a collection of links to free genealogical services, as well as to over 29,000 online resources.

- **Genealogy Spot** (http://www.genealogyspot.com)   This is a free portal with links to online genealogy resources for beginners and experts alike. Sites featured here are hand selected by an editorial team for quality, content, and utility.

- **GeneaNet** (http://www.geneanet.org)   Based in France, this is a genealogy database site you can search by name or geographic location. It is not based on GEDCOM, but rather has its own database format. Other resources are available, such as a list of genealogy books, genealogy news briefs, and more. Much of the emphasis is on French history, genealogy, and research, but there are other resources, too.

- **DMOZ Genealogy page** (http://www.dmoz.org/Society/Genealogy/Directories/)   This is part of an edited catalog of the Web, so real people have gathered, verified, and edited the links here.

- **Linkpendium** (http://www.linkpendium.com)   This site has a goal to index every genealogy, "geneology," family history, family tree, surname, vital records, biography, or otherwise genealogically related site on the Internet. Built and maintained mainly by RootsWeb founders Brian Wolf Leverich and Karen Isaacson, it is updated often and definitely worth a bookmark.

- **Marston Manor** (http://freepages.genealogy.rootsweb .ancestry.com/~dickmarston/)   This personal genealogy site offers numerous useful items for online genealogists, including a chart for calculating family relationships and a detailed discussion of the terms "proof" and "evidence" as they relate to genealogy.

- **The USGenWeb Project** (http://www.usgenweb.com)   This is a noncommercial project with the goal of providing websites for genealogical research in every county and every state of the United States.

Supplies, Books, Forms, and More

- **Global: Everything for the Family Historian** (http://www .globalgenealogy.com)   This is the Global Genealogy Supply website. Shop online for genealogy supplies—maps, forms, software, and so forth—and subscribe to the *Global Gazette*, a free e-mail newsletter covering Canadian genealogy and heritage.

- **Family Chronicle** (http://www.familychronicle.com)   This is the website for the *Family Chronicle* magazine, which is dedicated to families researching their roots. Check out their offerings and request a free sample of the magazine.

- **Genealogical.com** (http://www.genealogical.com)   This site has genealogy supplies, articles about research, and books and CD-ROMs.

Wrapping Up

- Thousands of websites exist to help with genealogy.

- Some of the most useful websites are collections of links to other sites, such as Cyndi's List and RootsWeb.

- A number of websites are more specific with genealogies submitted by users.

- Several websites have data such as land records, family bible entries, and transcribed census data (for example, AfriGeneas, The Library of Virginia, and the Bureau of Land Management).

- Other pages have good information on how to proceed with your research (for example, DearMYRTLE and the Adoptee Search Resource page).

Part IV

Appendixes

Appendix A

Genealogical Standards from the National Genealogical Society

Genealogical Standards

Standards For Sound Genealogical Research

Recommended by the National Genealogical Society

Remembering always that they are engaged in a quest for truth, family history researchers consistently—

* record the source for each item of information they collect.
* test every hypothesis or theory against credible evidence, and reject those that are not supported by the evidence.
* seek original records, or reproduced images of them when there is reasonable assurance they have not been altered, as the basis for their research conclusions.
* use compilations, communications and published works, whether paper or electronic, primarily for their value as guides to locating the original records, or as contributions to the critical analysis of the evidence discussed in them.
* state something as a fact only when it is supported by convincing evidence, and identify the evidence when communicating the fact to others.
* limit with words like "probable" or "possible" any statement that is based on less than convincing evidence, and state the reasons for concluding that it is probable or possible.
* avoid misleading other researchers by either intentionally or carelessly distributing or publishing inaccurate information.
* state carefully and honestly the results of their own research, and acknowledge all use of other researchers' work.
* recognize the collegial nature of genealogical research by making their work available to others through publication, or by placing copies in appropriate libraries or repositories, and by welcoming critical comment.
* consider with open minds new evidence or the comments of others on their work and the conclusions they have reached.

Genealogical Standards

Guidelines For Using Records Repositories And Libraries

Recommended by the National Genealogical Society

Recognizing that how they use unique original records and fragile publications will affect other users, both current and future, family history researchers habitually—

* are courteous to research facility personnel and other researchers, and respect the staff's other daily tasks, not expecting the records custodian to listen to their family histories nor provide constant or immediate attention.
* dress appropriately, converse with others in a low voice, and supervise children appropriately.
* do their homework in advance, know what is available and what they need, and avoid ever asking for "everything" on their ancestors.
* use only designed work space areas and equipment, like readers and computers, intended for patron use, respect off-limits areas, and ask for assistance if needed.
* treat original records at all times with great respect and work with only a few records at a time, recognizing that they are irreplaceable and that each user must help preserve them for future use.
* treat books with care, never forcing their spines, and handle photographs properly, preferably wearing archival gloves.
* never mark, mutilate, rearrange, relocate, or remove from the repository any original, printed, microform, or electronic document or artifact.
* use only procedures prescribed by the repository for noting corrections to any errors or omissions found in published works, never marking the work itself.
* keep note-taking paper or other objects from covering records or books, and avoid placing any pressure upon them, particularly with a pencil or pen.
* use only the method specifically designated for identifying records for duplication, avoiding use of paper clips, adhesive notes, or other means not approved by the facility.
* return volumes and files only to locations designated for that purpose.
* before departure, thank the records custodians for their courtesy in making the materials available.
* follow the rules of the records repository without protest, even if they have changed since a previous visit or differ from those of another facility.

Genealogical Standards

Standards For Use Of Technology In Genealogical Research

Recommended by the National Genealogical Society

Mindful that computers are tools, genealogists take full responsibility for their work, and therefore they—

* learn the capabilities and limits of their equipment and software, and use them only when they are the most appropriate tools for a purpose.
* do not accept uncritically the ability of software to format, number, import, modify, check, chart or report their data, and therefore carefully evaluate any resulting product.
* treat compiled information from on-line sources or digital databases in the same way as other published sources--useful primarily as a guide to locating original records, but not as evidence for a conclusion or assertion.
* accept digital images or enhancements of an original record as a satisfactory substitute for the original only when there is reasonable assurance that the image accurately reproduces the unaltered original.
* cite sources for data obtained on-line or from digital media with the same care that is appropriate for sources on paper and other traditional media, and enter data into a digital database only when its source can remain associated with it.
* always cite the sources for information or data posted on-line or sent to others, naming the author of a digital file as its immediate source, while crediting original sources cited within the file.
* preserve the integrity of their own databases by evaluating the reliability of downloaded data before incorporating it into their own files.
* provide, whenever they alter data received in digital form, a description of the change that will accompany the altered data whenever it is shared with others.
* actively oppose the proliferation of error, rumor and fraud by personally verifying or correcting information, or noting it as unverified, before passing it on to others.
* treat people on-line as courteously and civilly as they would treat them face-to-face, not separated by networks and anonymity.
* accept that technology has not changed the principles of genealogical research, only some of the procedures.

Genealogical Standards

Standards For Sharing Information With Others

Recommended by the National Genealogical Society

Conscious of the fact that sharing information or data with others, whether through speech, documents or electronic media, is essential to family history research and that it needs continuing support and encouragement, responsible family historians consistently—

* respect the restrictions on sharing information that arise from the rights of another as an author, originator or compiler; as a living private person; or as a party to a mutual agreement.
* observe meticulously the legal rights of copyright owners, copying or distributing any part of their works only with their permission, or to the limited extent specifically allowed under the law's "fair use" exceptions.
* identify the sources for all ideas, information and data from others, and the form in which they were received, recognizing that the unattributed use of another's intellectual work is plagiarism.
* respect the authorship rights of senders of letters, electronic mail and data files, forwarding or disseminating them further only with the sender's permission.
* inform people who provide information about their families as to the ways it may be used, observing any conditions they impose and respecting any reservations they may express regarding the use of particular items.
* require some evidence of consent before assuming that living people are agreeable to further sharing of information about themselves.
* convey personal identifying information about living people—like age, home address, occupation or activities—only in ways that those concerned have expressly agreed to.
* recognize that legal rights of privacy may limit the extent to which information from publicly available sources may be further used, disseminated or published.
* communicate no information to others that is known to be false, or without making reasonable efforts to determine its truth, particularly information that may be derogatory.
* are sensitive to the hurt that revelations of criminal, immoral, bizarre or irresponsible behavior may bring to family members.

Genealogical Standards

Guidelines For Publishing Web Pages On The Internet
Recommended by the National Genealogical Society

Appreciating that publishing information through Internet web sites and web pages shares many similarities with print publishing, considerate family historians—

* apply a title identifying both the entire web site and the particular group of related pages, similar to a book-and-chapter designation, placing it both at the top of each web browser window using the <TITLE> HTML tag, and in the body of the document, on the opening home or title page and on any index pages.

* explain the purposes and objectives of their web sites, placing the explanation near the top of the title page or including a link from that page to a special page about the reason for the site.

* display a footer at the bottom of each web page which contains the web site title, page title, author's name, author's contact information, date of last revision and a copyright statement.

* provide complete contact information, including at a minimum a name and e-mail address, and preferably some means for long-term contact, like a postal address.

* assist visitors by providing on each page navigational links that lead visitors to other important pages on the web site, or return them to the home page.

* adhere to the NGS "Standards for Sharing Information with Others" regarding copyright, attribution, privacy, and the sharing of sensitive information.

* include unambiguous source citations for the research data provided on the site, and if not complete descriptions, offering full citations upon request.

* label photographic and scanned images within the graphic itself, with fuller explanation if required in text adjacent to the graphic.

* identify transcribed, extracted or abstracted data as such, and provide appropriate source citations.

* include identifying dates and locations when providing information about specific surnames or individuals.

* respect the rights of others who do not wish information about themselves to be published, referenced or linked on a web site.

* provide web site access to all potential visitors by avoiding enhanced technical capabilities that may not be available to all users, remembering that not all computers are created equal.

* avoid using features that distract from the productive use of the web site, like ones that reduce legibility, strain the eyes, dazzle the vision, or otherwise detract from the visitor's ability to easily read, study, comprehend or print the online publication.

* maintain their online publications at frequent intervals, changing the content to keep the information current, the links valid, and the web site in good working order.

* preserve and archive for future researchers their online publications and communications that have lasting value, using both electronic and paper duplication.

Genealogical Standards

GUIDELINES FOR GENEALOGICAL SELF-IMPROVEMENT AND GROWTH

Recommended by the National Genealogical Society

Faced with ever-growing expectations for genealogical accuracy and reliability, family historians concerned with improving their abilities will on a regular basis—

* study comprehensive texts and narrower-focus articles and recordings covering genealogical methods in general and the historical background and sources available for areas of particular research interest, or to which their research findings have led them.
* interact with other genealogists and historians in person or electronically, mentoring or learning as appropriate to their relative experience levels, and through the shared experience contributing to the genealogical growth of all concerned.
* subscribe to and read regularly at least two genealogical journals that list a number of contributing or consulting editors, or editorial board or committee members, and that require their authors to respond to a critical review of each article before it is published.
* participate in workshops, discussion groups, institutes, conferences and other structured learning opportunities whenever possible.
* recognize their limitations, undertaking research in new areas or using new technology only after they master any additional knowledge and skill needed and understand how to apply it to the new subject matter or technology.
* analyze critically at least quarterly the reported research findings of another family historian, for whatever lessons may be gleaned through the process.
* join and participate actively in genealogical societies covering countries, localities and topics where they have research interests, as well as the localities where they reside, increasing the resources available both to themselves and to future researchers.
* review recently published basic texts to renew their understanding of genealogical fundamentals as currently expressed and applied.
* examine and revise their own earlier research in the light of what they have learned through self-improvement activities, as a means for applying their new-found knowledge and for improving the quality of their work-product.

Appendix B

How to Find a Professional Genealogist

Most of the fun of genealogy, online and offline, is the solving of puzzles and learning about your family's place in history, but sometimes you hit a brick wall.

You may need a consultant on a specific research problem or help finding a missing relative. Maybe you need a record translated from a foreign language or some handwriting deciphered. Maybe you need an experienced eye to look over what you have and help you develop a plan for what to do next. Maybe you want to surprise your mother with a genealogy for Christmas, or maybe there's just one whole branch of the tree you know you'll never find time for.

All of these are good reasons to use a professional genealogist. Professional genealogists can prove you are a descendant of someone for organizations such as the Daughters of the American Revolution. Professionals can help you with genealogy chores as simple as searching some records you cannot get to online or travel to physically, or they can take what information you have and trace the ancestry as far back as you are willing to pay for.

But hiring a professional genealogist is not as simple as a Google search. Genealogical research is a science requiring skillful analysis and intellectual concentration, as well as years of experience and education.

"I would not discount local history and genealogy experts in the areas where an ancestor once lived, but I find this is a touchy area," advised DearMYRTLE, the genealogy columnist and lecturer. "It is so difficult to evaluate the reliability of research when a person one might hire hasn't been certified or [is not an] accredited genealogist."

So, the solution, she said, is to look for someone certified as a researcher. First, there is the Certified Genealogist (CG) designation from the Board for Certification of Genealogists (www.bcgcertification .org). This organization tests and certifies researchers and teachers (the latter is a Certified Genealogical Lecturer, or CGL). A list of those certified is maintained on the website. The board has a Code of Ethics and Genealogical Proof Standard that the members must adhere to. Another such certification body is The International Commission for the Accreditation of Professional Genealogists (ICAPGen), which certifies genealogists through comprehensive written and oral examinations.

The ICAPGen website is http://www.icapgen.org, which offers the following: The agreement between the Accredited Genealogist (AG) professional and ICAPGen outlines the responsibilities of each

AG researcher to ICAPGen, to the researcher's clients, and to the genealogical community. Should a dispute or client complaint occur, the agreement outlines the arbitration process. Out of a desire to protect the consumer, ICAPGen tests the competence of genealogists and provides assurance to those who want to hire a professional in the field. You can find a list of ICAPGen members on the website.

The Family History Library of the Church of Jesus Christ of Latter-day Saints (LDS) also has a staff of professional genealogists. The staff will test for AG status by the Genealogical Department of the LDS Church. Examinations include specialized areas such as American Indian, Southern, United States, England, and Germany. These genealogists are not necessarily members of the LDS church, nor do they limit themselves to LDS clients. Accredited Genealogists sign an ethics agreement and agree to adhere to a code of conduct; they are required to renew their accreditation every five years.

Choosing a DNA Test Provider

As discussed Chapter 10, different tests can answer different questions when it comes to DNA for genealogy. Choosing the company to test your DNA for genealogical information can depend on which questions you are asking.

For example, to research a specific surname, search the Web for DNA and the surname. If you find a project, see which company and/or test they are using. For example, both a POWELL and a SPENCER YDNA project are using Family Tree DNA. If you are a female with those surnames, as I am, you would need to have some male relative do the test that those projects are working from. If your brick wall is in a maternal line, you can search for the surname and mtDNA project.

For male adoptees, autosomal DNA can help augment YDNA tests. And if you are just interested in overall ancestral origins, migration patterns, and so on, you could just choose the autosomal DNA test that fits your budget.

No matter which you choose, you may then want to hire a professional genealogist to use the data to track down and find those ancestors!

You can get a roster of these by sending a self-addressed stamped envelope (SASE) with the geographic or topical specialization needed to:

Family History Library
35 North West Temple Street
Salt Lake City, UT 84150-1003

Another organization to consult is the Association of Professional Genealogists (APG). Ethical conduct is extremely important to members of this association. Every member of APG signs a code of professional ethics, stating that the professional will

- Promote a coherent, truthful approach to genealogy, family history, and local history.

- Clearly present research results and opinions in a clear, well-organized manner, with accurately cited references.

- Advertise services and credentials honestly.

- Explain without concealment or misrepresentation all fees, charges, and payment structures.

- Abide by agreements regarding project scope, number of hours, and deadlines or reporting schedules.

- Refrain from knowingly violating or encouraging others to violate laws and regulations concerning copyright and right to privacy.

- Give proper credit to those who supply information and provide assistance.

These are good things to ask any professional genealogist to provide.

Also, various certification boards in other countries may be of help, as the following sections explain.

Australia

Australian Association of Genealogists and Record Agents
P.O. Box 268
Oakleigh, Victoria 3166, Australia

Send five International Reply Coupons for a roster. Tests and certifications in Australian and New Zealand records.

Canada

Genealogical Institute of the Maritimes
Universite de Moncton, Moncton
New Brunswick, E1A 3E9, Canada

Send SASE (with Canadian postage or two International Reply Coupons) for a roster. Tests and certifications for specialized research areas in Canada.

England

Association of Genealogists and Researchers in Archives
Hon. Secretary
31 Alexandra Grove
London N12 8HE, England

Send five International Reply Coupons for a roster. Peers recommend those listed as competent by long experience.

France

Chambre Syndicale des Genealogistes – Heraldistes de France
74, Rue des Saints-Peres
75005 Paris, France

Send five International Reply Coupons for a roster.

Ireland

Association of Professional Genealogists in Ireland
c/o The Genealogical Office
30 Harlech Crescent
Clonskeagh, Dublin 14, Ireland

Send two International Reply Coupons for a roster. Membership is based on independent assessment and experience.

New Zealand

Genealogical Research Institute of New Zealand
P.O. Box 36-107 Moera
Lower Hutt 6330, New Zealand

Send a large envelope and two International Reply Coupons for a roster. Members sign a code of ethics.

Scotland

Association of Scottish Genealogists and Record Agents
51/3 Mortonhall Road
Edinburgh EH9 2HN, Scotland

Send two International Reply Coupons for a roster. Members sign a code of practice.

Set Terms

Hiring a genealogist is a bit like hiring a contractor: You must have a clearly defined project and budget in mind before you sign a contract. You need to present to the genealogist a letter of agreement that lists

- The scope of work to be performed

- How many hours to be worked for you, with some provision for time extensions under specified circumstances

- A definition of fees for various actions

- Definition of what the retainer covers and how it will be applied toward final payment

- How you will agree on more research activities after the original work is finished

It is also a good idea to define who holds the copyright to the written research reports. Often, the professional genealogist wants to retain those rights, which means you cannot publish the report without the researcher's permission.

Note

What if something goes wrong? If your researcher is a member of the Association of Professional Genealogists and you believe he or she has not worked within the code of ethics, you can file a grievance with the organization. APG will work with you and the professional to mediate the disagreement.

Ask at genealogy societies and clubs for the names of good local professional genealogists before contacting one. Once you find one to talk to, it never hurts to ask for and check references. If the professional is reluctant to provide this, use your best judgment in deciding whether you want to hire this person. It's also a good idea to begin with a short, simple assignment, such as a research chore in a city you just cannot travel to. See how quickly and accurately the candidate can work and how important your business is. Then you can judge whether you have the confidence to agree on a larger project.

Most genealogists charge by the hour; the fees can range from $10 to $95 per hour. An average is $30 to $50 per hour for the professional in the United States. However, you may find a researcher who prefers to charge a flat daily fee, such as $150 to $500 per day for their services. Indeed, several professionals prefer a minimum retainer (usually $350 to $500) for a research project. This gives the researcher a good block of time and some working capital for transportation, copies, and so on. It also gives the genealogist leeway to do a careful and thorough job on your project.

Once you have a specific list of research needs, a list of professional genealogists who meet your criteria in price and expertise, and you have checked their references, you can determine who to hire and sign an agreement. Then you give the researcher the information you have and the fees to begin.

Glossary

A

a.   About (or circa, in Latin), often used in front of uncertain dates.

AG (Accredited Genealogist)   Designation conferred by the Church of Jesus Christ of Latter-day Saints (LDS). In 1964, the Genealogical Department of the Church of Jesus Christ of Latter-day Saints established the Accreditation Program for Genealogists to credential genealogy researchers through comprehensive written and oral examinations that require the use of the highest professional genealogy standards and ethics. Administration of the program was transferred to an independent testing organization, the International Commission for the Accreditation of Professional Genealogists (ICAPGen), in 2000.

aggregator (also called feed reader, news reader, RSS reader)   Software or web application that collects syndicated web content such as news headlines, blogs, podcasts, and vlogs (video blog) in a single location for easy viewing.

ahnentafel   "Ancestor table" in German—a format is more than a century old. A way of listing a family tree, it includes the full name of each ancestor, with dates and places of birth, marriage, and death. The ahnentafel format organizes this information along a numbering scheme. If an individual's number in the table is X, then the father's number is 2X in the table; the mother is 2X + 1. So, all males in the table are even numbers and all females are odd numbers. If you are #1 in the table, your father is #2 and your mother is #3. Your father's father is #4, your father's mother #5, and so on.

allele (DNA)   One of two alternative forms of a gene that is located at a specific position on a specific chromosome.

Ancestral File (AF)   A searchable collection of genealogical data submitted to the LDS archives in GEDCOM format to help genealogists coordinate their research.

Android   An open-source operating system for smart phones and tablet computers developed by Google as an alternative to iOS.

anonymous FTP (File Transfer Protocol)   The process of connecting to a remote computer, either as an anonymous or guest user, to transfer public files back to your local computer. (See also: *FTP* and *protocol*.) Anonymous FTP is usually read-only access; you often cannot contribute files by anonymous FTP.

app   A self-contained program to accomplish a particular function; a software application, especially as downloaded by a user to a mobile device.

Atom   A syndication format written in eXtensible Markup Language (XML) language used for web feeds and as a publishing protocol (APP is the acronym, but it is referred to as "AtomPub" for short) for creating and updating web resources. It is a form of "push" technology that allows the user to retrieve information without the problems of e-mail and web browsing.

B

backbone   A set of connections that make up the main channels of communication across a network.

BCG   Board for Certification of Genealogists.

blog   A "web log," or journal, is a website where someone posts regular articles and information for public use and reading. The articles may contain commentary, descriptions of events, or other material such as graphics or video. "To blog" is to write and maintain such a site.

browser   An Internet client for viewing the World Wide Web.

bulletin board   A way of referring to online message systems where you must log onto the site or Internet service provider (ISP) to read and post messages. Also called a message board, forum, or discussion board.

C

cadastre   A survey, map, or some other public record showing ownership and value of land for tax purposes.

catalog   A search page for the Web within an edited list, not the whole Internet.

CG   Designates a Certified Genealogist by the BCG.

CGI   Designates a Certified Genealogical Instructor by the BCG.

CGL   Designates a Certified Genealogical Lecturer by the BCG.

CGRS   Designates a Certified Genealogical Record Specialist by the BCG.

chat   When people type messages to each other across a host or network, live and in real time. On some commercial online services, this is called a conference.

client   A program that provides an interface to remote Internet services, such as mail, RSS feeds, Telnet, and so on. In general, the clients act on behalf of a human end user (perhaps indirectly).

cloud (the)   An often-used metaphor for the Internet because of how it is shown in computer network diagrams of cloud computing and because it is a way to express the complex infrastructure the Internet conceals.

cloud computing   Internet-based development and use of computer technology.

collateral line   A family that is not in your direct line of ancestry but of the same genealogical line. For example, if you are descended from Patrick Henry's sister, his direct descendants are your collateral line.

compression   A method of making a file, whether text or code, smaller by various methods. This is so the file will take up less disk space and/or less time to transmit. Sometimes, the compression is completed by the modem; sometimes, the file is stored that way. The various methods to do this go by names (followed by the system that used it), such as PKZIP (DOS), ARC (DOS), TAR (UNIX), STUFFIT (Macintosh), and so forth.

conference   A usually large gathering with discussions, lectures, exhibits, and perhaps workshops. Genealogy conferences are held around the country every year.

D

database   A set of information organized for computer storage, search, retrieval, and insertion.

default   In computer terms, the "normal" or "basic" settings of a program.

directory   1. A level in a hierarchical filing system. Other directories branch down from the root directory. Also called a "folder." 2. A type of search site where editors choose the websites and services in the catalog instead of a robot collecting them indiscriminately. http://www.dmoz.org is one example.

domain name   The Internet naming scheme. A computer on the Internet is identified by a series of words, from more specific to more general (left to right), separated by dots: www.microsoft.com is an example (See also: *IP address.*)

Domain Name Server (DNS)   A computer with software to translate a domain name into the corresponding numbers of the IP address. "No DNS entry" from your browser means a name such as www .firstlast.org wasn't in the Domain Name Server's list of valid IP addresses.

downloading   To get information from another computer to yours.

E

e-mail   An electronic message, text, or data sent from one computer or person to another computer or person.

F

Family Group Sheet   A one-page collection of facts about one family unit: husband, wife, and children, with birth and death dates and places.

FHC   Family History Center, a branch of the Family History Library in Salt Lake City, found in a local LDS parish.

Firefox   A popular web browser. Originally called "Netscape."

firewall   Electronic protection against hackers and other unauthorized access to your files while you're connected to a network or the Internet.

flame   A message or series of messages containing an argument or insults. Not allowed on most systems. If you receive a flame, ignore that message and all other messages from that person in the future.

folksonomy   Categorizing things by common use, social networking, or other informal process. Based on the word "taxonomy," the practice and study of the classification of things or concepts, including the rules that underlie such classification, combined with the adjective "folk," or of the common people.

forensic genealogy   Using techniques such as DNA, knowledge of history and geography, and other science and technology tools to establish genealogical facts.

forum   A set of messages on a subject, usually with a corresponding set of files.

French Revolutionary Calendar   The French Revolutionary Calendar (or Republican Calendar) was introduced in France on November 24, 1793, and abolished on January 1, 1806. It was used again briefly during the Paris Commune in 1871.

FTP (File Transfer Protocol)   Enables an Internet user to transfer files electronically between remote computers and the user's computer.

G

gateway   Used in different senses (for example, mail gateway, IP gateway) but, most generally, a computer that forwards and routes data between two or more networks of any size or origin. A gateway is never, however, as straightforward as going through a gate. It's more like a labyrinth to get the proper addresses in the proper sequence.

GEDCOM   The standard for computerized genealogical information, which is a combination of tags for data and pointers to related data.

genotype   A person's complete genomic sequences.

Gregorian calendar Introduced by Pope Gregory XIII in 1582 and adopted by England and the colonies in 1752, by which time it was 11 days behind the solar year, causing an adjustment in September 1752.

H

hacker Originally, someone who messed about with computer systems to see how much could be accomplished. Most recently, a computer vandal.

hangout Video conference with two or more people using Google apps and technology. A hangout may be private or public, and can be recorded and posted to a site such as YouTube.

haplotype A collection of alleles arranged linearly along a person's DNA molecule.

hashtag A form of folksonomy using a pound sign (#) before one word to designate the topic of your Multimedia Message Service (MMS) message, tweet, or status entry.

host computer In the context of networks, a computer that directly provides service to a user. In contrast to a network server which provides services to a user through an intermediary host computer.

HTML (Hypertext Markup Language) A coding system to format and link documents on the World Wide Web and intranets.

hub A computer that collects e-mail regionally and distributes it up the next level. Collects the e-mail from that level to distribute it back down the chain.

I

IGI The International Genealogical Index, a database of names submitted to the LDS Church.

Instant Message (IM) A type of text communication that requires users to register with a server. Users build "buddy lists" of others using the same program and are notified when people on their buddy list are available for chat and messages.

institute   A week-long set of courses on a specific area, usually held at the same site every year, with class size ranging from 15 to 30 students, allowing personalized instruction. Genealogical institutes are held yearly in many sites in the United States and other countries.

Internet   The backbone of a series of interconnected networks that includes local area, regional, and national backbone networks. Networks in the Internet use the same telecommunications protocol (TCP/IP) and provide electronic mail, remote login, and file transfer services.

Internet Service Provider (ISP)   A company that has a continuous, fast, and reliable connection to the Internet and sells subscriptions to the public to use that connection. The connections may use TCP/IP, shell accounts, or other methods.

intranet   A local network set up to look like the World Wide Web, with clients such as browsers, but self-contained and not necessarily connected to the Internet.

iOS   The mobile operating system for smart phones and tablets for Apple products.

IP (Internet Protocol)   The Internet-standard protocol that provides a common layer over dissimilar networks, used to move packets among host computers and through gateways, if necessary.

IP address   The alpha or numeric address of a computer connected to the Internet. Also called "Internet address." Usually, the format is user@someplace.domain, but it can also be seen as *###.##.##.##*.

J

Julian calendar   The calendar replaced by the Gregorian calendar, which had also fallen behind the solar year.

K

Keychain   Apple's password management system.

L

LDS   Accepted abbreviation for the Church of Jesus Christ of Latter-day Saints, also known as the Mormons.

list (Internet)   Also called "mail list" or "mailing list." Listserv lists (or listservers) are electronically transmitted discussions of technical and nontechnical issues. They come to you by electronic mail over the Internet using listserv commands. Participants subscribe via a central service, and lists often have a moderator who supervises the information flow and content.

lurk   To read a list without posting messages yourself. It's rather like sitting in the corner at a party without introducing yourself, except it's not considered rude online. In fact, in some places, you're expected to lurk until you get the feel of the place.

M

mail list   Same as list.

marker (DNA)   A gene or DNA sequence with an established location on a chromosome that can be used to identify individuals or species.

metadata   Data about data. When you add keywords to your webpage or a hashtag to a post, that is metadata about the page or post.

microblogging   The posting of very short entries or updates on sites such as Twitter, Pinterest, or Facebook, usually with a smart phone or tablet.

MMS   A protocol for sending instant messages to a smart phone; "texting" is the most common synonym.

MNP (Microcom Networking Protocol)   Data compression standard for modems.

modem   A device to modulate computer data into sound signals and to demodulate those signals to computer data.

moderator   The person who takes care of a message list, newsgroup, or forum. This person takes out messages that are off topic, chastises flamers, maintains a database of old messages, and handles the mechanics of distributing the messages.

MOOC   A Massive Open Online Course (MOOC) is an online course (usually college level but not always) with open access on the Web and unlimited participation.

Mozilla   A nickname for Netscape or "Firefox" in its latest form. In the early days, Netscape's mascot was a little dragon-like creature called Mozilla.

mtDNA   The DNA inherited only from the mother's side of the family.

N

navigation bar   A set of words and/or images that appears on every page of a website, with links to other sections or pages of the same website.

NEHGS   New England Historic Genealogical Society, founded in 1845. The website is http://www.newenglandancestors.org. Published quarterly since 1847, *The New England Historical and Genealogical Register* is the oldest and most respected journal of American genealogy.

NGS   National Genealogical Society, United States.

NIC (Network Information Center)   An NIC provides administrative support, user support, and information services for a network.

O

offline   The state of not being connected to a remote host.

online   The state of being connected to a remote host.

OPAC   Acronym for Online Public Access Catalog, a term used to describe any type of computerized library catalog.

P

PDF (Portable Document Format) An Adobe-copyrighted format that allows a document to be saved to look a certain way, no matter what computer is used to display it. The computer, however, must use Adobe's Acrobat reader (a free program) to display the file.

pedigree chart The traditional way to display a genealogy, the familiar "family tree," where one person's ancestors are outlined. Other formats are the fan chart, decadency chart (starts with the ancestor and comes down to the present), and timeline.

Pedigree Resource File (PRF) Genealogical information submitted by users of FamilySearch.com.

phenotype The individuality that is formed by the combination of genes and environment.

phishing Posing as a legitimate company to fraudulently gain access to a consumer's data or financial information.

plat (v.) To draw a map of a piece of land by the description of a deed. (n.) The map of a piece of land as defined by the deed.

podcast A media file (sound, perhaps video) that is distributed to users though a "push" system such as syndication (Really Simple Syndication, or RSS) or downloaded from a site. Like "radio," this can mean either the content or the medium. A podcast is played with a program such as Windows Media Player, iTunes, or RealAudio.

post (n.) An entry in one's blog ("My post is on the use of Endnote for genealogy."). (v.) to display an entry to one's blog, status line, or website. ("He didn't post that yet.")

PPP (Point-to-Point Protocol) A type of Internet connection.

protocol A mutually determined set of formats and procedures governing the exchange of information between systems.

push A communication protocol where the request for a given transaction originates with the creator of content, and the user receives it with a special client (See: *Atom* and *RSS*). E-mail is a "pull" technology; RSS readers use "push" technology.

Q

query   A request for genealogical information. To be effective, it must have at least one name, one date, one geographical location, and your contact information.

R

register style   A format for a genealogy created for the NEHGS publication. It is a narrative style that assigns each ancestor a superscript number representing a generation. The first ancestor (the "primary") is 1, and each descendant of the primary individual is assigned a consecutive number; children are assigned lowercase roman numerals as well as Arabic numbers. The result looks much like an outline, as we were taught to do when learning how to write a research paper.

remote access   The capability to access a computer from outside another location. Remote access requires communications hardware, software, and actual physical links.

research log   A record of what sources were searched, where they were found, and what they contained.

RSS   Really Simple Syndication is a family of web feed formats used to publish frequently updated content, such as blog entries, news headlines, or podcasts. Atom is a similar format. They allow the user to retrieve content without the problems of spam and pop-ups that often accompany e-mail and web browsing.

S

search engine   A program on the World Wide Web that searches parts of the Internet for text strings. A search engine might search for programs, webpages, or other items. Many claim to cover "the whole Internet," but that's a physical impossibility. Getting more than 40 percent of the Internet is a good lick.

seminar   An educational event highlighting the interaction and exchange of information, typically among a small number of participants. Genealogy seminars (sometimes called workshops) are often held by local organizations.

server   A computer that allows other computers to log on and use its resources. A client (see the previous definition) program is often used for this.

shareware   The try-before-you-buy concept in microcomputer software, where the program is distributed through public-domain channels and the author expects to receive compensation after a trial period. Brother's Keeper, for example, is shareware.

signature   A stored text file with your name and some information, such as names you're searching or your mailing address, to be appended to the end of your messages. Your signature should contain only ASCII (text-only) characters, no graphics.

SMS   The data system used to send text messages from one mobile phone to another.

social bookmarking   A way to share, organize, search, and manage bookmarks for website resources.

social networking   A rather redundant term for the interaction of users of services such as Facebook, Twitter, and others, where people connect as "Friends" or "followers" to share links, thoughts, messages, and files.

Social Security Death Index (SSDI)   A searchable database of records of deaths of Americans with Social Security numbers, if that death was reported to the Social Security Administration. It runs from the 1960s to the present, although a few deaths prior to the 1960s are in it. The records give full name, place and date of death, where the card was issued, and birth date. Many websites have online searches of the SSDI, some with Soundex (see the following definition).

Soundex   An indexing system based on sound, rather than on the spelling of a surname.

spider   A program that gathers information on webpages for a database, usually for a search engine.

study groups   People creating their own online course on a subject. They "meet" via video chat and help each other. Often, there is a leader, but sometimes not. You could think of it as a small open online course (instead of a MOOC).

sysop   The system operator (manager) of an online community, or forum. The sysop sets the rules, maintains the peace and operability of the system, and sometimes moderates the messages.

T

tablet computer   A mobile device, often with Internet connectivity, that runs smaller programs than a desktop.

tag   A notation of keywords to associate with a resource, page, message, tweet, blog post, or status. Often preceded by a pound sign, but not always.

tag cloud   Also known as a word cloud, this is a weighted list shown in a visual representation of user-generated tags, or simply the word content of a site. The more often a tag appears in the resource, the larger the word appears in the visual depiction.

tagline   A short, pithy statement tagged on to the end of an e-mail message. Example: "It's only a hobby, only a hobby, only a...." Taglines are rarely seen on commercial networks, such as AOL, MSN, and CompuServe.

taxonomy   The science of finding, describing, classifying, and naming things, especially organisms, in a hierarchical system.

TCP/IP (Transmission Control Protocol/Internet Protocol)   A combined set of protocols that performs the transfer of data between two computers. TCP monitors and ensures correct transfer of data. IP receives the data from TCP, breaks it up into packets, and ships it off to a network within the Internet. TCP/IP is also used as a name for a protocol suite that incorporates these functions and others.

Telnet   An Internet client that connects to other computers, making yours a virtual terminal of the remote computer. Among other functions, it enables a user to log in to a remote computer from the user's local computer.

terminal server   A computer that connects terminals to a network by providing host Telnet service.

thread (message thread)   A discussion made up of a set of messages in answer to a certain message and to each other. Sometimes, worthwhile threads are saved in a text file, especially on Yahoo! groups.

Tiny Tafel (TT)   A standard way of describing a family database so the information can be scanned visually or by computer. All data fields are of fixed length, with the obvious exceptions of the surnames and optional places. Many TTs are extracted from GEDCOMs.

Trojan horse   A type of malicious code. This is usually a program that seems to be useful and harmless. In the background, however, it might be destroying data or breaking security on your system. It differs from a virus in that it rarely propagates itself as a virus does.

U

upload   To send a file or message from your computer to another. (See also: *download.*)

USB (Universal Serial Bus)   A connection to a computer. Unlike a parallel port (where your printer probably plugs in) or a serial port (where your modem probably plugs in), a USB port enables you to "daisy-chain" peripherals. If you have a USB printer, modem, and CD-ROM drive, you could plug only one into the USB port, and the rest connect by USB cables in a chain (in theory, say, computer to modem to printer to CD-ROM). In practice, however, sometimes it's a little tricky to get them in an order that makes all the peripherals happy.

V

video chat   Audio and video interaction in real time between users at different locations using a computer, tablet, or smart phone. Examples of software to do this are FaceTime, Skype, and Google Hangouts, and those systems are often used as verbs for the activity (e.g., "I Skyped with my grandkids at Christmas"). Most often, video chat is one-to-one communication, but not always.

videoconferencing Audio and video interaction in a business setting with three or more participants at different locations.

virtual seminars (webinars) A presentation, lecture, workshop, or seminar that is transmitted over the Web. The format is interactive—the presenter can give, receive, and discuss information. However, often a webinar (and the comments from attendees) is saved and available as a webcast.

virus A program that installs itself secretly on a computer by attaching itself to another program or e-mail and then duplicates itself when that program is executed or e-mail is opened. Some viruses are harmless, but most of them intend to do damage, such as erasing important files on your system.

vital records The official records of birth, death, marriage, and other events of a person's life.

vlog A blog that uses videos for posts instead of text and/or pictures.

VOIP Voice Over Internet Protocol, or phone calls using the Internet instead of phone lines or towers.

W

web feed (or news feed) A data format used for providing users with frequently updated content, usually in RSS form.

webinar See: *virtual seminar.*

wiki A website or other online resource that allows users to add and edit content collectively.

workshop See: *seminar.*

World Wide Web (WWW or the Web) A system to pull various Internet services together into one interface called a browser. Most sites on the Web are written as pages in HTML.

worm A computer program that makes copies of itself and spreads through connected systems, using up resources in affected computers or causing other damage.

X

XML eXtensible Markup Language, or XML, is a specification developed by the World Wide Web Consortium (W3C). It is designed especially for web documents. It allows designers to create their own customized tags, enabling the definition, transmission, validation, and interpretation of data between applications and between organizations. Most "push" technology on the Internet is written in XML.

Y

YDNA The DNA inherited only from the father's side of the family.

Index

B

H

I